FEMALE CRIME IN INDIA

FEMALE CRIME IN INDIA and Theoretical Perspectives of Crime

DR. SMRITI BHOSLE

KALPAZ PUBLICATIONS
DELHI-110052

Female Crime in India : And Theoretical Perspectives of Crime

Rs. 750

ISBN: 81-7835-712-7

Published in 2009 in India by
Kalpaz Publications
C-30, Satyawati Nagar,
Delhi-110052
E-mail: kalpaz@hotmail.com
Phone : 9212729499

Laser Type Setting by: Rudra Computer Graphics, Delhi
Printed at : G. Print Process, Delhi

In Memory of
My Father

Shri S.J. Sarang
with love

Contents

Preface

"Female crime in India and the Theoretical perspectives of crime" is an attempt to increase our understanding of female criminality as well as to know the sociological context of female crimes.

This book is a publication of my Ph.D. thesis titled- "Under-trial Female Criminals in Mumbai: A Sociological Study". It provides the theoretical perspectives of criminality and also analyses the most recent research findings. It also highlights the changing profile of female crime and criminals. Besides that, additional chapters like- 'Feminist Perspectives in Criminology', 'Gender Differences in Crime', 'Women in Prison', and 'Prison Visiting System in India', have also been included to provide more information on the related issues.

This book aims at revealing the trends in female criminality in general and in Mumbai in particular. I hope that each chapter of this book will stimulate further thinking on this issue and prove useful for the development and implementation of policy.

The book would also be useful to the students of Sociology, Criminology and Gender Studies course. Likewise it will also be of considerable interest to students of Social Sciences, Social Work and Law.

DR. SMRITI BHOSLE

Acknowledgements

A quest for knowledge led to a scientific inquiry and provided an insight into the phenomenon of deviance that touches human lives. It aroused curiosity to search into these human concerns. Having accomplished academic requirements in a University set up, there was a spontaneous urge to be in touch with the ground realities. The experience has been enriching and refreshing. To achieve a goal, along with personal motivation one requires necessary support and guidance from several corners.

Every author has the pleasure of acknowledging those who have helped in the creation and production of a book. I am grateful to Prof. Dr. Rajendra B. Patil who had supervised my research work and always encouraged me to generate my own creative thinking. I must express my thanks to Dr. S. Salunkhe, Dr. J.B. Ambekar, Dr. Shrikant and Dr. S.N. Pawar who have shown interest in my work. All of them have a very supportive and co-operative attitude. I am also thankful to the Staff of Shivaji University, Kolhapur, for their cheerful cooperation.

My data collection wouldn't have been possible without the permission and support given by Shri Ashok Kinninge, the Deputy Inspector General (DIG) of Prisons, Mumbai and without the co-operation and unstinting assistance of the authorities of the prison departments and other personnel of the Arthur Road Central Prison, Mumbai. I owe special thanks to all of them. Above all, gratitude is owed to the under-trial female criminals of Arthur Road Central Prison, who confided in me and communicated freely during interviews.

I sincerely acknowledge the help rendered by the Librarians and staff of the libraries of the Tata Institute of Social Sciences, Mumbai; Research Centre on Women's Studies, Juhu Campus, S.N.D.T. Women's University, Mumbai, and the Mumbai University. Thanks are also due to the library staff of L.J.N.J. College, VileParle(E), Mumbai, for their efficient library services.

This study was greatly enriched as a result of the suggestions and creative insights of a number of sociologists. Let me thank in particular Prof. D.N. Dhanagare, Ex-President of 'Indian Sociological Society' and former Vice-Chancellor, Shivaji University, Kolhapur, and Late Prof. S.D. Punalekar, former Director, Centre for Social Studies, Surat for giving me encouragement and very useful advice.

It is my duty to thank my family members for their support, whithout which it would have been impossible to accomplish this task, especially my daughter Shashwati and my husband Shri Ashok Bhosle. I forever remain indebted to my mother, a devoted teacher, Smt. Kamal Sarang who has constantly inspired me in my work. I would also like to express my thanks to all my friends who have encouraged me in writing this book.

I would like to offer my sincere thanks to 'Kalpaz Publications' who not only offered to publish the book but did so in commendably short time.

Finally, I would like to thank the almighty for providing me with the strength to face any difficulties which came my way and to overcome them.

Dr. Smriti Bhosle

1

Crime in India, Female Criminals and Justice Process

1.1 Introduction

Crime is common to all countries and to all societies. Crime presents itself basically as a manifestation of the dysfunctioning of a social system. The fact that social structures and value systems have been changing in most developing countries had a pronounced effect on both, the nature and the composition of crime.

In India, recognizably, the problems are predominantly economic-deep-seated poverty, destitution, high dependency ratio and unemployment. All these lead to lack of social services, illiteracy and ill health. Industrialization, urbanization and migration to other parts and outside the country also contribute substantially to the alienation and anomie and resultant crime. These take place when peasants, traditional, rural and tribal artisans and unemployed youth cluster together in urban slums. Due to the breakdown of primary group relationships the structure of people's lives collapses and thereby delinquent and criminal behaviours increase.

With the increasing urge for materialistic development, consequent industrialization, urbanization and prevailing inequality, changes can be observed in every walk of life with a considerable erosion of certain egalitarian and secular values. Such changes especially in occupational structure, the consequential stress and strain in the network of social relationships, cultural pattern and gradual destruction of traditional ways of life in the wake of industrialization, urbanization and economic recession post industrialization phase often lead to non-conformity or deviance as individuals try to grapple with such disruptions of life. In other words, to cope with such situations People tend to resort to differential unusual means which constitute deviance. The social and economic imbalances, and other related deprivations in the development process give rise to this social pathology which is of major concern. Crime is not just a symptom of the development process but may prove to be an obstacle to its future development.

Contemporary sociological analysis on crime in India is usually based upon certain sociological factors, such as broken homes in rural areas and urban slums, caste rivalries in rural areas, religious fundamentalism in urban areas, and sexual and pathological behaviour patterns of certain category of individuals. Some groups of people do not accept the legal norms of society. They perceive different standards of what is appropriate behaviour and these standards conflict with those of dominant cultures. An individual from a slum learns values such as belief in fate toughness and desire to become "rich". In particular castes and political groups in India, violence and crime are encouraged under certain conditions for self-preservation and the destruction of their opponents.

1.2 Definitions of Terms

1.2.1 Crime

Crime is an acute form of deviance which means digressing from what is considered normal. The legal definition of crime is that, it is behaviour or an activity in violation of the legal code.

Hall Jerome has defined crime as, *"legally forbidden and intentional action which has a harmful impact on social interests, which has a criminal intent, and which has legally - prescribed punishment for it".*[1]

Crime has also been defined in social or non-legal terms. The social definition of crime is that it is behaviour or an activity that offends the social code of a particular community.

Caldwell has explained it as *"an act or a failure to act that is considered to be so detrimental to the well-being of a society, as judged by its prevailing standards, that action against it cannot be entrusted to private initiative or to haphazard methods but must be taken by an organized society in accordance with tested procedures".*[2]

Criminologists have drawn attention to situations in which people who engage in 'criminal' behaviour are either not caught or are acquitted by the courts because of inadequate evidence or legal loopholes or pressures. Taking a reconciliatory position between legal and social definitions of crime, *Reid* has said that, *"legal definition may be used for compiling statistics on crime and for assigning the label 'criminal', but, the studies undertaken for studying causation of crime should include such persons also in the sample of 'criminals' as admit their crime and were not convicted by the court".*[3]

Bonger has classified crimes into four groups on the basis of their motives:*"economic, sexual, political and miscellaneous* (with vengeance as chief motive)'.[4] But it cannot be maintained that all crimes are committed only with one motive. The classification is thus clearly inadequate.

Lemert[5] has classified crimes as situational and systematic. The former are those which are committed because of the pressure of situation while the latter are those which are committed in a planned and systematic way. This classification is important in the treatment of criminals.

1.2.2 A Criminal

Legally speaking, a criminal is one who is convicted by a court for violating the law of the land. A person who is arrested by the police but is let off by the court cannot be designated as a criminal, i.e., technically the term criminal cannot be applied to one who has not been convicted of a crime. However, the law has never specified whether the criminal status of person ends after completing the term of imprisonment imposed upon him, i.e., when the status begins and when it ends. A serious problem thus occurs when society refuses to erase the label of criminal. In practice, a person who is once labeled as a criminal is often not permitted to forget the status.

1.2.3 Female Criminality

Crime and criminal both have become the focus of attention in the present society. Crime is increasing at rapid rate. In India, crime has been considered a male behaviour. But today the former notion is proved wrong. Women, like men, suffer from tensions, frustration, jealousy enmity and hatred, which motivate them to criminality. They indulge in all sorts of crimes. The changing social norms and values as well as the impact of other cultural patterns culminating in the complexity of life are largely responsible for this change.

Female criminality is indeed a serious social problem, it may be considered a crucial problem because of its impact on family, upbringing of children and the overall fabric of society.

As women's roles change and become more open to opportunities and tensions associated with the male-role, their criminal activities will be transformed in kind and degrees.

The predominant factors which are found to determine criminal tendencies in Indian women are economic insecurity, social deprivation and emotional disturbances. Besides, family and domestic quarrels and destitution may also significantly affect the criminality of women. Social environment and deviance are highly relevant to the subject of criminality. Migration from rural areas to urban areas and the inbalance in their adjustment to city life may also result in an increase of crime in cities. It is obvious now that female criminals do not form an isolated group from the normal population.

We have seen the image of women in various media as the preservers of social norms, traditions, customs, morality and family cohesiveness. But today, Westernized Indian culture, industrialization and urbanization have contributed in increasing crime rate among women.

The increasing crime rate among females in recent years has drawn the attention of researchers. An earlier Indian study on criminals has concentrated on male criminality. Within the past few decades, professional interest in female criminality has increased along with interest in the general topic of women.

The present study is a study of women who have been arrested for crime. The term *'undertrial criminal'* is applied to a person whose trial has begun.

1.2.4 Other Terms

In referring to persons arrested and detained in penal custody, but not yet convicted by a criminal court, various terms are found to be in vogue in both literature and practice. Although some of these are used interchangeably, it is important to distinguish between the sub-categories in this usually large group of persons; such a distinction can communicate both the nature of custody, as well as the stage at which the proceedings are:

(1) ***'Suspect'*** is often used for a person detained in police custody (However, a suspect is also said to be 'remanded' to police custody).

(2) **'Remand'** may refer to an individual detained in prison, whose trial is yet to commence.

(3) **Trial/Undertrial/Unconvicted criminal** could include (2) above, but might more appropriately be applied to a person whose trial has begun.

The distinction of primary significance is between convicted and unconvicted criminals. The term *'undertrial criminal'* is being used in the present study-generally to refer to unconvicted persons in prison custody. The term *'undertrial'* rather than unconvicted has been preferred because of its widespread usage in India.

For the purposes of the present study, the term is defined in the following words:

"Any women who violates the law, is reported to the police, gets arrested and prosecuted, shall be included in the category of criminals".

The above definition has been adopted in order to analyze female crime phenomenon in Mumbai. No doubt there is a loophole in the above definition For example, all undertrials may not be convicted and it is not correct to consider them as offenders. Morally too, it is incorrect to consider 'undertrials' as 'offenders'. But there is no choice other than to keep in mind the margin of error and analyze the situation

The Model Prison Manual (1976) defines undertrial as, "a person who has been committed to pending trial or investigation by competent authority".[6]

The Bombay Jail Manual (1935) describes that, undertrial and awaiting trial are synonymous terms and refers to persons committed to prison whilst the charges against them are under judicial investigation.[7]

The problem of undertrials has posed a great challenge to prison administration. Due to the increasing number of unconvicted prisoners the problem of overcrowding in prisons has reached unmanageable proportions. The large number of undertrials contribute to serious problems of congestion in jails due to insufficient space and produces sub-human conditions of living.

Since undertrials are a floating population, there are administrative problems. The government spends much more on undertrials than it spends on covicted prisoners.

The long detainment of undertrials in the prisons is due to the slack procedures of the police in investigation of the cases and filling the charge-sheets, and later of the courts in delaying the trials of the undertrial prisoners.

Custodial function becomes the prime function of prison. Right from the introduction of modern prison system, undertrial prisoners are kept in the prison. We thus see considerable increase in undertrial prisoners. The undertrial prisoners are in the Judicial custody of the Magistrates but are under the control of the executive organization i.e., prison.

The undertrials are detained in the prison and are subjected to general prison discipline. Undertrial prisoners are generally confined in separate yards/wards in district/central prisons. Section 27 of the Prison Act, 1894 provides that criminal prisoners who are not convicted are to be kept apart from convicted criminal prisoners. They are given more concessions than convicted criminal prisoners. They are allowed to supplement their diet from outside, permitted to use their own clothes and not required to do labour. The rules in the 'Maharashtra Prison Manual'[8] make generous provisions to ensure that detention does not hamper the undertrial prisoner in preparing his defence.

The definition of an undertrial for this study is "under trials are persons who are alleged to have committed offences under IPC and detained in prisons, facing a trial in a court of law".

1.3 Crime in India: An Overview

Crime in India during the year 2000

The latest available data of Crime in India 2000[9] is published by National Crime Record Bureau (N.C.R.B.). This is an official publication of the Government of India and it is the source of information and statistics on crime. This annual report covers mainly the crime figures under different heads for various states, followed by an analysis of trends in the past few years. 'Crime in India' reports contain data on rates of crime (volume of crime per 100,000 population).

1.3.1 Characteristics of Crime in India:

(1) The total cognizable crimes in the country have been steadily increasing. It is however keeping pace with the

increase in population, though at varying rates, over the past 50 years. The incidence (No. of cases) increased by 5.5 percent over the decade with a compound growth rate of only 1.0 percent per annum.

(2) The IPC (Indian Penal Code) crimes have reported higher increase to the tune of 10.4 per cent during the decade compared to lower increase in SLL (Special Local Laws) crimes (3.1 per cent).

(3) The 17,71,084 IPC crimes were reported in the country during the year, as against 17,64,629 during 1999 recording marginal increase of 0.4 per cent only. The share of IPC crimes to total cognizable crimes in percentage terms, however, decreased to 34.3 from 35.9 per cent in 1999.

(4) The rate of crime defined as the 'incidence of crime' per lakh (1,00,000) of population is universally taken as a more realistic indicator since it balances the effect of growth in population. The rate of total cognizable crimes in the country during 2000 was 515.7. This crime rate increased marginally by 3.6 per cent over previous year. The crime rate in respect of IPC crimes decreased by 1.2 per cent and SLL crime rate increased by 6.2 per cent during the year.

(5) The IPC crime rate of 176.7, compared to crime rate (194.0) in 1990 recorded a decline of 8.9 per cent. The decadal (1990-2000) variation showed a compound decreasing rate of 1.0 per cent per annum. The crime rate during the year also decreased by 3.0 per cent over the quinquennial average (1995-99) rate of 182.1. Compared to 1999, it is observed that the IPC crime rate at All-India level also decreased by 1.2 percent.

(6) 17.7 laks IPC crimes, 34.0 lakhs SLL crimes reported during the year, 0.4 per cent increase in IPC crimes; 7.9 per cent increase in SLL crimes over 1999.

(7) 3 IPC crimes, 6 SLL crimes reported on an average in 1 minute in the country.

(8) 79.0 per cent IPC cases were investigated and 78.4 per cent of them were charge-sheeted. The 18.3 per cent cases tried, 41.8 per cent of them resulted in conviction.

(9) 30.7 percent of trials completed within 1 to 3 years. 24.2 per cent completed between 3 to 5 years.

Graph 1.1
State-wise Percentage Contribution to Total IPC Crimes During 2000

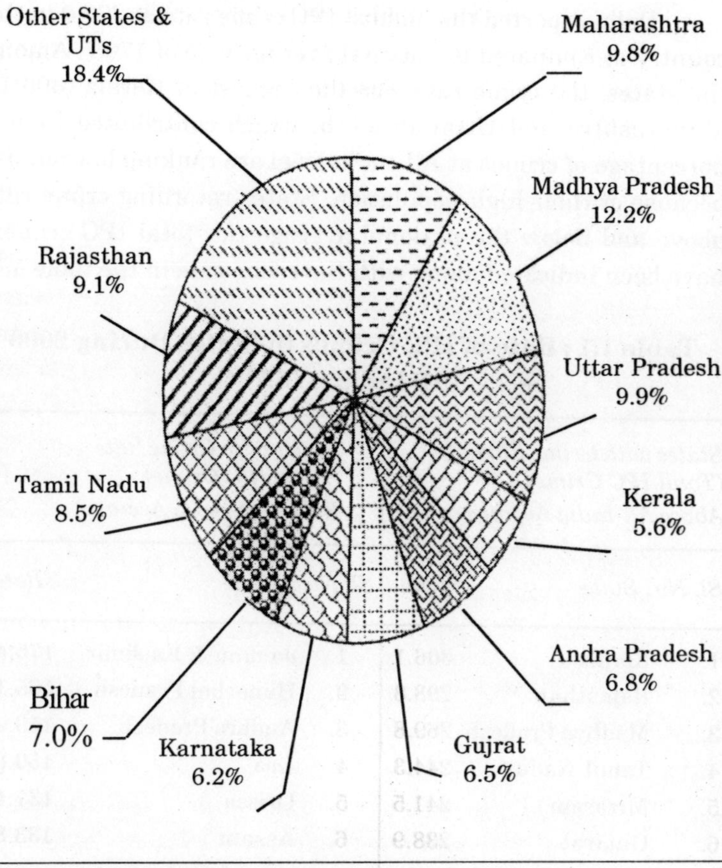

Source: Crime in India, 2000, pg. 34.

(10) Madhya Pradesh reported the highest incidence with 2,16,441 cases, accounting for 12.2 per cent of the total IPC crimes followed by (Uttar Pradesh 9.9 per cent) and Maharashtra (9.8 per cent). These three states together accounted for 22.1 percent of the total cognizable IPC crimes reported in the country during the year.

The state-wise percentage contribution to total IPC crimes during 2000 is shown in the Graph 1.1.

1.3.2 Crimes in States and Union Territories

Delhi reported the highest IPC crime rate at 399.0 in the country as compared to national average rate of 176.7. Among the states, the crime rate was the highest in Kerala (306.1). Maharashtra and Uttar Pradesh, which contributed higher percentage of crimes at All-India level are ranking low mainly because of their high population. States recording crime rate above and below the national average (for total IPC crimes) have been indicated along with the crime rate in the table 1.1.

Table 1.1 : Rate of IPC Crimes in States During 2000 (All India: 176.7)

States with Crime Rate (Total IPC Crimes) Above All-India Average			*States with Crime Rate (Total IPC Crime) Below All-India Average*		
Sl. No.	*State*	*Rate*	*Sl. No.*	*State*	*Rate*
1.	Kerala	306.1	1.	Jammu & Kashmir	175.4
2.	Rajasthan	298.8	2.	Himachal Pradesh	165.1
3.	Madhya Pradesh	269.8	3.	Andhra Pradesh	159.9
4.	Tamil Nadu	244.3	4.	Goa	150.8
5.	Mizoram	241.5	5.	Orissa	137.4
6.	Gujarat	238.9	6.	Assam	133.8

(Contd.)

(Contd. Table 1.1)

States with Crime Rate (Total IPC Crimes) Above All-India Average			*States with Crime Rate (Total IPC Crime) Below All-India Average*		
Sl. No.	*State*	*Rate*	*Sl. No.*	*State*	*Rate*
7.	Karnataka	209.2	7.	Bihar	123.4
8.	Haryana	198.2	8.	Punjab	103.2
9.	Arunachal Pradesh	197.3	9.	Uttar Pradesh	102.4
10.	Maharashtra	189.7	10.	Manipur	101.7
			11.	Tripura	88.6
			12.	West Bengal	83.0
			13.	Nagaland	80.7
			14.	Sikkim	76.9
			15.	Meghalaya	69.4

Source: Crime in India, National Crime Records Bureau, Ministry of Home Affairs, Govt. of India, New Delhi, 2000, p.33.

1.3.4 Crime-wise Analysis

- The highest number of burglary cases (17,245) were reported from Madhya Pradesh followed by Maharashtra (14,930) and Uttar Pradesh (9,569). Together, these three states accounted for 39.5 per cent of the total burglary cases reported in the country during the year. Punjab reported highest increase (30.1 per cent) as compared to previous year.
- The incidence of theft cases also reported a continual declining trend over decade with a decline of 26.8 per cent over 1990, 8.7 per cent over quinquennial average of 1995-99 and 4.9 per cent over the previous year. Though in A & N Islands, the number of theft cases increased from 51 to 89 reported the highest increase of 74.5 per cent in

such cases. The significantly higher rate (149.6) was reported at N.C.T. of Delhi followed by Chandigarh (119.8) against the national average rate of 25.8.

- The states of sikkim (44.3 per cent) and Lakshadweep (22.6 per cent) reported higher decline in the reporting of crimes as compared to previous year. A & N Islands reported (24.7 per cent) increase in the reporting of crimes.
- The incidence of cheating showed a steep rise of 70.4 per cent over the decade 1990-2000, 16.3 per cent increase over the quinquennial average. However, cheating cases remained almost constant when compared with the previous year. the crime rate of cheating was the highest (19.4) in UT of Chandigarh followed by N.C.T. of Delhi 13.8, while it was the lowest at 0.7 in Tripura against the national average of 4.2.
- There was significant increase of counterfeiting cases of 70.7 per cent in cases over previous year at national level. Karnataka reported the highest number of cases 685 and the highest crime rate at 1.3.
- Hurt cases showed continual increasing trend over last 5 years with increase of 6.6 per cent over quinquennial average and 1.8 per cent over previous year. Madhya pradesh recorded the highest incidence (33,080) followed by Andhra Pradesh (29,987). The crime rate as highest 55.4 in Kerala against the national average of 24.0.
- Out of 672 Police Districts in India during 2000,as many as 86 districts registered more than 5,000 cognizable IPC crimes. Of these, 11 Police Districts, viz., Hyderabad, Ahmedabad, Bangalore, Ernakulam, Trivendrum, Bhopal, Indore, Mumbai, Jaipur, Kolkata and Delhi registered more than 10,000 cognizable IPC crimes each. Of the above 11 districts, Mumbai Commissionerate registered the highest IPC cases (29,238) during the year, amongst all the Police districts in India.

1.3.5 Crimes in Mega Cities

The term 'Mega City' refers to cities which have a population of over 10 lakhs as per 1991 census. Based on prescribed standards (population size, male working population engaged in non-agricultural pursuits and density of population), these cities, have been categorized as 'A-Class' and 'B-Class'.

On account of peculiar problems such as unchecked migration, illegal settlements, diverse socio religion-cultural disparities, uneven distribution of incomes, etc., Mega Cities are facing increased criminal activities.

Table 1.2: Classification of Cities

	'A' Class			*'B' Class*	
SI.No.	*City*	*Estimated Mid-year (2000) Population (in lakhs)*	*SI.No.*	*City*	*Estimated Mid-year (2000) Population (in lakhs)*
1.	Ahemdabad	42.8	1.	Bhopal	16.9
2.	Bangluru	57.1	2.	Coimbatore	13.0
3.	Chennai	67.5	3.	Indore	14.6
4.	Delhi	120.6	4.	Jaipur	22.1
5.	Hyderabad	71.5	5.	Kochi	18.3
6.	Kanpur	24.8	6.	Ludhiana	17.3
7.	Kolkata	130.6	7.	Madurai	12.8
8.	Lucknow	26.7	8.	Patna	13.0
9.	Mumbai	187.1	9.	Pune	35.9
10.	Nagpur	20.9	10.	Surat	24.4
			11.	Vadodara	16.6
			12.	Varanasi	13.1
			13.	Visakhapatnam	17.8
Grand Total: Metropolitan Cities: 23			**Population: 985.4 lakhs**		

Source: Crime in India, 2000, p.113.

The population of 23 Mega Cities constitutes only 9.8 per cent of the country's population in contrast to share of 25.7 per cent of urban population in the country's population as per 1991 census. Mega Cities of the country are covering approximately 38.1 per cent of the urban area. The mid-year population of the cities for the year 2000 is cstimated on the basis of their 1991 population.

Incidence of Crimes under the Indian Penal Code (IPC)

A total of 2,55,276 cognizable crimes under the IPC were reported in the 23 mega cities during the year as compared to 2,54,499 crimes during 1999, thereby reporting a negligible increase of only 0.3 per cent, following the state scenario. The crime headwise incidence and the percentage share of each crime in the total crimes is shown through table 1.3.

Table 1.3: Incidence of Crimes under the Indian Penal Code (IPC) and the Percentage Share of Each Crime

Sl. No.	*Crime Head*	*Incidence* 1999	2000	*Percentage Share 2000*	*Percentage Variation in 2000 over 1999*
1.	Murder	2747	2620	1.03	-4.62
2.	Attempt to Commit Murder	2868	2743	1.07	-4.36
3.	C.H. not amounting to Murder	202	196	0.08	-2.97
4.	Rape	1008	1078	0.42	6.94
5.	Kidnapping and Abduction	3046	2935	1.15	-3.64
	(i) Of Women and Girls	1939	1895	0.74	-2.27
	(ii) Of others	1107	1040	0.41	-6.05
6.	Dacoity	461	457	0.18	-0.87

(Contd.)

(Contd. Table 1.3)

Sl. No.	*Crime Head*	*Incidence 1999*	*2000*	*Percentage Share 2000*	*Percentage Variation in 2000 over 1999*
7.	Preparation and Assembly for Dacoity	289	330	0.13	14.19
8.	Robbery	3559	3579	1.40	0.56
9.	Burglary	19199	18738	7.34	-2.40
10.	Theft	77121	73368	28.74	-4.87
	(i) Auto theft	25376	26036	10.20	2.60
	(ii) Other theft	51745	47332	18.54	-8.53
11.	Riots	5253	5507	2.16	4.84
12.	Criminal Breach of Trust	3215	3231	1.27	0.50
13.	Cheating	11885	11422	4.47	-3.90
14.	Counterfeiting	-416	1150	0.45	176.44
15.	Arson	252	251	0.10	-0.40
16.	Hurt	23277	22823	8.94	-1.95
17.	Dowry Deaths	547	512	0.20	-6.40
18.	Molestation	2059	2066	0.81	0.34
19.	Sexual Harassment	1845	1328	0.52	-28.02
20.	Cruelty by Husband or Relatives	4156	4353	1.71	4.74
21.	Importation of Girls	1	33	0.01	3200.00
22.	Other IPC Crimes	91093	96556	37.82	6.00
	Total Cognizable Crime under IPC	**254499**	**255276**	**100.00**	**0.31**

Source: Crime in India, 2000, p.114

It is observed that, percentage variation in 2000 over 1999 was significantly higher in the incidence of crimes, viz. Importation of Girls followed by Counterfeiting, as compared to only one case of the crime under the heading "Importation of Girls" in the year 2000, registering steep jump.

Graph 1.2 Percentage Distribution of IPC Crimes in Mega Cities During 2000

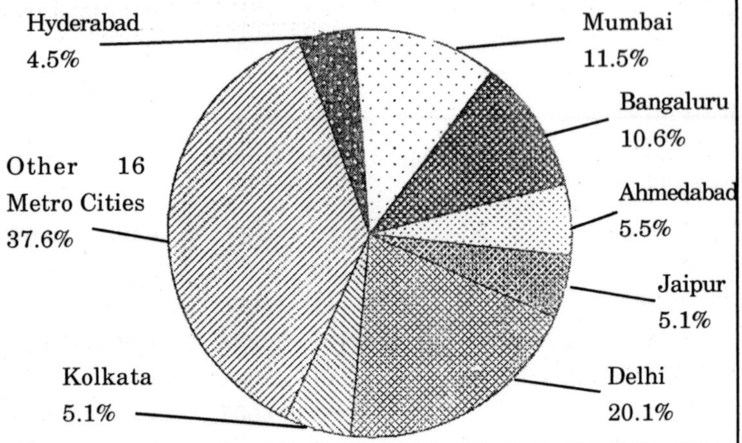

Source: Crime in India, 2000, p.115.

Incidence of Crimes under Special and Local Laws (SLL)

The statistics related to the incidence of crimes under 'Special and Local Laws' (SLL) highlighted that in 23 mega cities, 14,13,500 cases were registered in the year 2000, reporting marginal decline of 1.7 per cent over 1999.

Table 1.4 : Total Crimes under Special and Local Laws (SLL)

Incidence of Total Cognizable Crimes under SLL 1999	*2000*	*Percentage Share 2000*	*Percentage Variation in 2000 over 1999*
14,38,599	14,13,500	100.0	-1.74

Source: Crime in India, 2000, p.120.

Crime in India report indicated that, no case was reported from these 23 cities under 'Terrorist and Disruptive Activities Act' (TADA) and 'Sati Prevention Act' during the year 2000.

The percentage distribution of total cognizable IPC crimes in the 23 mega cities during the year is depicted through the graph (1.2). It is seen that share of crimes reported in Delhi was highest (20.1 per cent) followed by Mumbai (11.5 per cent).

Rate of Crime (IPC)

The rate of crime i.e., incidence of crime per lakh population for cities is based upon estimated mid-year population of cities during the year. The crime rate for IPC as obtained for each city is compared with the corresponding crime rate of the domain state which is depicted through table 1.5.

Table 1.5: Comparative Rate of Crime (IPC) in Cities and States

Sl.No.	*City*	*Rate of Crime (IPC)*	
		City	*Domain State*
1.	Ahmedabad	330.5	238.9
2.	Bangaluru	476.4	209.2
3.	Bhopal	650.1	269.8
4.	Chennai	92.1	244.3
5.	Coimbatore	281.9	244.3
6.	Delhi	425.6	399.0
7.	Hyderabad	162.0	159.9
8.	lndore	735.3	269.8
9.	Jaipur	586.2	298.8
10.	Kanpur	271.0	102.4
11.	Kochi	300.2	306.1
12.	Kolkata	99.4	83.0
13.	Lucknow	280.1	102.4
14.	Ludhiana	94.0	103.2
15.	Madurai	299.5	244.3
16.	Mumbai	156.3	189.7

(Contd.)

(Contd. Table 1.5)

Sl. No.	*City*	*Rate of Crime (IPC)*	
		City	*Domain State*
17.	Nagpur	457.5	189.7
18.	Patna	441. 0	123.4
19.	Pune	248.8	189.7
20.	Surat	161.0	238.9
21.	Vadodara	341.2	238.9
22.	Varanasi	145.9	102.4
23.	Visakhapatnam	189.8	159.9
	Total	**259.1**	**176.2**

Source: Crime in India, 2000, p.115.

From the above table, it is observed that the crime rate in cities was generally higher than the corresponding crime rate of domain state. Only in case of Chennai, Mumbai, Kochi, Ludhiana and Surat, the crime rate was lower than the rate of the respective state. The average crime rate in a city (259.1) was significantly higher than the average crime rate of the country (176.2).

1.3.6 Duration of Trials for IPC Crimes by Various Courts during 2000

It is observed that out of 9,32,774 completed trials at various levels of courts from all the States/UTs, only 3.4 per cent were completed after 10 years of trial, 12.4 per cent between 5 to 10 years, 24.2 per cent between 3 to 5 years, 30.7 per cent within 1 to 3 years, 18.1 per cent between 6 months to a year and 11.2 per cent within 6 months (excluding information for Sikkim state).

1.3.7 Arrests during 2000

A total of 26,75,923 persons were arrested by the Police under various IPC crimes during 2000 against 26,00,876 persons in 1999. Thus, the number of total arrcstees increased by 2.9 per cent during 2000 over 1999.

The state-wise percentage distribution of persons arrested under IPC crimes during 2000 (Graph 1.3). The arrest rate at All India level increased by 1.3 per cent in 2000 from 263.6 to 267.0 over 1999. The percentage of femalės arrested under IPC crimes at All-India level was '5.2.

Table 1.6 provides the sex-wise details on number of persons arrested under different crimes (IPC) in States, UTs and Cities.

Prom table 1.6, it is observed that, Himachal Pradesh (10.9 per cent) followed by Goa (9.5 per cent), Gujarat (8.9 per cent) and Maharashtra (8.7 per cent) recorded comparatively higher share of females in total arrests in the state.

Table 1.6 : Persons Arrested under IPC Crimes during 2000 (State, UT and City-wise and Sex-wise)

Sl.No.	*State / UT / City*	*Total Cognizable Crimes under IPC*			*Percentage of Female to Total*
		Male	*Female*	*Total*	
	States:				
1.	Andhra Pradesh	172922	13385	186307	7.2
2.	Arunachal Pradesh	2774	72	2846	2.5
3.	Assam	49270	1600	50870	3.1
4.	Bihar	228326	9297	237623	3.9
5.	Goa	2766	289	3055	9.5
6.	Gujarat	151689	14830	166519	8.9
7.	Haryana	58580	2596	61176	4.2
8.	Himachal Pradesh	15248	1860	17108	10.9
9.	Jammu & Kashmir	20145	1032	21177	4.9
10.	Karnataka	152278	10724	163002	6.6
11.	Kerala	141018	4872	145890	3.3

(Contd.)

(Contd. Table 1.6)

Sl.No.	State / UT / City	Total Cognizable Crimes under IPC Male	Female	Total	Percentage of Female to Total
	States:				
12.	Madhya Pradesh	328463	4620	333083	1.4
13.	Maharashtra	239611	22957	262568	8.7
14.	Manipur	1156	42	1198	3.5
15.	Meghalaya	1531	17	1548	1.1
16.	Mizoram	4640	126	4766	2.6
17.	Nagaland	1117	42	1159	3.6
18.	Orissa	75382	2824	78206	3.6
19.	Punjab	34045	2640	36685	7.2
20.	Rajasthan	203156	15831	218987	7.2
21.	Sikkim	510	34	544	6.3
22.	Tamil Nadu	208107	14391	222498	6.5
23.	Tripura	4057	161	4218	3.8
24.	Uttar Pradesh	295015	6613	301628	2.2
25.	West Bengal	89093	5161	94254	5.5
	Total (States)	**2480899**	**136016**	**2616915**	**5.2**
Union Territories:					
26.	A & N Islands	817	75	892	8.4
27.	Chandigarh	3489	197	3686	5.3
28.	D & N. Haveli	771	25	796	3.1
29.	Daman & Diu	358	17	375	4.5
30.	Delhi	45592	2531	48123	5.3
31.	Lakshadweep	23	1	24	4.2
32.	Pondicherry	4824	288	5112	5.6
	Total (UTs)	**55874**	**3134**	**59008**	**5.3**
	Total (All-India)	**2536773**	**139150**	**2675923**	**5.2**

(Contd.)

(Contd. Table 1.6)

Sl.No.	*State / UT / City*	*Total Cognizable Crimes under IPC*			*Percentage of Female to Total*
		Male	*Female*	*Total*	
	States:				
33.	Ahmedabad	15074	1307	16381	8.0
34.	Bangalore	12571	1129	13700	8.2
35.	Bhopal	12798	469	13267	3.5
36.	Chennai	5711	305	6016	5.1
37.	Coimbatore	3814	246	4060	6.1
38.	Delhi	40713	2146	42859	5.0
39.	Hyderabad	9235	362	9597	3.8
40.	Indore	10946	481	11427	4.2
41.	Jaipur	12109	837	12946	6.5
42.	Kanpur	8584	499	9083	5.5
43.	Kochi	6620	163	6783	2.4
44.	Kolkata	8354	139	8493	1.6
45.	Lucknow	7150	84	7234	1.2
46.	Ludhiana	2067	140	2207	6.3
47.	Madurai	3930	182	4112	4.4
48.	Mumbai	25535	1579	27114	5.8
49.	Nagpur	9101	292	9393	3.1
50.	Patna	13710	54	13764	0.4
51.	Pune	10545	1332	11877	11.2
52.	Surat	5052	291	5343	5.4
53.	Vadodara	6267	780	7047	11.1
54.	Varanasi	2682	30	2712	1.1
55.	Vishakhapatnam	2867	37	3238	11.5
	Total (Cities)	**235435**	**12318**	**248653**	**5.3**

Source: Crime in India, 2000, p.328.

Table 1.7 : Persons Arrested under SLL Crimes during 2000 (State, UT and City-wise and Sex-wise)

Sl.No.	*State / UT / City*	*Total Cognizable Crimes under IPC*			*Percentage of Female to Total*
		Male	*Female*	*Total*	
	States:				
1.	Andhra Pradesh	503884	9669	513553	1.9
2.	Arunachal Pradesh	34	1	35	2.9
3.	Assam	4074	60	4134	1.5
4.	Bihar	15085	505	15590	3.2
5.	Goa	1925	165	2090	7.9
6.	Gujarat	153964	37019	190983	19.4
7.	Haryana	27969	217	28186	0.8
8.	Hlimachal Pradesh	4189	705	4894	14.4
9.	Jammu & Kashmir	3591	149	3740	4.0
10.	Karnataka	37962	2929	40891	7.2
11.	Kerala	35165	717	35882	2.0
12.	Madhya Pradesh	293967	609	294576	0.2
13.	Maharashtra	204581	23949	228530	10.5
14.	Manipur	1126	81	1207	6.7
15.	Meghalaya	231	4	235	1.7
16.	Mizoram	2382	328	2710	12.1
17.	Nagaland	572	85	657	12.9
18.	Orissa	8248	404	8652	4.7
19.	Punjab	27051	1200	28251	4.2
20.	Rajasthan	37613	835	38448	2.2
21.	Sikkim	6253	36	6289	0.6
22.	Tamil Nadu	552857	91988	644845	14.3
23.	Tripura	110	0	110	0.0
24.	Uttar Pradesh	503497	2676	506173	0.5
25.	West Bengal	1318918	6558	1325476	0.5
	Total (States)	**3745248**	**180889**	**3926137**	**4.6**

(Contd.)

(Contd. Table 1.7)

Sl.No.	State/UT/City	Total Cognizable Crimes under IPC Male	Female	Total	Percentage of Female to Total
	Union Territories:				
26.	A & N Islands	3147	426	3573	11.9
27.	Chandigarh	1069	44	1113	4.0
28.	D & N. Haveli	52	0	52	0.0
29.	Daman & Diu	2	1	3	33.3
30.	Delhi	12689	2015	14704	13.7
31.	Lakshadweep	10	0	10	0.0
32.	Pondicherry	884	106	990	10.7
	Total (UTs)	**17853**	**2592**	**20445**	**12.7**
	Total (All-India)	**3763101**	**183481**	**3946582**	**4.6**
Cities:					
33.	Ahmedabad	16049	1609	17658	9.1
34.	Bangalore	3730	1157	4887	23.7
35.	Bhopal	5174	19	5193	0.4
36.	Chennai	58073	13632	71705	19.0
37.	Coimbatore	3488	296	3784	7.8
38.	Delhi	11683	1953	13636	14.3
39.	Hyderabad	58505	1453	59958	2.4
40.	Indore	5721	31	5752	0.5
41.	Jaipur	2952	85	3037	2.8
42.	Kanpur	28650	99	28749	0.3
43.	Kochi	2085	16	2101	0.8
44.	Kolkata	1296838	3479	1300317	0.3
45.	Lucknow	12578	43	12621	0.3
46.	Ludhiana	1228	33	1261	2.6
47.	Madurai	27878	750	28628	2.6
48.	Mumbai	18041	5322	23363	22.8

(Contd.)

(Contd. Table 1.7)

Sl.No.	State/UT/City	Total Cognizable Crimes under IPC Male	Female	Total	Percentage of Female to Total
Union Territories:					
49.	Nagpur	5544	246	5790	4.2
50.	Patna	660	14	674	2.1
51.	Pune	8696	2831	11527	24.6
52.	Surat	16257	7006	23263	30.1
53.	Vadodara	8374	1263	9637	13.1
54.	Varanasi	8698	40	8738	0.5
55.	Vishakhapatnam	62090	140	62230	0.2
	Total (Cities)	**1662992**	**41517**	**1704509**	**2.4**

Source: Crime in India, 2000, p.342.

Graph 1.3 State-wise Percentage Distribution of Persons Arrested Under IPC Crimes During 2000

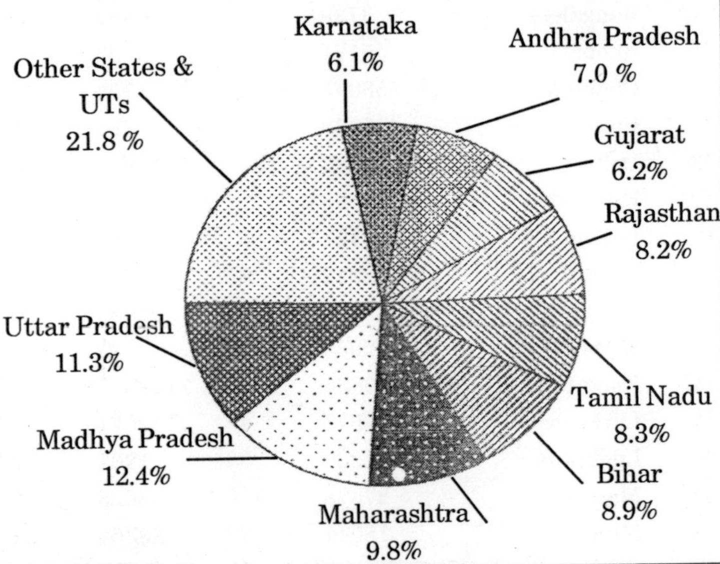

Source: Crime in India, 2000, p.308

The State, UT, City-wise and Sex-wise details of number of persons arrested in various SLL crimes are given in table 1.7. Gujarat (19.4 per cent) and Himachal Pradesh (14.4 per cent) recorded comparatively higher female arrestees percentage than the national average of 4.6 per cent. Maharashtra (10.5 per cent) also recorded higher female arrestees percentage than the national average. It is found necessary to present the account of involvement of females in different crimes in India.

Table 1.8, gives crime head-wise and sex-wise break-up of persons arrested for IPC crimes during the year 2000. The female criminality in the total IPC crimes amounted to 5.2 per cent, which was 3.4 per cent in 1991. Of the total number of persons arrested during the year 2000 under IPC crimes, the significant involvement of women was under the head of Dowry Deaths (21.3 per cent) followed by Cruelty by husband and relatives (20.6 per cent) and Kidnapping and abduction of women and girls (8.8 per cent). On the other hand very negligible number of females were involved in the crimes of preparation and assembly for Dacoity (0.1 per cent), Sexual harassment (0.6 per cent) and Robbery (0.9 per cent). Not a single woman is found involved in the crime of 'Importation of Girls' (0.0 per cent).

Table 1.9, presents sex-wise and crime head-wise information of persons arrested and the percentage of arrestees during 2000. The percentage of females arrested under SLL crimes at All-India level was 4.6 per cent against 5.2 per cent of IPC crimes, Percentage of female criminals arrested under SLL crimes in 1991 was 4.2 per cent. The percentage of female criminals under the Immoral Traffic (Prevention) Act (87.2 per cent) and Indecent representation of women (prevention) act (82.3 per cent) is found to be a significant involvement. As against this merely 0.1 per cent females were arrested under Arms Act and also under Gambling Act. The above table shows zero per cent involvement of women in Terrorist and Disruptive Activities Act (TADA) and Antiquity and Art Treasurers Act.

To conclude, in a country like India with a population above one billion and extreme level of poverty, one would expect

Table 1.8 : Persons Arrested under IPC Crimes during 2000 (Crime Head-wise and Sex-wise)

Sl. No.	Crime Heads	Male	Female	Total	Percentage to Total Male	Percentage to Total Female
1.	Murder	74390	3788	78178	95.2	4.8
2.	Attempt to commit Murder	72077	2836	74913	96.2	3.8
3.	C.H. not amounting Murder	6692	171	6863	97.5	2.5
4.	Rape	19980	320	20300	98.4	1.6
5.	Kidnapping and Abduction	27308	2014	29322	93.1	6.9
	(i) Of Women and Girls	15638	1507	17145	91.2	8.8
	(ii) Of Others	11670	507	12177	95.8	4.2
6.	Dacoity	22758	118	22876	99.5	0.5
7.	Preparation and Assembly for Dacoity	6840	4	6844	99.9	0.1
8.	Robbery	28718	248	28966	99.1	0.9
9.	Burglary	66610	1355	67965	98.0	2.0
10.	Theft	162793	4074	166867	97.6	2.4
	(i) Auto Theft	24805	168	24973	99.3	0.7
	(ii) Other Theft	137988	3906	141894	97.2	2.8
11.	Riots	409340	21253	430593	95.1	4.9
12.	Criminal Breach of Trust	14218	330	14548	97.7	2.3
13.	Cheating	37447	1543	38990	96.0	4.0
14.	Counterfeiting	2111	25	2136	98.8	1.2
15.	Arson	14420	258	14678	98.2	1.8
16.	Hurt	432062	23270	455332	94.9	5.1

(Contd.)

(Contd. Table 1.8)

Sl. No.	*Crime Heads*	*Male*	*Female*	*Total*	*Percentage to Total Male*	*Percentage to Total Female*
17.	Dowry Deaths	14532	3923	18455	78.7	21.3
18.	Molestation	41281	453	41734	98.9	1.1
19.	Sexual Harasment	13586	76	13662	99.4	0.6
20.	Cruelty by Husband and Relatives	83794	21753	105547	79.4	20.6
21.	Importation of qirls	156	0	156	100.0	0.0
22.	Other IPC Crimes	985660	51338	1036998	95.0	5.0
Total Cognizable Crimes under IPC		**2536773**	**139150**	**2675923**	**94.8**	**5.2**

Source: *Crime in India, 2000, p.315.*

Table 1.9 : Persons Arrested under SLL Crimes during 2000 (Crime Head-wise and Sex-wise)

Sl. No.	*Crime Heads*	*Male*	*Female*	*Total*	*Percentage to Total Male*	*Percentage to Total Female*
1.	Arms Act	64875	55	64930	99.9	0.1
2.	Narcotic Drugs and Psychotropic SubstancesAct	23864	1262	25126	95.0	5.0
3.	Gambling Act	301657	229	301886	99.9	0.1
4.	Excise Act	122430	5481	127911	95.7	4.3
5.	Prohibition Act	425060	111319	536379	79.2	20.8
6.	Explosive and Explosive Substances Act	6161	16	6177	99.7	0.3

(Contd.)

(Contd. Table 1.9)

Sl. No.	Crime Heads	Male	Female	Total	Percentage to Total Male	Percentage to Total Female
7.	Immoral Traffic (P) Act	1782	12088	13870	12.8	87.2
8.	Indian Railways Act	52534	2982	55516	94.6	5.4
9.	Registration of Foreigners Act	2226	415	2641	84.3	15.7
10.	Protection of Civil Rights Act	1178	82	1260	93.5	6.5
11.	Indian Passport Act	585	45	630	92.9	7.1
12.	Essential Commodities Act	6466	27	6493	99.6	0.4
13.	Terrorist and Disrup -tive Activities Act	43	0	43	100.0	
14.	Antiquity and Art Treasurers Act	48	0	48	100.0	
15.	Dowry Prohibition Act	5519	1192	6711	82.2	17.8
16.	Child Marriage Restraint Act	235	97	332	70.8	29.2
17.	Indecent Representa -tion of Women (P) Act	421	1952	2373	17.7	82.3
18.	Copyrights Act	3673	15	3688	99.6	0.4
19.	Sati Prevention Act	0	0	0	-	3.1
20.	SC/ST (Prevention of Atrocities) Act	25933	840	26773	96.9	
21.	Forest Act	9546	44	9590	99.5	0.5
22.	Other SLL Crimes	2708865	45340	2754205	98.4	1.6
	Total Cognizable Crimes under SLL.	**3763101**	**183481**	**3946582**	**95.4**	**4.6**

Source: Crime in India, 2000, p. 330.

more crimes than what the statistics indicate. Despite the tremendous increase in population, the crime rate in India has not increased very much.

1.4 Facilities Available for the Undertrial Prisoners

In general the accused should be produced before a magistrate by the police within 24 hours from the time of her arrest excluding the traveling time. At this time, the accused is said to be in under police custody. If the police require the accused for further investigation, the magistrate can pass orders accordingly. If the police have completed their investigation then the magistrate can remand the accused to judicial or prison custody and is given a court date. If the accused is able to get out on bail then she must appear in court for her trial on the given date. But if the accused is not able to get out on bail she is detained in prison.

As an undertrial there are certain facilities available for her in prison. According to the Maharashtra Prison Manual, the facilities are as follows:

(a) In every prison, in which women are confined there shall be one or more women jailors and/or matrons, who shall maintain discipline in the women's section of the prison. No woman undertrial shall be removed from the women's section except with the special permission of the superintendent and for the purpose of being taken to court, interviews, release or transfer.

(b) No male officers, including Superintendent and Deputy Superintendent shall on any pretext enter the women's section without the women Jailor or Matron, and the two shall not separate whilst in the section.

(c) A register shall be maintained at the gate of the women's prison or women's section of a prison. Whenever any woman undertrial is taken out, an entry shall be made in the register. Whenever any visitor enters the section, an entry indicating name of the visitor, day and time of such visit shall also be made in the register.

(d) Undertrial prisoners should be admitted during usual working hours of the prison. On admission they shall be examined by the medical officer for marks of violence, birthmarks, etc. And a printed card should be sent to the undertrial's family giving information about the inmate's institutional number and address, brief summary of rules regarding interviews, letters, etc.

(e) It is the duty of every prison officer to find out whether an undertrial prisoner has been previously convicted and such information should be immediately forwarded to the concerned Superintendent of Police for necessary action.

(f) When an undertrial prisoner has been notified by the trying magistrate or the police as an approver or a confessing accused, she should be kept separate from others concerned in the same case.

(g) Children of women undertrials may be admitted if suitable arrangements for their care cannot be easily made outside.

(h) Private clothing to meet reasonable requirements should be allowed to undertrial prisoners. An undertrial prisoner who has no sufficient clothing of her own may be provided with the same at government cost.

(i) Food from outside may be allowed. Prisoners allowed to receive outside food, shall not be given prison food. Undertrial prisoners should not be allowed to cook their food separately in the institution.

(j) Four letters per calendar month, two at her cost, and two at government cost, shall be allowed to be written by an undertrial prisoner. There shall be no limit on the number of incoming letters to prisoners.

(k) One interview per calendar week with family members or relatives or close friends or lawyers may be allowed.

(l) No newspapers shall be supplied to undertrials at government cost.

(m) Unless she so desires, no undertrial prisoner shall be allotted any work except that it shall be her duty to keep her bedding, clothing and yard clean.

(n) An undertrial prisoner may make purchases from the canteen as per canteen rules.

(o) Women undertrial prisoners should normally be escorted by women police. Separate conveyance should be provided for the transport of women undertrial prisoners.

(p) Every Superintendent of a Prison shall, on the first day of each month, submit to the sessions Judge or the Chief Presidency Magistrate a statement of cases of all undertrial prisoners pending for more than three months in the court of the Judicial Magistrate.

(q) Undertrial women prisoners accused of the offence of traveling ticketless released on bail should be paid traveling allowance if the Superintendent considers that it is necessary to do so in the interest of the released woman prisoner.

As far as possible women undertrial prisoners should be handed over to their relatives after release. If this is not possible a woman police or woman prison guard should escort the released woman undertrial prisoners to the nearest station or bus stand.

Children of the Women Undertrial

Women undertrial having children below 4 years of the age can keep the children along with them in the prison, while children above 4 years of age for whom no arrangements can be made outside, are placed in Children's Homes.

For the children, milk, banana and rice is provided. Medical facilities are also extended to them. But there are no educational or recreational facilities for these children.

1.5 Criminal Justice Process

The criminal Justice Process is the entire system of criminal prevention, detection, apprehension, adjudication and punishment. It includes all those agencies such as the police, correctional institutes, courts and legislatures that are responsible for enforcing crimininal laws.

The right to life and liberty guaranteed in the constitution is the primary source of criminal law. This right is then translated into 'Indian Penal Code', 'Criminal Procedure Code and Evidence Act' and also in Local and Special Laws (non-code legislation). The Directive principles of state policy set down the responsibility of the state to provide for free legal aid where required (for reasons of economic or other disabilities). This is to ensure equal justice for all citizens and to further the guarantee of equality before the law, as provided in Article 14 of the Constitution. There are also departmental rules, special manuals and standing orders to guide the functioning of the courts, as well as the police, prisons and social welfare departments. Relevant court decisions, too, are integrated into these regulations, as they identify gaps in the system - situations not specifically defined for whatever reason.

The criminal justice process, is being viewed under the following stages:

1.5.1 The Police System

N.C. Pal has stated that the 'Police is the first agency for the administration of criminal justice and is considered to be the first line of defense against-crime'.[9] The law relating to the sphere of police work in India has remained unamended even after independence. Modern Police System in India was established by the British Government. The Indian Police Act, 1861 provided for a uniform system of police force in India. The powers and functions are derived from this statute. Besides power of arrest, search, seizure and investigation of offences have been conferred on the police by the code of criminal procedure. The Police Act has continued to regulate the functions of the police. The Criminal Procedure Code, 1898, which had undergone minor changes from time to time was later repealed and replaced by the code of criminal procedure 1973.

1.5.2 The Alleged Offence

The criminal justice process, in the case of a cognizable offence, may be set into motion either on the complaint of an aggrieved individual, or citizen (as witness), or by the police itself on receipt of information. In the case of non-cognizable offences, which are generally viewed as disputes of a civil nature (for instance, family or neighborhood quarrels), the police cannot act unless a formal accusation has been lodged with them.

In short, offences are divided under the Criminal Procedure Code into two categories: Cognizable and Non-Cognizable. A cognizable offence is one for which any police officer may arrest without a warrant. When he does not have that power under the law, the offence is non-cognizable. Cognizable offences are more serious and more severely punished. As the accused may try to do away with the evidence of the crime or hide himself, the police officer is empowered to arrest without a warrant and investigate without seeking the court's permission, considering the time factor involved and non-coonizable offences are minor offences. So the person hurt has to move the court by lodging a complaint.

1.5.3 Arrest

Arrest is the act of taking a person into custody in order to make a criminal charge against the person. The arrested person must be informed of the ground of his arrest, his right to bail and to engage a counsel/lawyer. But some officers are not conscious of their duty and they do not inform the accused of the grounds of her arrest. They usually assume that the accused is aware of such rights.

A person arrested without a warrant cannot be detained for more than 24 hours from the time of his arrest exclusive of traveling time from the police station to the court. Usually investigation cannot be completed within 24 hours, so the magistrate may authorize detention of the accused in police custody for not more than 15 days. This is known as remand.

1.5.4 Police Custody

When the police decide to take a suspect into custody to pursue further inquiry or prevent the commission of further violation. It is known as arrest or police custody. This can be done under judicial sanction with warrant or without warrant.

The police may identify possible suspects on the basis of evidence or suspicion. In order to pursue the inquiry or to prevent the commission of further violation, the police may decide to take a suspect into custody (that is arrest him or her). Ordinarily judicial sanction is required for an arrest, in the form of a warrant. However, arrest without warrant is also permissible in certain cases. This is rationalized on the grounds that quick action is necessary to prevent a suspect from escaping, tampering with evidence, or committing another offence.

Police custody is not free from fear and anxiety. Offenders always remain in constant fear of possible torture and abuse. The first offenders also face mental and emotional shock and damage to their reputation. The offenders during police custody have to face accommodation, diet and other difficulties.

The offender's first encounter with the criminal justice process is in a police lock- up where he is temporarily confined before being produced before a magistrate or on remand of police custody.

Once an arrest has been affected and remand taken, the suspect is detained in the police lock-up, so as to be available to the police for its investigation. If the offence is bailable, the suspect can make arrangements for bail through persons related or otherwise known, or lawyers. But if the offence is non-bailable and bail is rejected by the court, or cannot be arranged for by the prisoner, the latter continues to remain in custody (but may ask for a transfer to prison as an undertrial).

1.5.5 Police Investigation

Under Chapter XII of the Criminal Procedure Code, the police has a statutory right to carry on investigation.

Investigation generally through interviews and Interrogation is most important in criminal trial. The scientific investigation can help in arriving at correct conclusions. Investigation of an offence is the field exclusively of the police department. The police has the bounden duty to investigate and it is their duty to collect the evidence for the purpose of providing the evidence. These statutory rights and duties of the police cannot be interfered with by any magistrate nor is any sanction required from a magistrate to investigate into a cognizable offence.

1.5.6 Filling the Charge-sheet

Information relating to the commission of a cognizable offence which is given orally must be written down by a police officer. This is known as the 'First Information Report' (FIR) and it must be signed by the informant and must be entered in a prescribed book by the officer. When a police officer has completed investigation, he must make an official report to the magistrate. The completed report is known as charge-sheet. A charge-sheet consists of the police reports, the first information report and all documents relating to the offences and confessions and statements of witnesses, etc. A copy of the charge-sheet is also given to the accused. Once the charge-sheet is submitted the power of the police to investigate comes to an end. The police cannot now interfere with the investigation of the magistrate court. But according to a new provision in the Criminal Procedure Code i.e., Section 173(8), even after submission of the charge-sheet, a police officer may make further investigation in respect of an offence and send to the magistrate any further reports regarding any additional evidence obtained by him.

1.5.7 Prosecution

This process starts when the state begins the formal process of inquiry and detection of crime in a criminal case. Action is taken by a prosecuting attorney, government official whose duty is to initiate and maintain criminal proceedings on bebalf of the government against persons accused of committing crimes.

1.5.8 Prison Custody

When the police no longer require the individual for the purposes of investigation, he/she is given prison custody.

As mentioned earlier, if a prisoner in police custody is not released on bail, he or she may request a transfer to prison custody. This may occur even otherwise, when the police no longer require the individual for the purposes of investigation. While in prison, the undertrial continues to be remanded and produced in court on the next date given. This process of giving remands may go on for weeks or months before the hearing actually starts.

1.5.9 Detention

Detention in prison between arrest and trial, either because the judge has refused bail or the defendant cannot meet the requirements of bail. Generally the purpose is to assure the presence of the accused at trial.

1.5.10 Court

Legal aid is the right of the suspect and free legal services are the constitutional right of every accused person who is unable to engage a lawyer and secure 1egal services on account of reasons such as poverty or some other reason. State has to provide a lawyer to an accused person if the circumstances of the case and the needs of justice so require.

1.5.11 Trial

From now on, the role of the court begins. The criminal court is the core of the criminal justice process. It has the duty to supervise the work of the police, prosecutor and defence counsel and implement the laws. A trial is a court proceeding during, which the judge listens to the evidence as presented by the defence and the prosecution, and determines whether the defendant or accused is guilty beyond a reasonable doubt or not. On completion of investigation, the police must file charges in court. The charge-sheet becomes the basis of the trial.

A fair trial implies a speedy trial. Speedy trial is the essence of the criminal justice. However, there is no specific criterion of promptness. The Indian Constitution does not specifically guarantee to the accused the right to a speedy trial. But Article 21 along with Articles 14,38, 39 and 39-A make it a necessary concomitant of social justice promised in the preamble. Right to speedy trial is also recognized in Article 3(i) of the Universal Declaration of Human Rights. It says that arrest and detention constitute restrictions on the right of personal freedom.

1.5.12 Appeal

An accused person may apply to a higher court for release on bail, or modification of bail conditions stipulated by the police or lower court. He or she may also appeal against the decision of the trial court. In the case of a death sentence, the final appeal for mercy lies with the President of India.

1.5.13 Bail

Money or property posted by the defendant after arrest and before trial to guarantee that he or she will appear for trial, sentencing or imprisonment. If the defendant does not appear, the money cr property is forfeited to the state. Liberty is a most valuable right and when the accused applies for bail, he seeks this right from the court. In offences which are specified in the code of bailable, bail is a matter of right. And if the offence is specified as non-bailable, bail is a matter of discretion. Bail may be granted by the court or by the officer-in-charge of a police station. If the person fails to appear in court on the given date or tampers with the evidence witnesses then the bail order can be revoked and he will be arrested and imprisoned.

1.5.14 Police Escort

While in custody, a prisoner is taken from one place to another for various reasons, for instance, from lockup to court or hospital and back. All these visits must necessarily be under police escort, even when the person is transferred to prison as an undertrial. Women constables are required to be present for escorting women prisoners to court.

1.5. Legal Aid

Legal aid is crucial for a suspect and each individual has the right to obtain it. The Supreme Court has even held that free legal services are the "constitutional right of every accused person who is unable to engage a lawyer and secure legal services on account of reasons such as poverty, indigence or incommunicable situation and the state is under a mandate to provide a lawyer to an accused person if the circumstances of the case and the needs of justice so require". It is also important to note here that legal aid is urgent for the suspect from the moment of detention, and not only during the trial.

In short, the complexities of substantive and procedural laws require a specialized mediator - lawyer. Menon has stated that, *"the legal process is quite cumbersome and presents a financial liability to the accused particularly when he is poor and illiterate"*.[10] If the right to counsel is essential to fair trial, it is important that the accused has the necessary means for his defence. So Section 304 of the Criminal Procedure Code deals with legal aid to the accused at the expense of the state.

1.6 Legal Provisions For Women Prisoners

Specific legal and administrative provisions exist with respect to women suspects and prisoners. These provisions are intended to provide directions to the police, courts and prison authorities in the handling of this group of women prisoners.

1.6.1 Prison Act, 1894

(1) Section 24(3) provides that in the case of female prisoners, the search and examination (on admission) shall be carried out by the matron under the general or special orders of the Medical Officer.

(2) Section 27(1) provides that in a prison containing female as well as male prisoners, the females shall be imprisoned in separate buildings, or separate parts rof the same building, in such manner as to prevent their seeing, or conversing or holding any intercourse with male prisoners.

(3) Section 46 states that no female shall be liable to the imposition of any form of handcuffs or letters, or to whipping, as punishment for prison offences.

1.6.2 Criminal Manual Issued by the High Court of Bombay, 1960

Women accused of any offence if arrested soon after childbirth, cannot be at once taken before the magistrate as this may cause personal suffering and risk to health. They should not ordinarily, be removed until they are in a proper condition to travel. In such cases, sanction must be obtained by the police from the nearest magistrate for their detention at their homes. or in the dispensary beyond a period of 24 hours allowed by Section 61 of the Criminal Procedure Code.

1.6.3 Criminal Procedure Code. 1973

(1) Sections 51(2) and 100(3) make it obligatory that a woman should be searched by woman, and with strict regard to decency.

(2) Section 160(1) Criminal Procedure Code prohibits the police from requiring any woman to appear at any place other than the place of her residence for the purpose of examination by police.

(3) Section 53(2) states that the meclical examination of a female accused should be conducted only by or under the supervision of a woman medical practitioner.

(4) Section 437 provides that in the case of a non-bailable offence, a court (not being the sessions or high court) may direct a woman accused to be released on bail.

(5) Section 360(1) provides that a woman of any age, if convicted of an offence (not punishable with death or imprisonment for life), and with no previous conviction, may be released on probation for good conduct instead of serving the sentence (in contrast, a man would have to be below 21 years of age to obtain this benefit; or, if over 21 years, to be convicted of an offence punishable with fine only or with imprisonment for seven years or less).

(6) Section 416 enacts that if a woman sentenced to death is found to be pregnant, the High Court shall order the execution of the sentence to be postponed and may, if it thinks fit, commute the sentence to imprisonment for life.

1.6.4 Maharashtra Prison Manual, 1979

This has a separate chapter dealing with women prisoners. References to women are also found in other chapters. While it is not feasible to transcribe all these provisions here, the subjects covered are as follows: search, segregation, clothing, ornaments, facilities in barracks, pregnancy, childbirth, care of children of women prisoners, medical aid, interviews, limits of cellular confinement for women, educational and vocational training, release, women staff and their duties.

These provisions refer on the whole, to convicted female prisoners, but would be applicable to undertrials confined in the women's section. Where undertrials are specially mentioned, the regulations are generally inclusive of both men and women -contrasting the treatment of undertrials with that of convicts.

References

1. Hall Jerome. "General Principles of Criminal Law", pp. 8-18.
2. Caldwell, R.G. "Criminology", p.114.
3. Reid, Sue Titus. "Crime and Criminology", p.5.
4. Bonger. "Criminality and Economic Conditions", pp. 36-37.
5. Lemert. "Social problems", pp. 141-49.
6. The Model Prison Manual, 1976.
7. The Bombay jail Manual, 1935.
8. Maharashtra Prison Manual, 1979.
9. Crime in India, National Crime Record Bureau, 2000.
10. Menon, N.R.M. "Legal Aid in the Criminal Proceedings", Soci al Defence, Vol. XIII, No. 50, p. 16.

2

Female Crime: A Theoretical Perspective

2.1 Introduction

Theories about crime have been propounded from time to time. Many writers have explained the deviant behaviour of a person. We have writers of the biological school, the psychological school as well as of the sociological school. Writers of the biological school explain deviant behaviour in terms of inherited traits- physical and mental. According to the psychoanalytical school, deviance is not problematical because this theory starts with the postulate about human nature according to which the tendency to deviance is 'given'. But sociologists look at it as problematical and as a tendency that is not given but learned. They explain deviant behaviour as the function of social environment and as one which is learned through group associations. We shall consider in this chapter major theoretical explanations of criminal behaviour.

2.2 Lombroso And Ferrero

Lombroso postulated a biological theory of crime. Cesare Lombroso and William Ferrero wrote 'The Female Offender'. It gives us an account of their much debated analysis about 'female criminality'.

Lombroso and Ferrero[1] applied the thesis that crime was biologically predisposed and recognizable by physical stigmata to female criminality. The criminal was a primitive breed, recognizable by physical, atavistic qualities. Women were, on the whole less inclined to criminality because of constitutional and psychological factors. Women, in Lombroso's scheme of things, are less likely to be born a criminal type and are more likely to display the characteristics of an occasional criminal. This type only committed crime under the influence of a male or in a situation of extreme temptation - but most of such female criminals are not entirely deficient in the moral sense. The small majority of female criminals whom Lombroso described as "born criminal" type tended to display greater criminal propensities and perversities from the psychological and behavioural standpoint than the male born criminal type. In this sense, when a woman is bad or worse, she is really worse or more perverse than man. The criminal woman, said Lombroso, is a monster who surpasses man when she wants to be wicked, cruel or diabolical. As criminal, she is an exception among criminals and her perversity knows no bounds.

More critiques have been written on Lombroso than on any other theorist in the field. The criticism, as Pollak[2] said focuses on two main categories: inadequacies in his methodology; and his general theoretical assumptions. His study of female criminals was based on a small sample of incarcerated female offenders. His theory that a Woman criminal was more terrible than a male was only a reflection of the common stereotype of women. When a murderess was described as more depraved than a murderer, it was because she had deviated from the norms of female behaviour. Traditional norms and attitudes about how a woman should behave influenced Lombroso to impose artificial double standards for men and women.

Bowker observed that, "Lombroso unfortunately utilized unrepresentative samples of incarcerated female offenders who had often suffered long periods of confinement under terrible conditions, and who, therefore, showed signs of physical deterioration that were partially the result of the criminal justice system "treatment" rather than the cause of criminality"[3]. Lombroso also focused too much on exceptionally severe cases, again generalizing inappropriately to criminals as a whole. These errors were compounded when he accepted the current sexist stereotypes of womanhood as true and interpreted female criminality in that light.

Lombroso's work on female criminality has served to create an ideological framework in which later, more contemporary studies have developed variations on the belief in biological determinism, on the sexist beliefs in the inferiority of women; and an implicit support of double standards of morality, coupled with the failure to take into account of the socio-economic, political and legal context in which crime occurs, all appear in later works on female criminality.

2.3 W.I. Thomas

Thomas's most important work in regard to female criminality is 'The Unadjusted Girl'. Thomas[4] lays emphasis on individualistic, psycho-physiological and socio-cultural approach. However, he failed to consider the secondary and low social status of women.

Thomas deals with female delinquency as a normal response under certairn social conditions, using assumptions about the nature of women. He rejects economic causes as a possibility at all, denying its importance in criminal activity.

Thomas offered an explanation for delinquency on part of young females which characterizes them engaging in departures from lines of conduct that are biologically and psychologically normal for women. Every human, he believed, has certain basic desires. The desire for new experience and the desire for response influenced criminality. A woman enters prostitution to satisfy a desire for excitement and response. For a woman, prostitution is, in one form or another, a means to satisfy these needs. Thomas did not altogether ignore environmental factors.

Pollak[5] criticizes Thomas for liberal paternalism. It was argued that his theories were sexist in that females were identified as offenders through sexual behaviour. The criticism related to some of the unproved assumptions, such as the maternal instinct and the female's greater need for response. Thomas did make several important observations such as that crime was one representation of the same creative drives that produced legitimate innovations.

Thomas's theory was primarily a pseudo-psychological justification for continuing rehabilitative methods to treat offenders and make only minor changes in the structure of society. The works of Thomas, said Carol Smart[6] still herald the development of a liberal tradition in criminology. This liberalism, she said, rests upon the individualization of social problems and ultimately on methods of individual treatment and cure. She further observed that this liberalism carries over from Lombroso's work in the sense that like Lombroso, Thomas too believes that criminality or deviance is pathology. But Thomas differed with Lombroso when he preferred to treat it as a biological abnormality. His work on delinquent girls incorporates the familiar nature-nurture debate, in which nature is viewed as a supportive of environmental factors. Thomas believed that women had varieties of love in their nervous system and consequently their desire for response is more intense than that of men. Thomas argued that the inherent maternal instinct in women, buttressed by the intense need to give and feel love, leads women to crime, particularly of a sexual nature, including prostitution. Refering to the treatment of offenders, Thomas finally suggested that they be treated as unsocialized, as not fully adapted to social issues of society which represent their interest, and ultimately as being sick rather than inherently evil or rationally opposed to the dominant values of society.

2.4 Otto Pollak

In his book 'The Criminality of Women', Pollak[7] has challenged the so-called disproportion between male and female criminality. He claimed that women engage in hidden crimes like abortions, murders by poisoning, offences against children, etc., because of their greater skill at deceit and cunning behaviour acquired through sexual socialization. Besides the superstitious and cunning nature of women acquired through differential socialization process, Pollak also suggested that biological factors including lesser physical strength, as well as psychological concomitants of menstruation, pregnancy, etc. enter into the etiology of female crime.

Pollak's major concern was the "masked" character of female criminality. This masked character is achieved in three ways: *firstly*, female criminality is concealed by the under-reporting of offences committed by women; *secondly,* by the lower detection rates of female offenders compared to male offenders; and *thirdly*, by the greater leniency shown to women by police and courts. Keeping in mind the masked character of female crime, Pollak advanced the theory of the "hidden" female criminal to account for what he considered unreasonably low official crime rates for women. A major reason for the existence of hidden crime, as he sees it, lies in the nature of women. Women are instigators rather than perpetrators of criminal activity. He believed that if the amount of hidden crime is added, the female figures would surpass the figures for males. He believed that law enforcement officers as well as judges are much more lenient towards women than towards men which is why the official statistics and records of female criminality do not reflect the real number of crimes committed by women. The masked character of female criminals, Pollak observed, results in gross under-reporting and bolsters the official belief that females are a very low risk for crime. Generalizing on the basis of arrest data on female crime, he maintained that women offenders have lesser chance to be reported to be arrested, to be convicted and to be committed than men.

Carol Smart[8] believes that, Pollak's theory is heavily influenced by Freudian analysis and therefore is subject to the same criticism that has been raised against the Freudian theory. The 'sexual passivity' in females, said Smart, has no proof and is poorly chosen for use in a casual theory. The criticism of Pollak's views on female criminality revolves round the fact that he made no substantial departure from the Lombroso tradition and displayed a kind of common-sensical approach to the study of female crime. With all his limitations, we should not forget that the history of female criminological theories cannot be completed without a mention of Pollak's contribution.

2.5 An Overview

The theories on female criminality, as Pollak[9] rightly said, are generally contaminated by popular stereotypes and myths regarding women. Both classical and contemporary criminologists have failed to dismantle the sexist notions and common sense perceptions about women in general and female offenders in particular. The shared proposition of all these scholars is that female crime is the result of physiological or psychological characteristics of individuals. They have not given any importance to socio-cultural factors but have viewed the biological characteristics as pathological distortions or departures from the normal inherent nature of women. Obviously the assumptions in all these explanations about biological and psychological traits of 'normal' and criminal women are questionable.

Thus it is clear that the theoretical basis of female criminality still depends on biological determination and foundation. However, at the same time, classical theories of female criminality are not only pioneering theories but also are relevant today,

After the analysis of the viewpoints of the scholars of past decades, we can now turn to the major important theories which explain the causes of female criminality which are as follows.

2.6 Theory of Anomie

American sociologist Robert Merton, borrowed ideas from the French Sociologist Emile Durkheim.[10] Durkheim defines crime as acts which *"offend strong and definite states of the collective conscience"*. Crime for him is a social fact. It is normal and universal in its varying forms, in all cultures and societies, at all stages of their development. A certain amount of crime is inevitable, normal and healthy in *any* society. Crime is inevitable because not every member of society can be equally commited to the collective sentiments, the shared values and ethics of society. Since individuals in society are exposed to various influences, it is impossible for all to be alike. Durkheim further argues that crime is not only inevitable, it can also be functional. Social change begins with some form of deviance and society itself generates deviance for its own well-being. Repressing criminal behaviour completely is not desirable, for that would create a situation that is inimical to innovation and social change.

Robert Merton[11] borrowed ideas from Emile Durkheim. According to Merton, criminality is caused by pressure or tension. The source of this tension is stimulated aspirations to achieve certain goals coupled with obstacles to their achievement. Frustrated individuals turn to crime either to release this tension or to achieve their goals via illegitimate avenues. Merton used the word 'Anomie'. To Merton, anomie was not a state of normlessness which precipitated anti-social behaviour, but the condition experienced by individuals taught to want the goals of their culture but denied access to them.

Merton distinguished between social and cultural structures. Cultural structures refer to goals and interests men pursue, while social structures refer to means or approved methods which regulate and control the pursuit of goals and interests. The cultural system of society enjoins all men to strive for goals by means of normatively approved forms of behaviour. However, opportunities to reach these goals through socially approved means are unequally distributed. Deviant behaviour occurs when social structure restricts or completely closes a person's access to the approved models of reching these goals. Some social structures exert a definite pressure on some persons to engage in non-conformist rather than conformist conduct.

This theory has been criticized by Cohen Clinard and Lemert. Their main arguments are (1) only structure has been given importance and the individual's personality ignored, (2) tensions do not necessarily lead to deviant behaviour, (3)Merton's assumption that deviant behaviour is disproportionately more common in lower classes is not correct, (4) Merton has failed to account for 'non-utilitarian' crime and Juvenile delinquency in which people engage only for fun and not to meet specific goals of the society, (5) it does not take into account the social-psychological variables or the social structural elements, which might explain the priority of one adaptation over the other by individuals.

2.7 Strain Theory

American Social Scientist Albert Cohen,[12] in his work, "Delinquent Boys", took up Merton's idea of 'strain' explicitly to explain the different patterns of male and female crime, in particular the crimes of youth. He interpreted strain as the main catalyst in the formation of delinquent gangs by male working-class American youth. Cohen unintentionally extends this theory by proposing that when their aspirations for status are frustrated in the middle-class milieu, lower class boys tend to set up a delinquent structure, whereas Cloward and Ohlin[13] intentionally extend Merton's theory by suggesting that whether the potentially delinquent lower-class youth will actually delinquent depends on the factor of differential illegitimate opportunity.

This theory has been criticized for lacking in empirical support, for ignoring value pluralism, and for slighting the fun element in delinquency. But the theory has been praised for replacing the psychological approach with the sociological approach to deviance and for offering a valid premise concerning the aspiration opportunity gap.

2.8 Theory of Differential Opportunity

Instead of discussing pressures and motivations leading to criminal acts, this theory gives importance to adoption of particular kind of criminal act. This theory is presented by Richard Cloward and Lloyd Ohlin[14] The theory attempts to answer the question why different criminals adopt different forms of crime to express or fulfill their wishes or resistance. They consider that all individuals live in two kinds of opportunity structures. One is the legitimate opportunity structure and other is the illegitimate opportunity structure. As some people in society have limited access to achieve goals by legitimate ways or means, they may turn to illegitimate opportunities. A person may even directly turn to illegitimate opportunities. But the nature or pattern of illegitimate behaviour depends upon the access to a learning environment of such behaviour. Describing the importance of theory of differential opportunity Cloward and Ohlin contended that the concept of differential opportunity structures permits us to unite the theory of anomie, which recognizes the concept of differentials in access to legitimate means and the "Chicago tradition", in which concept of differentials in access to illegitimate mean is implicit. We can now look at the individual not simply in relation to one or the other system of means but in relation to both legitimate and illegitimate systems.

Thus the theories of status frustration and opportunity draw our attention to structured inequalities, which lead to variations in crime rates. These theories also explain why a particular class of society turns to a particular kind of crime pattern. In short these theories analyze societal and structural roots of crime and criminal behaviour.

2.9 Labeling Theory

The most notable contribution about this theory is made by Franklin Tahnenbaum in his book 'Crime and the Criminality'. Criminologist Howard Becker has stated his theory in his volume 'The Outsiders'. According to the labeling theory, super cordinate parties apply the deviant label to subordinate parties; being labeled deviant produces unfavourable consequences for the individual so labeled; and labeling others as deviant generates favourable consequences for the individuals, groups or communities that do the labeling. But the labeling theory has been criticized by some sociologists for being unable to tell us the causes of deviant behaviour and for over- simplifying and exaggerating the influence of labeling on the development of a deviant career.

Becker[15] observed that society itself creates 'outsiders' by generating the rules that define crime and other kinds of deviance. He noted the importance of the process of stigmatization and labeling. He also tried to trace out political intentions working behind the process of law or rule-making.

2.10 Differential Association Theory / Learning Theory

Edwin Sutherland [16] introduced the theory of 'Differential Association'. He gave two explanations for criminal behaviour. Situational and genetic or historical. Situational crime is crime on the basis of the situation that persists at the time of crime and genetic crime on the basis of a criminal's life experiences. He himself used the second approach in developing the theory of criminal behaviour. Sutherland's main thesis is that individuals encounter many inharmonious and inconsistent social influences in their life-time and many individuals become involved in contact with carriers of criminalistic norms, and as a consequence become criminals. He called this process 'differential association'.

The theory states that criminal behaviour is learnt in a process of communication with other persons, principally in small intimate groups. This learning includes the techniques of committing the crime. The specific direction of motives, drives, rationalizations and attitudes is learned from definitions of the legal codes as favourable or unfavourable.

This theory states that a person will become a criminal if he or she associates more with criminal than with anti-criminal people and ideas. The first explicit application of differential association to females was by Ruth Morris in her effort to explain female conformity. She hypothesized that, "there is a relative absence of a deviant sub-culture for female delinquents, and absence of sub-cultural as well as cultural support for female delinquency".[17] Glaser[18] extends differential association theory by suggesting that 'differential identification' is the determining factor for turning the differential association into criminal action.

Sutherland's theory has been criticized for its failure to explain the behaviour of lone criminals, for offering an empirically vague concept and a tautological explanation, and for wrongly assuming the learning of special skills as necessary for committing crime and delinquency. But the theory has inspired substantial empirical research.

2.11 Control Theory

The control theory perspective suggests that, every person has bad and good qualities only because of the social environment, social values and norms around him. This theory states that what causes conformity is control and therefore the lack of control causes deviance. The group of control theorists consists of three sociologists - walter Reckless, Ivan Nye, and Travish Hirschi. Reckless[19] refers to the casual factor of conformity as containment, Nye[20] as 'social control' and Hirschi[21] as 'bond to society'. This theory has been well supported by empirical data, but it is applicable to unsophisticated delinquent behaviour only. This theory seems unable to explain more sophisticated adult deviant behaviour, aside from presenting an oversimplified view of social control. Control theory differs from both the anomie and the differrntial association theorists who approach the problem of explaining deviant behaviour asking 'What causes deviance?' Control theorists on the other hand approach the problem in a round about way and ask 'What causes conformity?' They will automatically find out what causes deviance. For, what causes deviance is simply the absence of what causes conformity. This control theory differs from Anomie theory.

The literature applying control theory to women is inconclusive. However, ever since *Hindelang* discovered that, *"the presence or absence of social bonds bore a weaker relation to female delinquency than to male delinquency"*[22] control theory would predict that, *"girls who are most like boys ('masculine' girls) would offend as much as boys & because of a similarity of strength of social bonds - which should be weaker than those of more feminine, more confirming girls"*.[23]

2.12 Masculinity Theory

This theory comprises of two ideas: Crime is symbolically masculine and masculinity supplies the motive for a good deal of crime. The qualities demanded of the criminal-daring, toughness, aggression all exemplify maleness. As an explanation of female behaviour, masculinity theory expounds the unsuitability of crime for women, thereby explaining their conformity. The masculinity theory of offending was first expounded by Talcott Parsons. Parsons offered an account of the greater delinquency of boys as compared to girls based on nuclear family. He stated that *"The tendency of girls seems to be more law-abiding than boys"*.[24] ln' contemporary criminology, there has been a remarkably high degree of fidelity to Parsons's original conception of sex roles among both feminist and more traditional writers. Criminologists assume that crime for females is a form of expression of gender role. Modern theorists speak in terms of the pernicious effects of the gender roles imposed on women and rather than regarding them as appropriate and functional, they advanced nevertheless a view of women at least as controlled, as conformist and as ineffectual as Parsons conceived.

2.13 Role Theory

Recently, criminologists have used role theory to explain women's crimes. While advocating this theory, it is pointed out by scholars like Frances Heidensohn[25] and Marie-Andree Bertrand[26] that owing to close supervision and social restrictions on women, socialization, development of consciousness, and self-perception vary considerably beteeen boys and girls. Girls are usually trained to be passive, domesticated and non-violent and are not allowed to learn how to fight or use weapons. Contrary to this, boys are aggressive, ambitious and out-going. Girls thus shrink from violence and do not possess the necessary technical ability or strength to engage in crimes of violence, armed robberies, gang fights, etc. At worst, they engage in petty or domestic offences. Different expectations of standards of behaviour appear to be important in the genesis of women's crime. Normally girls are expected to adhere strictly to moral standards whereas boys are considered as normal violators of moral standards. So it is seen that women are less involved in immoral behaviour.

The Role theorists highlight the way in which opportunity structures predispose males rather than females to delinquency. Woman's criminality can be theorized in terms 'contradictory or ill-defined roles in the family'. However, there are some inbuilt limitations to the role theory. *Carol Smart*[27] observes that, role theory fails to discuss motivation or intention as an integral part of female criminality. For example role theory does not explain why even though women are socialized into primarily conforming patterns of behaviour a considerable number of them still engage in crime.

2.14 Social Bond Theory

Ram Ahuja[28] has put forth an explanation from an Indian perspective for women's crime. His work attracted the attention of a number of sociologists and criminologists to the area of female criminality in India. This perspective is primarily concerned with the pattern of family relationships. Through analyzing the structural problems of family organization and the types of functional problems in women's families of procreation, crimes committed by women are examined in terms of maladjustment in interpersonal relationships within the family. This 'family-centred explanation' or more broadly the 'Pressure of primary relations perspective' can be explained through a following Diagram 2.1.(see pg. No. 68)

The diagram shows that factors endogenous or exogenous to family create provocation, temptation, strains and stresses in a woman's life. These provocations or stresses produce a desire or a need to deviate from social and/or legal norms. The personality structure or the biological and psychological characteristics like temperament attitudes, frustrations, deprivations or dominant underlying need prevent this deviation in some women, but fail to do so in other cases. Thus, both personality system and pressures of environment in which woman functions, contribute to woman's criminality.

This theoretical model focuses on "strength of character", "role conflict" (role collision, role incompatibility, role confusion), "opportunity", and "totality of situatibn" in family. Totality of situation includes varied situations in family taken together's. Suppose a woman fails to get her husband's love and affection (Situation S_1) and in-law's care and support (Situation S_2), and has illicit relations with a person (Situation S^3), it will be the totality of the three situations together (S_1+ S_2+ S_3) that will lead her to criminality (say, either Personality P_1+ or Personality P_2) will determine whether she will really commit murder (one type of behaviour) or suicide (other type of behaviour) or elope (third type of behaviour) or continue to live in the family (fourth type of behaviour).

Thus, the woman's "crime" (e.g., husband's murder) will be the outcome of interaction between her personality system

Diagram 2.1

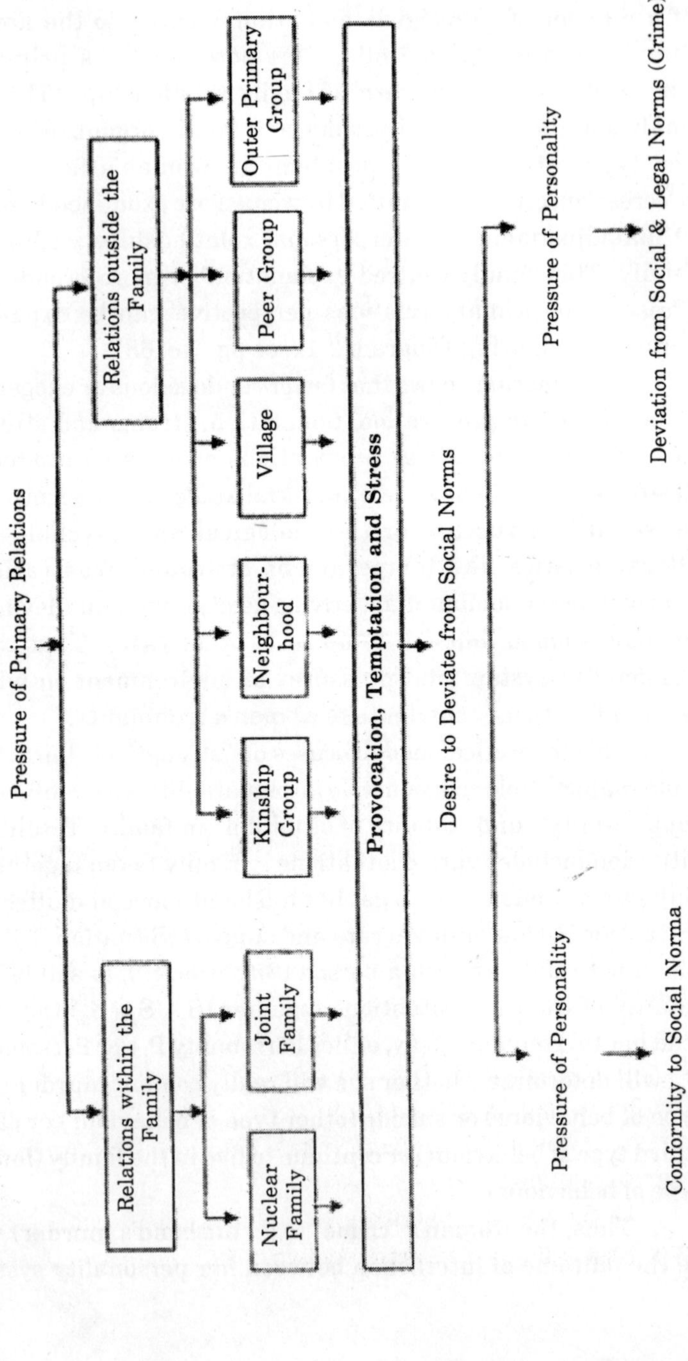
Pressure of Primary Relations
Relations within the Family
Relations outside the Family
Nuclear Family
Joint Family
Kinship Group
Neighbourhood
Village
Peer Group
Outer Primary Group
Provocation, Temptation and Stress
Desire to Deviate from Social Norms
Pressure of Personality
Pressure of Personality
Conformity to Social Norma
Deviation from Social & Legal Norms (Crime)

and totality of situations in her family. The crime will develop in interaction process over time through a series of stages. In this process of spread in time, the "criminal behaviour" will emerge not by the 'past' alone but by the 'current' situation and by triggering or precipitating circumstances too. In simplified form, conjunctive theoretical model in women's criminality accounts for differences in women's families and other institutional structures as well as in their personalities.

Ahuja has analyzed intra-family problems of relationships that is the structural problems of family organizations. He presented his theory on the basis of interaction of woman with their family members. He tried to explain etiology of female crime in terms of 'maladjustment' in interpersonal relationships within the family.

2.15 The Women's Liberation Thesis

The impact of the women's liberation movement on female crime has become the basis of a heated debate in the criminological literature on women. The catalyst was Freda Adler's 'Sisters in Crime: The rise of the New Female Criminal'. To Adler, "the liberation of women in western society is a 'fait accompli'. Women have fought and won their battle for equality. They have 'come of age' and the phenomenon of famale criminality is but one wave in this rising tide of female asserti veness".[29] Adler's analysis of the nature of the new female criminal seems to rest on two points. One is that women's liberation has brought out women's competitive instincts. Women are now more assertive, more aggressive, and, indeed, more 'masculine'. Her other argument is that women's liberation has opened up structural opportunities for women to offend. For example, women now have more opportunities to engage in crime in the workplace. Thus, liberation is causing women to engage in more crime.

Different theories and explanations for the causes of crime have been suggested by writers at different times. However, no single theory can explain all crimes and delinquency. Different patterns of crime require different explanations. Therefore, understanding criminal behaviour 'requires examining the individual and the situation because basically criminal behaviour depends upon how the individual perceives and interprets a situation.

Thus, the validity of any social science theory depends upon its verification based on the empirical data. Like other social science theories, criminological theories are always being challenged by new empirical evidence. *Naffine*[30] examines in his review various theories of criminality and explores the idea of 'female voice' for the construction of women in criminology. However, theories discussed above, have given the proper perspectives to researchers in understanding the nature of crime and criminals. These theoretical frameworks have been taken as guidelines for the present study.

References

1. Lombroso and Ferrero. 'The Female Offender', p. 1 09-112.
2. Pollak Otto. 'The Criminality of Women', p. 31-32.
3 Bowker, Lee H. 'Women and Crime in America', p. 2.
4. Thomas, W.I. 'The Unadjusted Girl', p.70-72.
5. Pollak Otto. 'The Criminality of Women', p. 45.
6. Smart Carol. 'Women, crime and criminology - A feminist critique', p. 37.
7. Pollak Otto. 'The Criminality of Women'. p. 48.
8. Smart Carol. 'Women, crime and criminology - A feminist critique', p. 50-52.
9. Pollak Otto. 'The criminality of women', p. 51.
10. Durkheim Emile. Suicide, tran. I.A. Spaulding and G. Simposons, p. 362.
11. Merton Robert. 'Social theory and social structure', p. 230-35.
12. Cohen Albert. 'Delinquent Boys', p. 75.
13. Cloward, R. and Ohlin, L. 'Delinquency and opportunity: A theory of Delinquent Gangs'. p. 50-52.

14. Ibid., pp. 50-52.
15. Becker Howard. 'Outsiders', p. 9.
16. Sutherland Edwin. 'Principles of Criminology', p. 61.
17. Morris, R. 'Female Delinquency and Relational Problems',p. 25l.
18. Glaser Daniel. 'Criminality theories and Behavioural Images', American Journal of Sociology, p. 433-44.
19. Reckless Walter. 'The crime problem', p. 522.
20. Nye F. Ivan. 'Family Relationships and Delinquent Behaviour', p. 5.
21. Hirschi, T. 'Causes of Delinquency', p. 32.
22. Hindalang, M.J. 'Causes of Delinquency: A Partial Replication and Extension', p. 47l.
23. Naffine, N. 'Female Crime', p.72.
24. Parsons Talcott. 'Family structure and the socialization of the child', in Family, Socialization and Interaction Process', p. 306.
25. Heidensohn Frances. 'The Deviance of Women: A Critique and an Enquiry', British Journal of Sociology, p. 170.
26. Bertrand, M.A. 'Self Image and Delinquency: contribution to the study of female criminality and women's image', p.71
27. Smart Carol. 'Women, Crime and Criminology - A Feminist Critique', p. 69.
28. Ahuja Ram. 'Women and Crime' in 'Crime and Corrections in India', pp. 126-127.
29. Adler Freda. 'Sisters in crime: The rise of the New Female Criminal', p. 10.
30. Naffine, N. 'Female Crime', p. 72.

3

Review of Literature

3.1 Introduction

A systematic review of literature provides an overview of crime scenario. Many studies have been conducted on criminals, male and female, throwing light on various factors - sociological, psychological and economic, which contribute to the criminal offences of the individual. However, there has been considerable change in the view taken by researchers about women indulging in crime.

During the 1960s and 1970s, not much attention was paid to incidence of female crime in India, rather it was almost a neglected field. Much of the writing has been in the field of criminological theory, criminal law and the Indian prison system. Some reviews on various aspects of women criminals are mentioned here in brief.

Rao, V. and Sethna, M.J. made attempts to study female criminality from sociological point of view. Rao[1] found that in rural areas, women may be guided by superstition to commit crimes. According to him, frequent murders of human lives as sacrifices to deities, are likely to be committed with the belief that human sacrifices reveal hidden treasures.

Sethna[2] explains that most crimes committed by Indian women occur in the house. It may be due to the fact that Indian women particularly in rural areas spend considerable period of their time in their houses. Therefore, their criminal feelings are likely to be focused on their own kith and kin and the devices by which they commit crimes may either be kitchen utensils or domestic tools.

Singh[3] has studied 75 females prisoners, convicted for murder and equal number of female prisoners convicted for other petty crimes. His study deals with the personality aspects of female prisoners. He conducted his study in the prisons of Punjab, Harayana and U.P. He also studied concepts about self and personality characteristics of criminals and found that criminals are significantly different from non-criminals. He described that, criminals had a lower self and social esteem indicating of a lack of self-regard thus exhibit neurotic traits such as anxiety, irritability, hostility, maladjustment and insecurity.

Sanyal[4] conducted a study of women convicts of 'Nari Bandi Niketan' in Lucknow. Twenty-five women convicts, convicted for murder were studied. He reported considerable depression among married female prisoners. He found female convicts suffering from feelings of anxiety, guilt and insecurity, low self esteem. Sanyal and Agarwal studied a sample of 69 female convicts. The study deals with the personality characteristics of the criminals. The author arrived at the conclusion that the inmates were found to be maladjusted in marital life and relations.

Rani, B.M.[5] studied 120 female convicts in Andhra Pradesh. She has indicated that, women also take part in all types of crimes, including the ones which involved physical power and use of strong weapons. While analyzing the female property related offences in particular, she found that majority of them have indulged in petty thefts and house-breaking. Rani analyzed that, in general, women murderers were either deprived of the care of their parents or husbands and in-laws or a combination of both. The analysis reveals that, while committing murders, women concentrate mostly on persons who lived closer to them. She also observed that in more than 70 per cent of cases domestic factors, victim's provocation and lover's/friend' s instigation contribute substantially to homicides by females. Rani revealed that urban areas provide more female offenders than rural areas. She found that more than 50 per cent female criminals were dependent and slightly more than 50 per cent belonged to backward castes.

Prasad, S.K.[6] found in his study that all the female offenders were highly frustrated in their conjugal life and sexual relations. He further revealed that more than 90 per cent offenders came from low income group. His findings have revealed that the major areas of female criminals' conflicts are: (1) Husbands having habits like drinking, gambling, drug addition. (2) Lack of interest in the family and lack of love. (3) A forced marriage. (4) Sexual incompatibility and maladjustment with husband. (5) Jealousy due to husband's illicit relations with other women. (6) Low income and excessive expenditure. (7)Conflicts over sex. (8) Jealousy over property.

Ghosh Shubhra[7] has studied 69 female offenders of Nari Bandi Niketan of Lucknow, with psycho-analytical tests. She observed that the variables such as emotional traits, self-esteem and attitude of a female convict are greatly related to each other. Also the physical atmosphere of the institution interacts with the psychological process, leading to the outcome of the prevailing emotions, self-esteem and attitude of a convict inside the penal world.

Devasia Leelamma and Devasia, V.V.[8] have edited a volume of research papers offering a perspective in female criminality and female victims from an Indian view-point. In this volume, prominent Indian criminologists have contributed research papers covering a wide variety of facets of female criminality in India. This volume gives an over all picture of female criminality.

The following are some notable sociological studies conducted on women criminals explaining various aspects of female criminality.

3.2 Kerawalla, Perin: 'A Study in Indian Crime'

Kerawalla's study, has made many comparative observations about male-female criminality. The inquiry was directed to ascertain structural patterns of criminal behaviour with a view to isolating major areas of change. Among the areas explored were the age composition of criminals, their occupational pattern, the committing of crime by minority and majority groups, the entry of literates into criminality and an examination of what distinguishes the crime situation in Bombay state. The primary data was gathered through interviews of the inmates of Arthur Road Prison, Bombay.

Kerawalla's main conclusion is that the crime situation is characterized by a higher growth rate for almost every type of crime, a rate of increase which is 'vastly more impressive' than the rate of growth of population. Co-related with the growing crime is the increasing failure of the administrative and judicial systems to cope with the increase in crime.

In her study, she has analyzed the distribution of offenders, based on age group, literacy, religious denomination and occupational background. It was found that the proportion of 22-40 age group was higher in the female prisoner sample. Literacy among women prisoners was found to be only slightly below its level in the normal population on urbanization. The extent of 'urbanity' was felt to be an important aspect, it could not be treated as a casual factor for higher or lower criminality between regions. Nor was it the only factor. Although generally dismissing women criminals as a negligible criminal group, Kerawalla does refer to the need for studying female criminality with reference to the recommendations emerging from the study.

3.3 Ahuja Ram: 'Female Offenders in India'

It is the earliest study which deals with the phenomenon of female crime in India. His study[10] was conducted in Rajasthan, Madhya Pradesh and Punjab. The purpose of the study was to discover a cluster of related traits of the criminal behaviour of females, to study nature and pattern of crime amongst women, to analyze role of family in family crime, to assess the process of adjustment of family members in the absence of a woman due to imprisonment, to evaluate rational system of sentencing and treating female offenders and to review policy towards women offenders and their families both when they are inside the prison and when they are under supervision or probation.

Ahuja has indicated that maladjustment in conjugal relations is a natural situation in the context of women in India where, not only are most women married, but the fact of continuing with the marriage is usually the only socially permissible alternative. Whereas this approach to marriage has seemingly managed to retain cohesiveness and permanence of family and marriage as institutions, it has most likely also been the cause of acute frustration at the personal level. In some cases, such frustration can lead to desperate or other kinds of unexpected or expected behaviour, particularly in women. Although, in the present study, this relationship was not significantly demonstrated, the general impression that female criminality is possibly a manifestation, among others, of maladjusted conjugal relationships is not improbable.

The major findings of the study are summarized as follows: Of total offences, about half involved physical harm to some one, one-sixth involved economic harm, one-ninth involved moral aberrance and one-seventh were minor offences. Murder was the dominant offence. Victims of murder, in three-fourths of the total cases, were the primary kin. The bulk of offenders belonged to younger age groups. Sixty-six per cent of the sample were under 35 years of age, Low economic level was found to be more influential than low caste factor in the offender's profile.

Urban background was more prominent. Urban areas produce more female offenders than rural areas. Most of the offences committed were related to emotion. Illiteracy is found closely related to crime as 79 per cent female criminals were found to be illiterate. Most criminals were married (76 per cent). However, 17 per cent were widows and 3 per cent were deserted.

Ahuja is of the view that only economic compulsions lead women to crimes like theft. He rejects physical and psychological factors and puts the responsibility of dragging women to crime on instability in family relationships or disintegration of family life, Ahuja's work thus covers a variety of aspects related to female offenders.

3.4 Shastri Tara: 'A Study of Women Prisoners and Their Families in Maharashtra'

Shastri Tara[11] examined the background factors that contribute to the criminality of the female offender, the effect of imprisonment on her family and to what extent community welfare services are utilized by the members of the family during thel prisoner's absence.

Among the aspects examined were socio-economic and cultural causes leading to crime among women, their general crime pattern, life of convicts in the prison after being sentenced, adequacy of training and other amenities provided in prison and the future plans of offenders after their release. She has studied 186 femal offenders. The principal findings of the study are summarized below:

1. One-fourth of female offenders were found to be habitual.
2. Offence of prostitution was higher than the rest of the offences.
3. Residents in densely populated urban areas showed higher recidivism (three times more).
4. More than half of the offenders belonged to the age group 16-30, when extended to 40, this group accounted for 80 per cent.

5. Ninety-four per cent respondents came from families which were totally uneducated or partly educated.
6. Economic deprivations' are main cause for the criminal activities.
7. A majority of convicts were from agricultural and labourer profession,deviant pursuits such as prostitution and black-marketing were next in importance.

Shastri recommended that, female offenders need to be recognized as a distinctive sociological group so that appropriate attention can be given to their treatment and rehabilitation, as well as to crime preventive policies. Employment in prison needs to be "eared to specific needs of women and there should be intensive after care to prevent recidivism of female offenders.

3.5 Bhanot, M.L. and Misra: 'Criminality Amongst Women in India'

This is a brief monograph. The object of the study[12] is to throw light on the nature and pattern of female criminality, with a view to help the criminologist, the social reformer and the police to reorient policies and programme for coping with 'increased criminality among women'.

Two types of data were utilized for the study-those of women offenders frompolice records and those available from a sample survey of 641 women convicts. The sample was drawn from convicts lodged in 3 Central Jails, viz., Lucknow, Delhi and Allahabad and 3 District Jails, viz., Fatehgarh, Mathura and Kanpur.

The study provides information on the socio-economic background of female convicts, their age, education, marital status, offence-type, duration and nature of sentence, etc. Conclusions worth noting are as follows:

1. In India, arrests of women offenders have been on the increase. There is an upward trend in the rate of criminality among women.
2. Offence distribution reveals that women are less prone to

committing violent crime. Theft and rioting form a majority of female offences apart from miscellaneous offences.

3. Maharashtra is observed to have the highest average annual incidence of female arrests for crime in India.

It is the only study of its kind and scale, i.e., one dealing with a sizeable sample, of women convicts and drawn from more than one prison and from more than one state in India.

3.6 Nagla, B.K.: 'A Sociological Study of Female Offenders in India'

Nagla[13] analyzed data regarding female offenders lodged in the Borstal Jail Hissar, Harayana. According to his analysis, most of them were drawn from 'young category (only 11.11 per cent of the total were in the age group of 50-60 years), also, around 96 per cent were in the 'married' category. This leads him to deduct that family discord or circumstances in the families or in the marriage were responsible for goading the women to commit crimes.

Nagla differentiates between the social roles ascribed to women and men by most cultures. The role of a wife, lover or girl-friend is important to a woman. Many female offenders engage in prostitution and property offences to earn money to support the drug habit or to get rid of debts incurred by husband and lovers. When couples are involved in robberies, the woman is usually the girl-friend or wife of the male robber.To a considerable extent, the criminal activity of women is influenced by the requirements of the men to whom they are emotionally attached. But now the pattern of role-behaviour is changing, so also the pattern of crime among women.

3.7 Sohoni Neera, K.: 'Women Behind Bars'

Female crime has not been adequately debated in this country. This book[14] attempts to understand female criminality through a close-up study of socio-demographic characteristics of women prisoners. The author concludes that there can be no stereotype of a female offender and the questionable link of criminality with poverty is also eroded. While focusing on 120 women prisoners in Pune, there is a discussion on current thinking in western countries regarding female crime and an attempt to gain from the insights of other studies of women prisoners in India.

3.8 Gote-Govhane: 'Female Criminality and Sociological Theories'

Gote-Gavhane's study[15] aims to trace out the factors responsible for female criminality, to identify the socio-economic problems of female criminals in India, to find out the characteristics and the patterns of female criminality and their comparison with western societies, to test the feasibility of the different female criminality theories and models, and to suggest definite measures to prevent and to rehabilitate the female criminals in India.

Gote-Gavhane has studied 50 female convicts of Yeravada Central Jail, Pune. She found that the age of the female criminal is co-related to criminality. The peak age of female convicts was found to be between 25 to 35 years. Therefore, it is inferred that younger the age, higher is the possibility of criminal behaviour among women. Low class culture was found to be crime-productive. More important, it was also found that the culture of the upper caste women is equally crime productive. The analysis of the data revealed that female criminality was more prevalent among illiterate women in Maharashtra.

Gote-Gavhane found in her study that the main cause of crime is family maladjustment and unsound interaction patterns and relationships within a family. The dowry system is also found to be a strong responsible cause. In Indian Society, habitual criminality of women is found to be adopting 'masculine' crime patterns like smuggling, terrorism. This indicates the changing nature of female criminality in india.

The interaction patterns of women in India are very limited. Due to this limited interaction patterns, they interact with very few. Hence, their victims are mostly found to be to their close relatives. Interaction patterns are such that the crimes have taken place in their houses or in the field of their routine activity. They were also found using household materials to commit crimes.

She has indicated that female offenders generally belong to economically and socially deprived class of society. Socio-economic problems were found to be responsible factors for their criminal behaviour. Thus female criminality in India is co-related to peculiar socio-economic status of women in Indian society in general and family in particular. Most female convicts were found to be non-habitual and situational criminals.

Gote-Gavhane has suggested that since most of the female convicts are non-habitual first-timers, they should be kept away from the habitual criminals in separate custodial facilities and surroundings. Family members who had discontinued their relationship with the female convicts should be persuaded to resume warm and sympethetic relationships with the female prisoners. This would help them to have hopes of resuming family life after their release.

3.9 Report of National Expert Committee (NEC) on Women Prisoners

The Government of India took up the initiative in 1986-87 and set up the National Expert Committee on Women Prisoners' to identify the gaps in or drawbacks of the existing facilities and services, and to evolve a more humane policy towards women offenders. This committee[16] studied the procedure for handling of women offenders in detention or in custody and reviewed conditions governing the treatment of women offenders in police lock-up and penal and correctional institutions. The NEC also examined the efficacy of institutional and other services for reformation and rehabilitation of women offenders and suggested legal, administrative and organizationl measures for ensuring fair, humane and effective handling of women offenders in various criminal justice processes.

3.10 Report of The National 'Workshop on Custodial Justice to Women

Addressing the forum of National workshop[17] on 'Custodial Justice to Women', Ms. Pramila Dandavate, President of Mahila Dakshata Samiti, observed that in the present gender biased society, 'Women in Custody' are the most invisible and exploited lot. She informed that the living conditions of women prisoners are deplorable, where more than 40 women, convicted of crimes ranging from petty to the most heinous, are made to share a room.Apart from living quarters, the absence of medical aid and absolete toilet facilities made conditions inhuman in prisons. Majority of women commit crimes due to poverty and most of them are abandoned by the family and become destitute. She emphasized the need to change attitudes of the operators of the criminal Justice system- the police, judiciary and the correctional system, the need for vocational training for rehabilitation of women prisoners, along with the identification of avenues for their employment.

She emphasized the need to change attitudes of the operators of the criminal Justice system, the police, judiciary and the correctional system. She also pointed out that the provision for women coming out of prisons and needing support for rehabilitation is an absolute necessity. The workshop endorsed the statement for a National Policy on Custodial Justice for Women and urged the Government of India to initiate action recommended in the policy statement.

3.11 An Overview

The review of literatures provides an overview of the crime scenario in India. The subject of female crime was generally neglected in Western and Indian Criminology until the 1950s.

In India, interest in woman offenders was manifested by very few scholars and only recently. Most of such work focuses on female offenders at the micro level with generally modest-sized samples drawn from a single prison. The only study entailing a reasonable sample-size, and more than one prison and region, is sponsored by the Bureau of Police Research and Development, Government of India.

Female criminality is socially viewed as more serious and it is reportedly on the increase. Analysis of these literatures reveal that women criminals are generally younger in age, married, illiterate and also come from low economic class on the basis of review findings, it may be seen that the main causes of crime in female offenders are family maladjustment, emotionalism, frustration and emotional insecurity.

In recent years in India, a few studies have been conducted on female criminality in general and homicides in particular. It is found that, in committing crimes like sale of illicit liquor, gambling, prostitution and dacoity, the women were helped actively by their men folk. Regarding the place for committing crimes, it is observed that most of the homicides committed by women took place within home and kitchen. The analysis reveals that while committing murders women concentrate mostly on persons who live closer to them.

It was predominantly found that women criminals were generally younger in age. Therefore, this is a problem related to young women. Most of the crimes committed by women are due to stressful family situations, marital maladjustment, disharmonious and often conflict - prone relationship with husband. It is clear that maladjustment in interpersonal relationship within the family is one of the most important causes of criminality amongst women.

All types of crimes are the result of human nature (adjustment), needs (biological, economic and social condition), and situation (environment) which turn into unnatural behaviour (role). It may be explained that poor women have real economic needs which are not being met, and in many cases engage in illegal activities as a viable economic alternative. In recent times, women have been participating in various aspects of social life and this growing participation could be one of the contributing factors for the increase of crime among them. It has been argued that, "the socio-economic vulnerability of women is the dominating factor which explains the rising trend of crime among women" .[18]

Nagla[19] has indicated that, the compound annual rate of growth among female offenders is increasing by 10 per cent as compared to 9 per cent in male offenders. In this context, there is need for research which will clarify the influence of female criminality upon the total crime scene, where it may have large, unexplored implications. Although the literature on female offenders has been comparatively limited, studies have heen made and, in fact, the development in the study of female offenders reflects the larger development of the study of criminal behaviour in general.

The study of female criminality was more or less neglected upto to 1950's. It was only in the late 60's and early 70's that the need for a new perspective for understanding female deviant behaviour was realized, and professional interest in female criminality has greatly increased along with general interest in women's studies. Thus, there has been a small group of writings specially concemed with women and crime in India. However, the complexities of female criminal behaviour have attracted the attention of sociologists, phychologists and criminologists. In this context, the researcher has decided to conduct a sociological study of female criminality in Mumbai. The present study attempts to throw some light on the social pathology of female crime in the city of Mumbai.

References

1. Rao, V. 'Factors of crime in India'.
2 Sethna, M.J. 'Society and criminals'.

3. Singh, A. 'Personality of female murderers', Indian Journal of Criminology, 9(2), July 1981.
4. Sanyal, S. 'Female Criminals in India'.
5. Rani, B.M. 'Female Criminality'.
6. Prasad, S.K.'A study of women murderers in Tamil Nadu', Reading in Criminology, Vo1.12, No.2, 1982, p.72.
7. Ghosh Shubhra. 'Female Criminals in India'.
8. Devasia, L. and Devasia, V.V. (eds.). 'Female criminals and female victims: An Indian Perspective'.
9. Kerawalla, P.c. 'A study in Indian Crime'.
10. Ahuja Ram. 'Female offenders in India'..
11 .Shastri Tara. 'A study of women prisoners and their families in Maharashtra' Social Defence, Xll-46.
12. Bhanot, M.L. and Misra, S. 'Criminality amongst women in India'.
13. Nagla B.K. 'Women, Crime and Law'.
14. Sohoni Neera, K. 'Women Behind Bars'.
15. Gotc-Gavhane. 'Female cdminality and sociological theories'.
16. Report of the National Expert Committee on 'Women Prisoners', Department of Women and Child Development., p.98-111.
17. Report of the National Workshop on 'Custodial Justice to Women'.
18. Simon Rita James. 'The contemporary women and crime', p.4.
19. Nagla, B.K. 'The criminality of women in India', the Indian Journal of Social Work, XL-III(3), 1982, p.36.

4

Methodology of the Study

4.1 The Research Problem

The researcher's interest in the study of female remand and undertrial female criminal prisoners arose out of M.Phil. research experiences connected with the study of Juvnile boys and girls in remand homes. The current study is in sharp contrast to earlier Indian studies on prisoners, which focused either on socio-economic background, cause of crime, post conviction prison experiences or problems of rehabilitation. Systematic documentation had not been undertaken of the pre-conviction stages of the crminal justice process. This is a significant period of time for an accused person and espccially for those who have been taken into custody.

The focus of the present study thus, is the unconvicted or undertrial female criminal prisoners. The study limits itself to an attempt at reconstructing a subjective view of the criminal justice system from the vantage point of the criminal. The researcher has cross checked the official records and statements of prison authorities. In the study of undertrial female criminal prisoners, the researcher has done a follow-up of the cases.

This is a study of the undertrial female criminal prisoners or accused persons in criminal cases. The observations are confined to a single prison for female criminals in the city of Mumbai.

4.2 Objectives of the Study

The objectives of the study are as follows:

1. To understand the changing form of female criminality.
2. To study the various crimes committed by women and to examine their nature.
3. To analyze the socio-economic background of female criminals in terms of their age, marital status, residence, religion, caste, education, occupation, income, etc.
4. To understand the causes of female criminality.
5. To understand the criminal's feelings towards the offence and Itheir attitudes towards society and stay in prison.

4.3 Design of Research

The present study is based on descriptive research design. The study has been conducted in the city of Mumbai. The study was conducted in two phases. While, the first was the enumeration phase and a base-line survey of records available with State Government's Departments of Prison, the second phase was of data collection with some sample cases consisting of detailed case studies.

4.4 Hypotheses

On the basis of the survey of literature done by the researcher, following hypotheses were put forward for this study:

1. Low socio-economic status of the family is an important factor in female crime.
2. Stressful situation within the family plays an important role in the life of female criminals.
3. Undertrial female prisoners are prone to certain feelings and attitudes.

4.5 Universe

The universe for the study consisted of all the female inmates in the female section of a jail in Mumbai. The target group was undertrial female criminals of Arthur Road Central Prison, Mumbai. Therefore, the universe of the study is the women's section of Arthur Road Central Prison. The researcher proposed to interview all women, arrested for crime.

4.6 Census Study

The present study is a census study. This study has been conducted with reference to the total population of female undertrials of Arthar Road Prison, Mumbai, in the State of Maharashtra.

Undertrials are a floating population. Therefore, there is a continuous turnover in the prison population, and the period of stay of any undertrial prisoner is unpredictable.

It was decided to cover all the female inmates of the prison. There were 102 female inmates, out of whom 90 inmates were interviewed. Owing to different reasons, 12 inmates were not interviewed. Out of them 10 were foreigners of violent nature who were constantly confined to their cells. They had been arrested under the NDPS Act (Narcotic Drugs and Psychotropic Substances) crime. Another 2 were from middle-east-countries and did not speak English or any Indian language.

Some case studies were prepared on the basis of the information received from the inmates and the prison authorities.

The field work was conducted from May 2002 to the end of July 2002.

4.7 Methods of Data Collection

The data was collected from primary and secondary sources. The primary sources of data were the undertrial criminals of prison and the police officials. The secondary sources of data collected from the official records of the jail, census reports, crime repots and the office of the Inspector General of Prisons, Government of Maharashtra, Pune.

The methods, including sources, tools and process of data collection are as follows:

1. Reference to prison records - The undertrial register and court warrants were especially useful in this respect.
2. Individual Interviews - The study has been conducted with the help or an interview schedule related to-the objectives of the study.

Interview schedule covers a number of aspects of the prisoners, such as their sociol-economic background, type and nature of crimes, factors responsible for crime committed by them and their attitudes towards the offence, society, stay in prison. The interview schedule used both close-ended and open-ended questions.

Provision for testing reliability of answer was, to some extent, built into the questionnaire. Information was obtained through replies to the questionnaire supplemented with whatever was obtained from the overall case study as narrated by the respondent. Prison records, wherever available, were drawn on to further corroborate the information collected from the respondent. Even personal impressions of supervisory and other staff were sought to help achieve a crystallized prisoner profile.

For the study of undertrial female criminals in Mumbai, it was necessary to restrict the scope of the study by interviewing only undertrial female criminals, who were detained in prison.

Only Arthur Road Prison in Mumbai city has a female yard, and so data was collected there. This central prison is essentially for undertrials, detenues and short-term convicts (those sentenced to less than a month or a few days in lieu of fine).

From the time of the Indian Jail Committee Report, the accused prisoner has featured as an undertrial. The majority of Indian prisons contain a large population of undertrial prisoners.

It was not possible to get detailed information from official records, because all of them are undertrial female criminals. At the outset, undertrial criminals were assured that the information would be kept confidential and that it would be used only for research purposes.

4.8 Analysis of the Data

The data so collected has been coded and tabulated for the purpose of analysis. Simple frequency tables and cross-tables have been made and the highlights of quantitative data have been presented.

4.9 Field Experiences

The researcher was assigned particular timings to visit the prison. Prior to starting the work, the researcher paid a few visits to the women's section, to get familiar with the place and the people, the researcher needed acceptance and formed relationships, so that she would not be seen as a threat by inmates.

Initially women were very hesitant to talk because they were under the impression that the researcher was going to publish their identity and experiences. Clarifications were made about the research work and interest. Some women thought that the researcher would help them in their cases. Some women were under the impression that she was a lawyer. After some time, they realized that the researcher was a student and that would not be able to help them. So, the researcher had to make repeated requests to female prisoners for interview. Constant persuading and humane treatment was essential while collecting data. Even then, some responded with suspicious attitudes. Through informal dialogue, the researcher was able to generate openness among female prisoners. Most of the inmates have expressed feelings that ever since they came to the jail, no one has talked to them so humanely and frankly. Thus, the researcher has tried her best to collect the required information.

The meetings with prisoners held inside the female yard (or wing) had several advantages. It allowed the researcher sufficient time for work and freedom to make a programme for the day. Most important, the researcher could collect the data in a natural way. The arrangement suited the administration too. The respondent and the researcher were permitted to talk together in a separate place. This arrangement ensured both privacy and quiet time except when a 'Mahila Hawaldar' or 'Mahila Rakshak' (Matron) might be around.

4.10 Limitations of the Study

Some of the limitations of the study are:

1. This study covers the undertrials. It was found that a study of undertrials was rather difficult in that they were busy with court cases and some of them were not in a mood to talk frankly. Since the charges leveled against them were not confirmed by court, they were opposed to any kind of labeling as criminals.
2. It was difficult to interview all the respondents in total privacy in the prison environment. Often the 'Mahila Hawaldar' or 'Mahila Rakshak' would present. So sometimes it was difficult for an undertrial to answer questions frankly.

5

Demographic Profile of Undertrial Female Criminals

Introduction

Today, the position of women has changed more drastically than in any previous period of civilization. The concept of women's emancipation has opened the doors to a free life for women, but at the same time this attainment brought its own evils.

Any sociological analysis should focus its attention on demographic variables which are peculiar to the population under study and which reflect the properties of the larger social system. The variables covered in this regard are age, education, residence, religion, caste, marital status and occupational background of the respondents.

This chapter presents an overview of the demographic characteristics of the undertrial female criminals who were surveyed for this study. These charactelistics are presented in the following manner:

5.1 Age

The process of socialization is related to age, so the study of age structure becomes most important. Table 5.1 shows the age distribution of the respondents.

Table 5.1: Age-wise Distribution of the Respondents

Age (in years)	*Frequency,*	*Percentage*
18-29	30	33.3
30-39	28	31.1
40 and above	32	35.6
Total	**90**	**100.0**

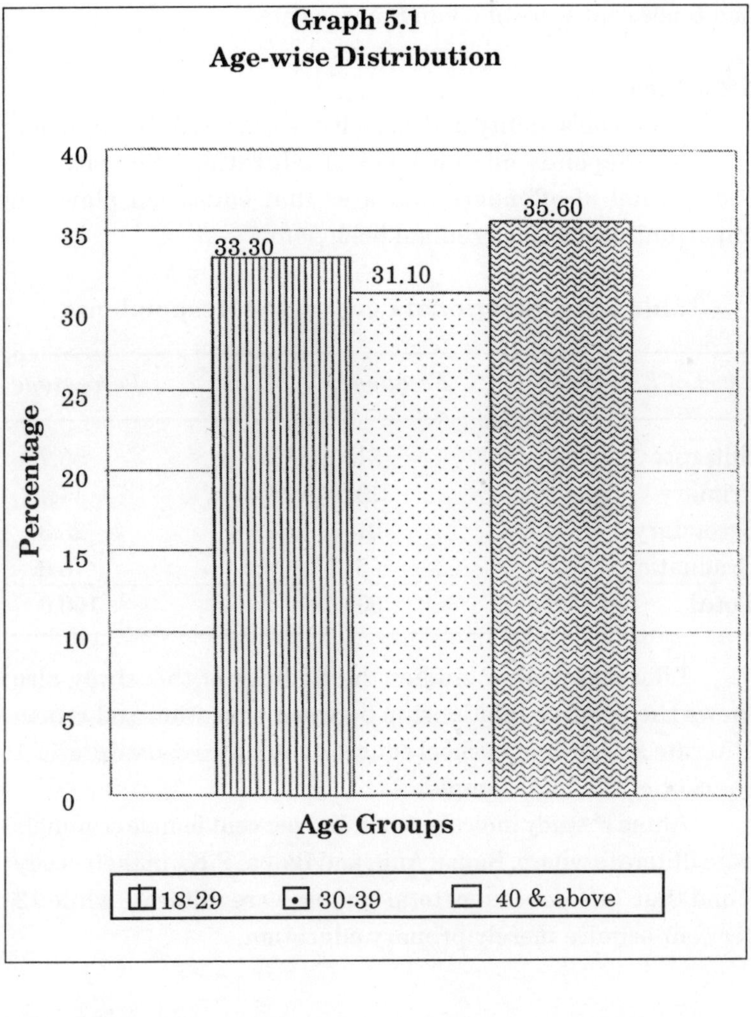

The table 5.1 shows that participation of women in criminal offences is more or less similar in all age groups. This clearly shows the rate of increase of crime in all age groups. While Ahuja's and Rani's[2] studies showed that predominantly women criminals are found in the age-group of 20-40 years. However, B.R. Sharma[3] studied 36 female ofenders in Tihar Jail, Delhi and Borstal Jail, Hissar (Harayana). Of these, 39 per cent were below 25 years of age, 39 per cent belonged to the age group 26-43 years, 16 per cent belonged to the age group of 44-53 years and 6 per cent were of 53 and more years.

5.2 Education

A person's ability and capacity to cope with the function of living depends on the level of education. Educational background of offenders indicates that education plays an important role in the criminal behaviour.

Table 5.2: Educational Level of the Respondents

Level of Education	*Frequency*	*Percentage*
Illiterate	51	56.7
Primary	13	14.4
Secondary	21	23.3
Graduation	5	5.6
Total	**90**	**100.0**

Like many other studies the findings of this study also shows the positive relationship between education and crime. llliterate and primary school education inmates constitute 71.1 per cent of the total sample.

Ahuja's[4] study indicated that 72.5 per cent female criminals were illiterate where, Bajpai Anju and Bajpai P.K.[5] in their study found that 74.4 per cent of total sample were illiterate while 13 per cent acquire merely primary education.

Low educational level indicates low economic conditions and low standard of life. Perhaps, education plays an important role in the development of personality. So far as the relationship between education and crime is concerned, we can affirm that, illiteracy and low level of education always dominates the crime scenario. It does not mean that educated people do not or least indulge in crime. Perhaps because crimes committed by educated people are white collar-crimes they mostly escape the eyes of the police and the law. However, the lack of education may create the problem of family adjustment, forcing a few women to take to deviant behaviour and also significant number of respondents had not completed secondary school. With regard to self-esteem and unemployment, which are consequences of low educational level, it has been observed that these factors affect the nature of crime.

Graph 5.2 Education Level

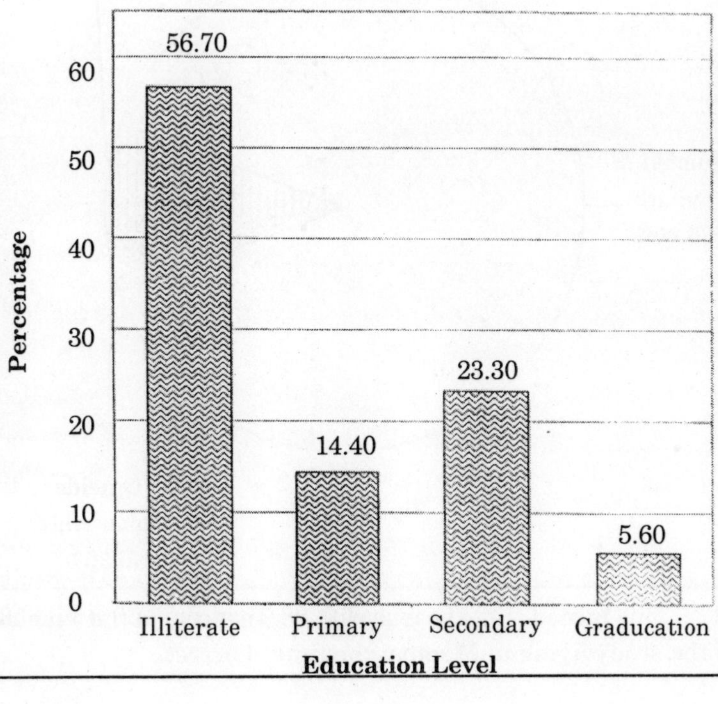

5.3 Residence

Though it is held that crime and criminals are not restricted to any geographical boundaries, yet the residence of the criminals has immense sociological importance in understanding the personality co-relates of the crime and criminals.

There was an expectation that as the prison from which the sample was drawn located in Mumbai, there will be greater representation of those living in Mumbai.

Graph 5.3
Residential Background

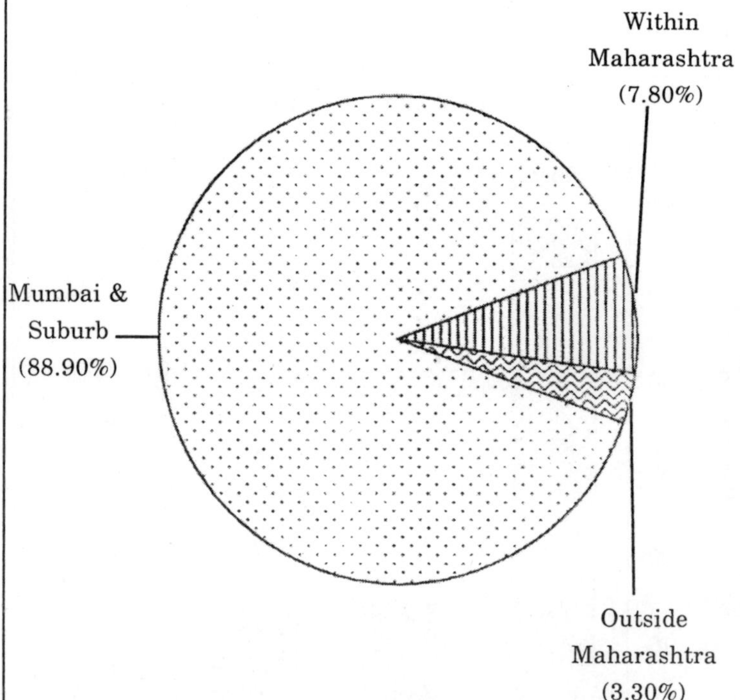

This turned out to be true with 88.9 per cent of the females in the study living in Mumbai the time of arrest.

Table 5.3: Residential Background of the Respondents

Residence	*Frequency*	*Percentage*
Mumbai and Suburbs	80	88.9
Within Maharashtra	7	7.8
Outside Maharashtra	3	3.3
Total	**90**	**100.0**

It is evident from the above that city-residents are most numerous in the sample. The city life is a manifestation of urbanization and modernization and our sample's distribution tends to affirm the association of crime with urban living. A generally higher percentage of criminals emanating from urban areas might be a result not only of greater urban pressures to take to deviance or crime but also, of the presence of a crime coping and detecting machinery, and to its proximity to the criminal. Most of the studies (Ahuja: 1969; Rani: 1983, etc.) reveal that urban areas provide more female offenders than rural areas.

The residential arrangements were also assessed with reference to type of dwelling.

Table 5.4: Type of Dwelling of the Respondents

Type of Dwelling	*Frequency*	*Percentage*
Slum Dwellers	49	54.4
Chawl Dwellers	31	34.4
Other than above	10	11.1
Total	**90**	**100.0**

Table 5.4 depicts that majority of the female criminals are slum dwellers. 34.4 percent are chawl dwellers, while the share of those residing in rented houses or owned houses and servant quarters is 11.1 per cent. The findings of the study show

that slums and chawls (88.8 per cent) produce more female criminals in urban area. A larger percentage of crimes are committed in cities by slum and chawl dwellers.

Slums and unauthorized structures, which are an outcome of irresistible inflow of population into the city and subsequent pressure on land and resources, not only reflect the range of disparity but also show inhuman living conditions and a declined quality of life. It may further be noted that such inhuman living conditions coupled with hardships in life, economic incapability, low education, health and mortality rate all are inter-relatcd and have a far reaching impact on the quality of life. Thus, the analysis reveals that the female criminals are partially a product of their living conditions.

Graph 5.4
Type of Dwelling

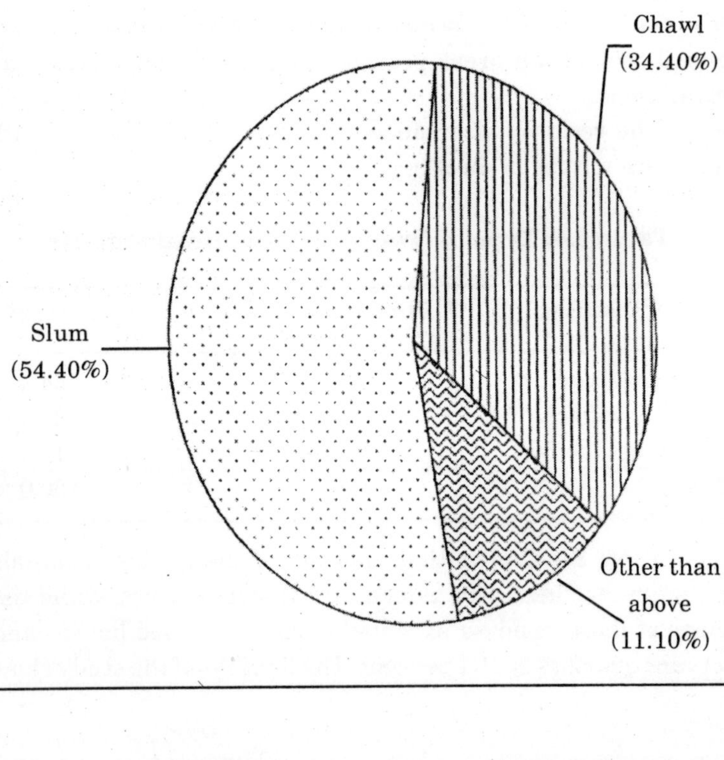

5.4 Religion and Mother Tongue

Religion forms the backbone of our systems and beliefs and is the influential force of social control. It was included in order to assess whether any religious group as abnormally represented in the study.

Table 5.5: Respondents' Distribution on the Basis of Religion

Religion	*Frequency*	*Percentage*
Hindu	52	57.8
Muslim	26	28.9
Others	12	13.3
Total	**90**	**100.0**

Graph 5.5
Religionwise Distribution

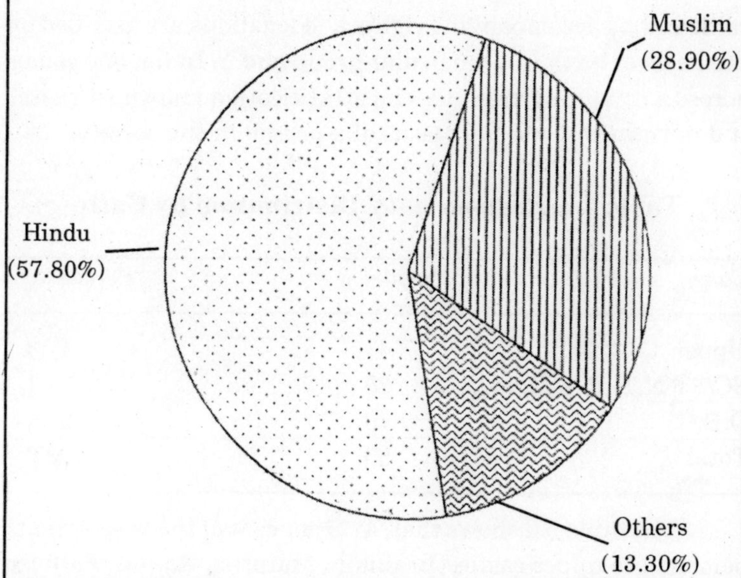

The table 5.5 reveals that majority of the sample consists of Hindus (57.8 percent) followed by Muslims (28.9 percent). Others constitute 13.3 per cent of the total sample i.e., Christians, Buddhist and Jains. Although there seems to be no direct link between religion and crime in present context yet it is imperative for the demographic analysis of the sample. No generalization can be made on the basis of this sample about the association of any particular religious group with criminality.

So far as mother tongue is concerned, in Maharashtra, most inmates either speak Marathi or in some cases understand and speak Hindi as well. However, since Mumbai is a cosmopolitan city situated in Maharashtra, out of the 90 respondents, i.e. 44.4 per cent respondents' mother tongue is Marathi, while 36.7 percent respondents' mother tongue is Hindi and 8.9 per cent spoke other languages. In Mumbai, Marathi and Hindi are dominant languages.

5.5 Caste

Religion and caste are important indicators of a person's status in Indian society. Caste is a system in which an individual's rank and its accompanying rights and legations are ascribed on the basis of birth in a particular group and in India, one comes across a unique system of social stratification known as 'caste'. It determines the social status of a person in the society.

Table 5.6: Respondents' Distribution by Caste

Caste	*Frequeny*	*Percentage*
Upper Castes	43	47.8
SC/ST/N.T. & D.T.	28	31.1
O.B.C.	19	21.1
Total	90	100.0

The table 5.6 shows that, 47.8 per cent of the respondents belonged to upper castes (Brahmin, Maratha, Rajput, Pathare

Prabhu, Saraswat, Bania, Pathan, Patel, Roman Catholic christians, Reddi and Gauda). This is followed by 31.1 per cent of SC/ST/N.T. & D.T., i.e., 18.9 per cent scheduled castes (Mahar, Mang, Chambhar,Garudi, Mang-Garudi, Telgu-Mochi, Meghwal, Nadia), 8.9 per cent scheduled tribes (Warli, Guriya), 3.3 per cent from N.T. & D.T. (Vadar, Kaikadi, Waghri) and 21.1 percent are other backward castes (Kunabi, Hajam, Darji, Vaishyavani, Shetty, Sutharia, Sunnai). Ahuja[6], in his study observed that the incidence of crime was low in backward castes whereas, Rani[7] found that a slightly more than 50 per cent of women criminals belonged to backward castes.

Graph 5.6
Castewise Distribution

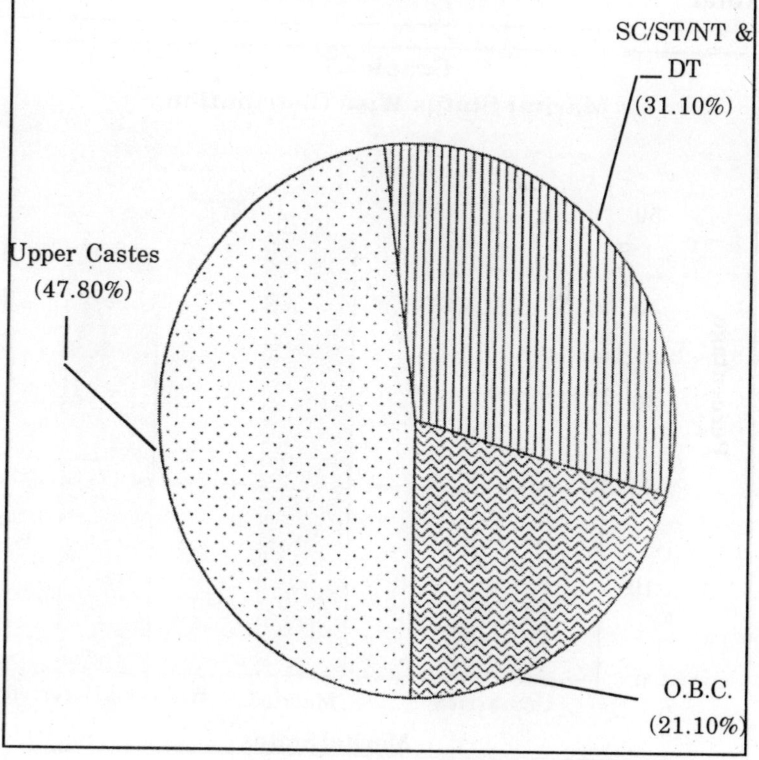

5.6 Marital Status:

Marital status, age at marriage and age difference between partners are crucial to the understanding of a person's most intimate and important interaction with life. Any sense of failure, frustration or victimization on this front may provoke unusual or deviant behaviour.

Table 5.7: Marital Status of the Respondents

Marital Status	*Frequency*	*Percentage*
Unmarried	9	10.0
Married	42	46.7
'Widowed / Deserted	39	43.3
Total	**90**	**100.0**

Graph 5.7
Marital Status Wise Distribution

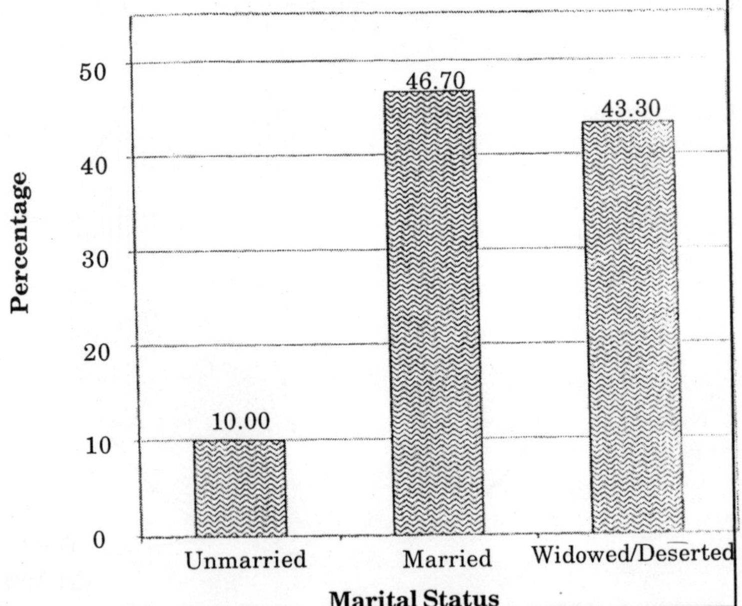

The present study shows that 46.7 per cent criminals were married, 43.3 per cent are widowed / deserted i.e., 17.8 per cent (16 respondents) and 25.6 per cent (23 respondents) respectively and only 10 per cent were unmarried. It may be legitimately inferred therefore that marital life in particular and family life in general in a female-criminal's career deserved special attention while analyzing the causes of female criminality.

In India, the outcome of marriage, if it ends in desertion or widowhood, carries respective strains and stigma for the woman. Marital status in the sample was thus a matter of great relevance and interest to the present study. Table 5.7 shows that very few respondents were unmarried. Marriage itself may not be a stabilizing element for women, as often assumed in India. In fact, in a culture like ours, most of the responsibilities attached to marriage and socio-cultural expectations are always much more attached to married than unmarried. When these responsibilities and socio-cultural expectations cannot be fulfilled within the framework of right means, the woman may enter the criminal world.

The details regarding age at the time of marriage are presented in Table 5.8.

Table 5.8: Age at the Time of Marriage

Age at the Time of Marriage	*Frequency*	*Percentage*
Below 18 yrs.	49	54.4
Above 18 yrs.	30	33.3
Don't know	2	2.2
Not Applicable	9	10.0
Total	**90**	**100.0**

Age at the time of marriage does affect person's ability to cope with married life. Keeping that in mind, this aspect was studied. Majority of the respondents have married before the age of 18. Young age at the time of marriage is a custom in India, and can cause strain on the health and personality of the woman, in some cases compelling some form of delinquent behaviour.

Age difference between spouses was studied and revealed no concentration of wide age differential between spouses. The fact that it barely figured as a cause of marital unhappiness only affirms the impression here that age difference between spouses as not consequential to the sample.

Table 5.9: Age Difference between Partners

Age Difference	*Frequency*	*Percentage*
Less than 5 yrs.	24	26.7
6 to 9 yrs.	22	24.4
10 and above	22	24.4
Don't know	13	14.4
Not Applicable	9	10.0
Total	90	100.0

Occupation

Details regarding occupation of the respondents are presented in Table 5.10.

Table 5.10: Distribution of the Respondents on the Basis of Occupation

Occupation	*Frequency*	*Percentage*
Service / Job	10	11.1
Domestic Servant	16	17.8
Business	19	21.1
Housewife	19	21.1
Any other	26	28.9
Total	**90**	**100.0**

A study of the occupations of the respondents reveals that only 19 (21.1 per cent) respondents were housewives. The rest 71 (78.9 per cent) respondents were engaged in some occupation and earned livelihood independently. 21.1 per cent were engaged in 'Business, e.g., vegetable vendors, retailers, etc. and the remaining 28.9 per cent wer engaged in different types of occupations like agriculture, labour work, social work, prostitution, beer-bar dancing, begging, collecting and selling old clothes, entertaining on the road.

In the total sample, 78.9 per cent of respondents were independent earners. In general, some impact on women of getting into employment and therefore, being exposed to the risk of getting into deviance of some kind is not improbable.

5.8 Income

Income is the indicator of economic well-being. It was therefore desirable to study the respondents' earnings and employment status. In studying this variable, the hypothesis was the probability of a low economic level, forcing a sense of despair and frustration and compelling respondents to resort to deviance. The relevant data is presented in Table 5.11.

The table below shows that, majority of the female criminals had an income below Rs.3000 per month. Even though economic condition does not necessarily indicate the role of

Table 5.11: Monthly Income of the Respondents

Monthly Income (in Rupees)	*Frequency*	*Percentage*
1000	22	24.4
1001-3000	27	30.0
3001-5000	9	10.0
5001 and above	7	7.8
Don't know & Not Applicable	25	27.8
Total	**90**	**100.0**

poverty in female crime, yet it is significant in the sense that low Income is an important contributory factor to family tensions and a combination of unsatisfactory social relationships and poverty leads to criminal behaviour.

Sharma B.R.[8] studied 36 female offenders in Delhi and Harayana and found 83 percent of them had monthly income of less than Rs.2000. Gote-Gavhane's[9] findings on 50 female convicts of Yeravada Jail, Pune in 1986 also proved that the incidence of female criminality is highest among the low income group and illiterates.

Graph 5.8
Monthly Income Wise Distribution

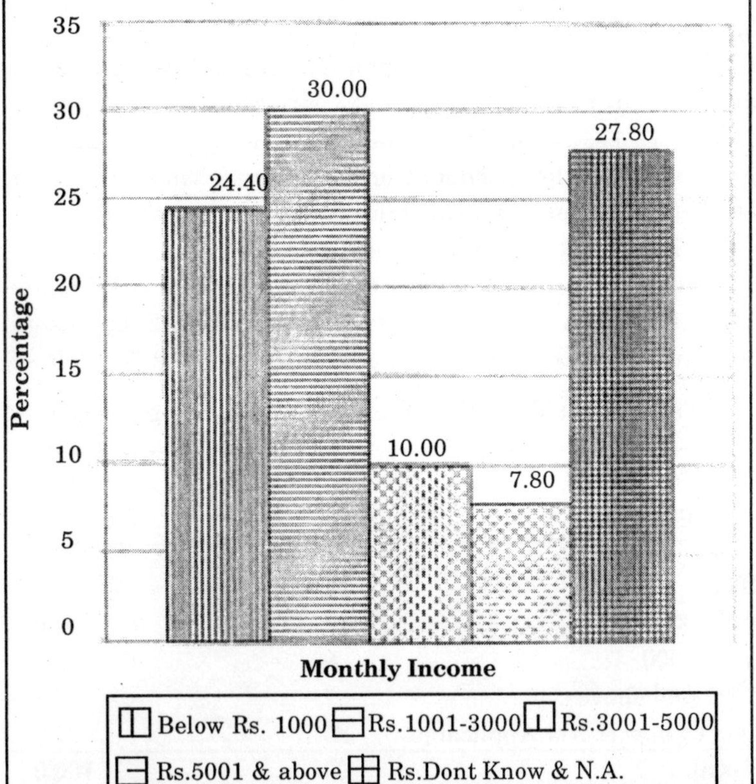

Therefore, it may be said that, female criminals are generally illiterate, slum dwellers, married, widowed or deserted, were married at early age and also come from low economic class. This reflects women's nature of adjustment, their economic and social conditions and environment situation for the explanation of crime and criminality.

References

1. Ahuja Ram - 'Female Offenders in India', p.10.
2. Rani Bilmoria - 'Female Criminality: An Empricial Study in Andhra Pradesh', p. 6.
3. Sharma B.R. - 'Crime and Women: A Psycho-Diagnostic Study of Female Criminality', p.130.
4. Ahuja Ram - 'Female Offenders in India', p. 25.
5. Bajpai Anju & Bajpai, P. K.- Female Criminality in India', p. 52.
6. Ahuja Ram - 'Female Offenders in India, p.18.
7. Rani Bilmoria - 'Female Criminality: An Empricial Study in Andhra Pradesh', p.73.
8. Sharma B.R. - 'Crime and Women: A Psycho-Diagnostic Study of Female Criminality', p.130.
9. Gote-Gavhane S. - 'Female Criminality and Sociological Theories', p. 229.

6

Socio-Economic Background of Undertrial Female Criminals

Introduction

The increasing crime rate in developing countries is a result of rapid socio-economic changes, industrialization and consequently urbanization.

The ill effects of development efforts are manifested in the industrialization and consequent urbanization viz., migration, increased mobility, population increase, unemployment, poverty, housing shortages, pressures on supplies, loss of values, cultural crisis and so on. Such a trend affects the social order and does not match with the principle of 'well-being' of humanity. It therefore calls for reconsideration of the development strategies and puts us into a condition of dilemma of deciding whether to go back to some of our traditional societal norms in a moulded way or to absorb more and more unfamiliar and valueless culture which is also the crux of development dilemma.

Such thoughts create an intellectual discomfort and provoke one to explore factors that are associated with deviance, their inter-relationships.Thus, the present study provides an overview of female criminality scenario in Mumbai, discusses the socio-economic background of the respondents. "Criminal behaviour is an integral part of social behaviour, which can be understood partly in relation to the person's social situation. The personality of the offender, the social world in which he lives and the previous experiences growing out of interactions between the individual and the environmental situation play a vital part in the social process leading to criminal behaviour".[1]

Family is the most important social group that exists in society. It not only gratifies an individual's essential needs but it also transmits cultural values which socialize an individual and train him in survival patterns. However, family situations vary from individual to individual. It is imperative on the part of the researcher to study the family background of undertrial female criminals in order to have an insight into the attitude, behaviour pattern, values and aspirations of female criminals.

6.1 Type of Family

The type of respondent's household is relevant to the respondent's social profile. The data is presented below:

Table 6.1: Type of Family

Type of Family	*Frequency*	*Percentage*
Nuclear	60	66.7
Joint	25	27.8
Not Applicable	5	5.6
Total	90	100.0

Table 6.1 shows that, majority of the respondents come from nuclear families while around one-fourth belong to joint families. Some of the respondents did not have family ties (either they lived alone or live with friends, neighbours or brothel-keeper). In Mumbai nuclear family seems to be a pattern of family structure. The majority of the respondents of the sample in Mumbai indicated the break-up of the traditional extended family network and emergence of nuclear family.

Graph 6.1
Type of Family

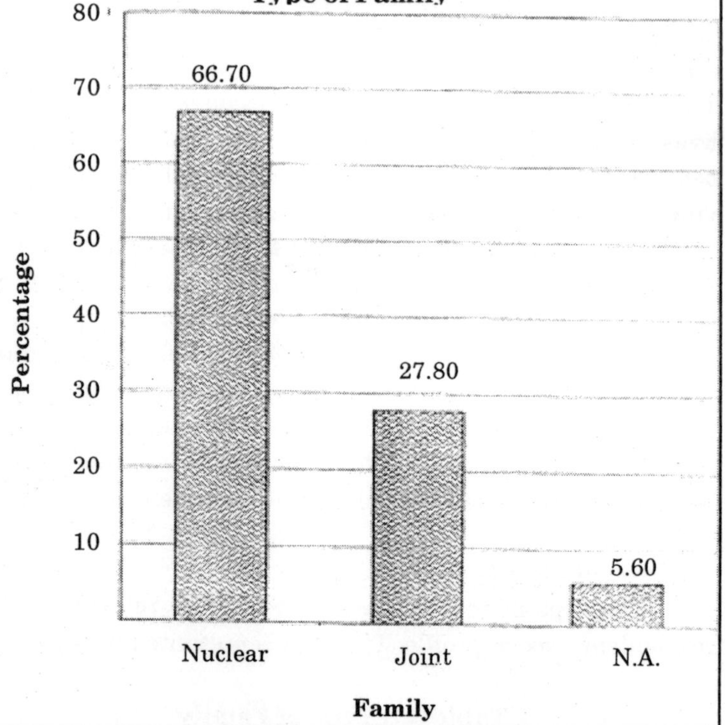

With change in family structure, family ties have probably weakened, with the consequent weakening of the family's ability to transmit moral values.

Table 6.2: Educational Level of the Family

Type and Educational Level of Family	*Frequency*	*Percentage*
Nuclear - more than 50% literate	35	38.9
Nuclear - more than 50% illiterate	25	27.8
Joint - more than 50% literate	13	14.4
Joint - more than 50% illiterate	12	13.3
Not Applicable	5	5.6
Total	90	100.0

Table 6.2, related to the literacy background of offenders' family, indicates that literate family members were more in number than the illiterate family members. These figures bring to light an interesting fact that in all these years illiterate family backgroundprovoked the individual for crime in greater proportion. However, the proportion of !iterates in the general population exhibits an increasing trend, while the illiterate proportion shows a declining trend both in general population in Mumbai and among the undertrials. Hence, it is clear that female criminals from literate family backgrounds are participating preponderantly in criminal acts.

The literacy rate in greater Mumbai in 1991 was - 78 per cent for males and 65.8 per cent for females assumes importance especially in the context of a developing nation like India where illiteracy is one of the major concerns.

6.2 Family Income

It is important to understand the economic status of the family. The normal expectation would be that criminality would be less where income is more.

Table 6.3: Monthly Family Income of Undertrial Female Criminals

Monthly Family Income in Rupees per month)	*Frequency*	*Percentage*
Below 1000	14	15.6
1001-3000	32	35.6
3001- 5000	22	24.4
5001 and above	14	15.6
Don't know & Not Applicable	8	8.9
Total	90	100.0

It is observed from Table 6.3 that, 8.9 per cent respondents either did not know their family income or they did not have family ties (both described together). This shows that female criminality is more a lower-class phenomenon. Almost all studies conducted in our country on crime and its relation to the socio-economic order, show that those belonging to the lower strata have been found to have committed the highest no. of crimes.

The present study points out that majority of the female criminals belonged to the families, the monthly incomes of which were less than Rs.3000. Low economic level of family indicates low standard of life. Thus, it proves that poverty is the factor, which creates an environment leading a person to commit a crime, e.g , if a person did not get required proper opportunities to earn more money through socially accepted ways, then there will be a possibility of violating the norms of society and turning

Graph 6.2
Monthly Family Income

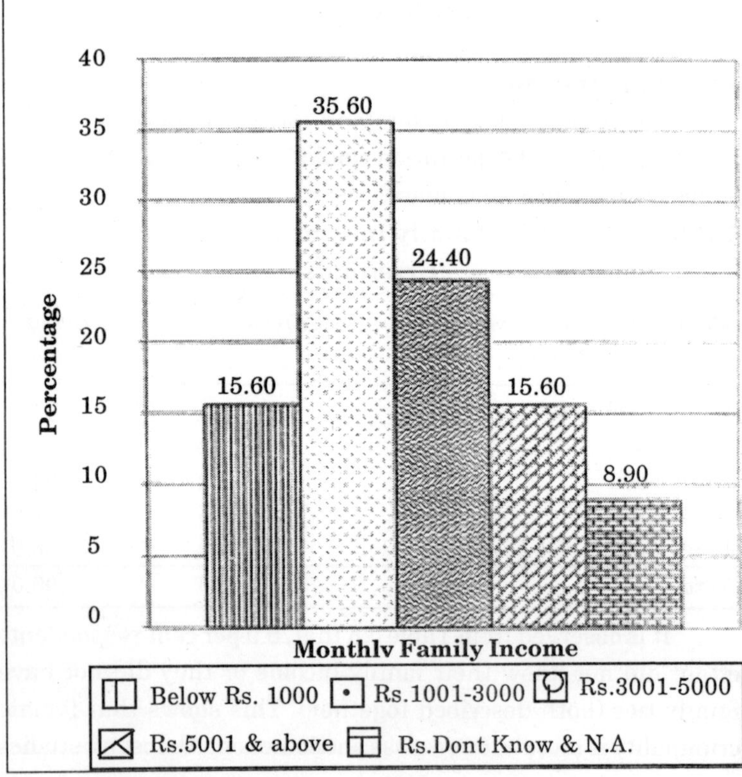

to deviant behaviour. In India, most of the population lives in poor economic to deviant conditions. We find that all of them do not turn to criminality because some other factors protect them from illegal ways. Thus, poverty can not be the sole factor responsible for generating criminality but still it plays a supporting role.

6.3 Bread-Winner of the Family

Table 6.4: Bread-Winner of the Family

Bread-Winner	*Frequency*	*Percentage*
Respondent	36	40.0
Husband	32	35.6
Any other	17	18.9
Not Applicable	5	5.6
Total	90	100.0

In India, the bread-winner of the family would be male and generally father or husband. In exploring this aspect, the interest was to ascertain whether the sample had any unusual distribution or female headed households. Female headed households were found to account for 40 per cent of the sample. 35.6 per cent households were headed by the husbands of the respondents, 18.9 per cent were headed by fathers, sons or daughters, sister-in-law, etc. and 5.6 per cent respondents did not have family ties. The respondents headed their households themselves either due to widowhood or desertion or spouses were non-earning dependents. Whatever the reason, the resultant strain and pressures must have been experienced by this particular segment in the present sample.

Childbearing, whether excessive, less or absent has a special bearing on a Woman's status in society.

6.4 Number of Children

Table 6.5 shows that, one-fourth of the respondents have more than 3 children. Those who had single child and who were childless accounted for equal percentage i.e., 12.2 per cent.

Nearly half of the respondents reported 2-3 children. However, this data included those who had children out of wedlock in the case of one unmarried mother and a prostitute.

Table 6.5: Distribution of the Respondents by No. of Children

No. of Children	*Frequency*	*Percentage*
Single Child	11	12.2
2-3 Children	38	42.2
More than 3 Children	23	25.5
No Child	11	12.2
Not Applicable	7	7.8
Total	90	100.0

6.5 Family Environment

Most studies have shown that crime is caused because of social environment, namely, family neighbourhood and peer group. Ahuja found that maladjustment in the family is a major cause of female criminality. Inter-relationships within the family, to a great extent, determines behaviour pattern of an individual and plays a significant role in the formation of behaviour which, in turn, effects inter-personal adjustment of an individual. It is often suggested that cordial family atmosphere provide an individual chances for his development.

Table 6.6: Information about Respondents' Family Environment

Family Environment	*Frequency*	*Percentage*
Members integrated emotionally	65	72.2
Quarrelsome nature	16	17.8
Members engaged in criminal acts	4	4.4
Not Applicable	5	5.6
Total	90	100.0

The majority of the respondents reported to have emotionally integrated family background, only 4.4 per cent have criminal background.

On the basis of review findings, it may be viewed that women are emotionally adjusted at familial levels. Majority of women have emotional ties and cordial relations with family members which bind them to their families as well as children. The one possibility behind it may be most of the respondents live alone with their children.

Table 6.7: Inter-Relationships within the Family

Inter -relationships	*Frequency*	*Percentage*
Cordial	68	75.6
Antagonistic	17	18.9
Not Applicable	5	5.6
Total	90	100.0

Table 6.7 indicates that, majority of the respondents had cordial interpersonal relationships within the family at the time of committing an offence, while one-fifth respondents reported antagonistic atmosphere.

Table 6.8: Treatment by Family Members

Nature of Treatment	*Frequency*	*Percentage*
Treated well	73	81.1
Harshly treated	12	13.3
Not Applicable	5	5.6
Total	90	100.0

Table 6.8 depicts that, majority of the respondents were treated well by their family members. Only few were harshly treated by their family members.

The above responses indicate that, there were no conflicts in interpersonal relationships within the family. It may be because, in India, women have to perform their roles as 'dharma' (religiously), so they don't expect too much from others. The ideal image delegated to woman does not allow her to express her feelings or frustrations at any time, instead they get accumulated. Therefore, most of the time they accepted the situation as it is.

6.6 Childhood Experience

Table 6.9: Respondents' Childhood Experience

Childhood Experience	*Frequency*	*Percentage*
Happy	43	47.8
Unhappy	45	50.0
Average	2	2.2
Total	90	100.0

In the present study half of the respondents experienced unhappy childhood. Psychologist Sidney Burman[2] relates the causation of delinquency to early childhood experiences, emotional deprivations, child rearing processes, etc., which influence the formation of the personality and the development of attitudes, values and life-style. The abnormal expression of behaviour expressed in an anti-social form, is the result of these factors. Childhood experience is related to family environment and family environment producing delinquent behaviour may be analysed with reference to a broken home, family tension, parental rejection, parental control and family economics.

Abrahamsen[3] also pointed out that, the youngster does not feel secure and content in the tension filled family environment and a home where tension exists is a good breeding ground for future delinquents.

Thus many sociologists and psychologists consider family as the most significant factor in the development of child. Half of the respondents did not feel happy in their childhood, may be because of either unsatisfactory relationship with their parents or they were not satisfied with the situation within their family. Satisfying their urges and impulses can take the form of anti-social behaviour.

6.7 Neighbourhood

Next to family, the person spends his/her time in the company of friends and neighbours. The neighbourhood can contribute to delinquency by blocking basic personality needs, engendering culture conflicts and fostering anti-social values.

Table 6.10: Friends of the Respondents

Type of Friends	*Frequency*	*Percentage*
Doing similar jobs/occupation	15	16.6
Doing different jobs/occupation	5	5.5
Neighbouring housewife	13	14.4
No friends	57	63.3
Total	90	100.0

Table 6.10 indicates that, the present study does not reinforce any influence in this respect. A majority of the respondents did not have friends. Hence the companion or group of peers was not found to be a supportive factor in committing crimes.

Table 6.11: Respondents' Relations with Neighbours

Nature of Relations	*Frequency*	*Percentage*
Friendly/ Good	78	86.7
Unfriendly /Bad	12	13.3
Total	90	100.0

The Table 6.11 indicates that, majority of the respondents had established good relations with their neighbours, while in urban areas neighbourhood is emerging as a secondary group. Therefore, like in rural areas, it is not an important agency of social control and does not contribute much to the development of the person. On the other hand, in urban areas neighbourhood can contribute to delinquency by fostering anti-social values. Only 13.3 per cent out of the total sample had unfriendly relations with neighbours, because they did not get along with them.

Tabie 6.12: Income Status of Neighbours (compared to respondents' income)

Income Status	*Frequency*	*Percentage*
Same income level	42	46.7
Higher income level	24	26.7
Lower income level	7	7.8
Income ranges varied	11	12.2
Don't Know	6	6.6
Total	90	100.0

About half of the neighbours' income status was similar to the income status of respondents. On the basis of table 6.10, 6.11 and 6.12, the present study depicts that, there was no direct influence of companions and neighbours. In other words, in India, female criminals did not engage in criminal gang activity *or* had any support from organized criminal gangs.

6.8 Decision Making in the Family

Table 6.13: Distribution of Respondents on the Basis of Decision Making in the Family

Matters decided without husband's consent	*Frequency*	*Percentage*
All	8	8.9
None	25	27.8
Only household matters	4	4.4
Upbringing of children	1	1.4
Purchasing of small thing	4	4.4
Not Applicable	48	53.3
Total	90	100.0

The above data is with reference to only married respondents in the sample. Therefore, responses of unmarried women, widows and those of deserted marital status were included in the table as 'not applicable'.

Table 6.13 shows that, 25 out of 42 married respondents were unable to decide any of the matter without their husband's consent. Only 8 respondents had decision making powers in their hands. The remaining 9 respondents took decisions on their own regarding household matters, upbringing of children and the purchasing of small things. It implies that in majority of cases (25 out of 42 married respondents) the decision making powers are entrusted entirely to the husbands. Sometimes it may lead to female crime because of the frustrations and stressful interpersonal relations with husband and other family members.

In a male dominated society, decision making also indicates family culture and understanding in the family. It is often claimed that women have equal rights in making family decisions but in practice they are just being informed about decisions which have already been taken. The analysis of the data depicted in the present study is no exception.

Table 6.14: Situation Created because of Serious differences in Opinion

Situation when respondent and her husband had serious differences of opinion	*Frequency*	*Percentage*
This was not very frequent	29	32.2
Frequent quarrels	6	6.7
Physical violence	7	7.8
Not Applicable	48	53.3
Total	90	100.0

Table 6.14, indicates that in the case of 29 respondents out of 42 married respondents, this situation of serious differences of opinion was not very frequent. In 6 cases there were frequent quarrels and in 7 cases respondents were victims of physical violence or being physically abused by their husbands. In India, society expects that a woman should be submissive. Therefore, there is a possibility that 29 out of 42 married

respondents did not have to face the situation of serious differences of opinion may be because they were unable to express their true feelings due to social pressures.

6.9 Marital Life

Nature of marital life and decision making power are intimate statements on a woman's status, sense of well-being and her self-esteem.

Table 6.15: Nature of Marital Life

Nature of Marital Life	*Frequency*	*Percentage*
Satisfactory	31	34.4
Unsatisfactory	7	7.8
Harrassment and torture	4	4.4
Not Applicable	48	53.3
Total	90	100.0

Table 6.15 indicates that, response of having satisfactory marital life was highest. The question was not applicable to unmarried, deserted and widowed respondents.

However, even the female offender understands her social roles as determined by society. In our society, woman's major role is that of a homemaker, dependent upon her husband. Once married, it is presumed that woman will spend most of her life in devotion and service to her husband and family. So, having no other alternative, there is a possibility that a woman tends to seek satisfaction in whatever situation she is in.

6.10 Surroundings

The analysis of environmental factors provides an insight into individual case histories. We will focus here on the role of family, friends and neighbours in provoking the individual to become a criminal.

Table 6.16 indicates that, majority of female criminals did not have criminal surroundings. Only in the case of one-fourth of respondents, their family members, friends or neighbours had committed offences.

Table 6.16: Offences Committed by Respondents Family Members/Friends/Neighbours

Offence Committed by	*Frequency*	*Percentage*
Family Members	3	3.3
Friends	4	4.4
Neighbours	15	16.6
Not Applicable	68	75.6
Total	90	100.0

The above analysis provides an understanding of the socio-economic background of the undertrial female criminals. The city reflects diversity, plurality, heterogeneity and disparity which are not only the symptoms of urban environment but also are some of the urban challenges. It may also be observed that only modernity or economic development not act as a buffer against deviance and ensure an overall well being.

In urban area, greater pressures provoke an individual to deviance or to commit crime. After independence, the position and status of women in India, especially in urban areas changed drastically. Modernization and industrialization transformed the process of socio-economic environment. More and more women started working outside and became able to supplement the income of their families. Therefore they gradually developed contacts beyond the control of their family members because of their employment away from home. Women became more independent and started imitating men in everything, even in crime. Although, crime is basically considered 'a male phenomenon' because it is the male who gets involved in criminal activities much more and much faster than a female. These sex differences in crime are due to socialization and unequal opportunities due to sex-role differences.

On the other hand, double burden of work and home responsibilities, the increasing rate of family breakdown, the psychological trauma of widowhood and desertion and also financial difficulties in rearing up children, all contribute to the incidents of female criminality.

Thus, socio-economic analysis of the present study conveyed that majority of respondents did not perceive themselves as unhappy, badly treated or victimized. In contradiction, nearly half of the respondents are found widowed or deserted and majority of married respondents were unable to decide any of the matter without their husband's consent. Poverty was found to be a significant factor in provoking a person towards delinquency and it may cause the root of marital or other frustrations. A poor home also fails to provide economic security to its members.

However, female crime is mostly related to the lower socio-economic status of the family. The people of lower socio-economic status face more deprivations throughout their life in comparison to people of higher or middle socio-economic status. It is difficult for them to satisfy their economic needs. Therefore, they are tempted to commit crimes. That is why the great majority of criminals come from poor economic conditions.

References

1. Chockalingam K.-'A Study of Relationship between Income and Expenditure and Past Life among Recidivists', p.114.
2. Sidney Burman - ' Anti-Social Character Disorder' in Ruth S. Cavan's, Readings in Juvenile Delinquency, p.142.
3. Abrahamsen David - 'The Psychology of Crime' , p. 43.

7

Nature and Causes of Female Crime

Introduction

The present study analyzes female criminality in the major city of Mumbai in Maharashtra. The worldwide statistics on the incidence of crime exhibit a general increase in the rate of female criminality in many countries. Women in India seem to be taking part in all types of crime. Thus, female criminality will remain a very significant area of studies. The crime trend seems to have increased in Mumbai. So it is necessary to understand what are the major crimes in which they are getting involved? The answer of this question will give a clear picture of female criminality.

7.1 Nature of Crime

This study of 90 undertrial female criminals, gives us the crime-wise picture.

Table 7.1: Nature of Crime/Offence (Offence under which respondents are on trial)

Crime / Offence	*Frequency*	*Percentage*
Murders	23	25.6
Thefts/Pick Pocketing	28	31.1

(Contd.)

(Contd. Table 7.1)

Crime / Offence	*Frequency*	*Percentage*
Kidnapping	2	2.2
Cheating	10	11.1
Assistance in Raping	5	5.6
Immoral Traffic (Prevention) Act	2	2.2
NDPS Act	11	12.2
Passport Act (Refugees)	9	10.0
Total	90	100.0

These crimes falls under Indian Penal Code (I.P.C.) as well as under special Local Laws (S.L.L.) applicable in Maharashtra. The undertrials were arrested by the police under sections of the IPC and other state/local laws as well as Central Government special laws such as Immoral Traffic Prevention Act, NDPS Act (Narcotic Drugs and psychotropic Substances Act) and Passport Act.

Table 7.1 highlights the following aspects:

Murders and Thefts are the two prominent crime activities in which females are getting involved. Theft activity is maximum (31.1 per cent) and occupies the first place, murders (25.6 per cent) occupy the second place. Considering the total female crime picture, in respect of murders and thefts, these two prominent crimes cover majority of the picture. This means that these are two activities in which women are getting involved to the maximum. NDPS crimes amount to 12.2 per cent followed by cheating (11.1 per cent). The other crimes like kidnapping, assistance in raping, immoral traffic and passport act crimes have comparatively very little share in the crime picture - only 20 percent of the total crime activities. According to role theory, girls are usually trained to be passive, domesticated and non-violent and are not allowed to learn how to fight. Girls thus shrink from violence and do not possess the necessary technical ability or strength to engage in crimes of

Graph 7.1

Nature of Crime/Offence

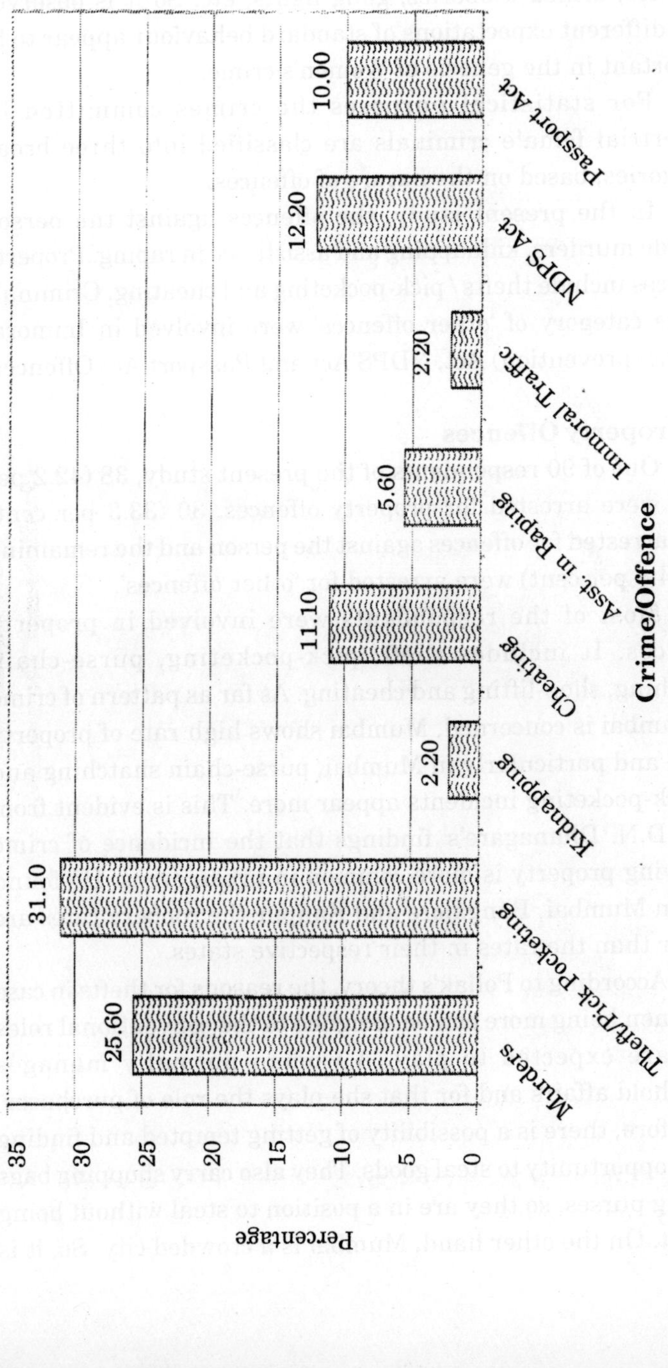

violence, armed robberies, gang fights, etc. So it is observed that different expectations of standard behaviour appear to be important in the genesis of Women's crime.

For statistical purposes the crimes committed by undertrial female criminals are classified into three broad categories, based on the nature of offences.

In the present study, the offences against the person include murders, kidnapping and assistance in raping. Property offences include thefts / pick-pocketing and cheating. Criminals in the category of 'other offences' were involved in Immoral Traffic (prevention) Act, NDPS Act and Passport Act Offences.

7.2 Property Offences

Out of 90 respondents of the present study, 38 (42.2 per cent) were arrested for property offences. 30 (33.3 per cent) were arrested for offences against the person and the remaining 22 (24.4 per cent) were arrested for 'other offences'.

Most of the respondents were involved in property offences. It includes theft, pick-pocketing, purse-chain snatching, shop-lifting and cheating. As far as pattern of crime in Mumbai is concerned, Mumbai shows high rate of property crime and particularly in Mumbai, purse-chain snatching and or pick-pocketing incidents appear more. This is evident from Prof. D.N. Dhanagare's[1] findings that the incidence of crime involving property is more common in urban areas. He found that in Mumbai, Bangalore and Kanpur the robbery rates are higher than the rates in their respective states.

According to Pollak's theory, the reasons for thefts in case of women being more can be assigned to the conventional roles they are expected to play. A woman normally manages household affairs and for that she plays the role of purchaser. Therefore, there is a possibility of getting tempted and finding ready opportunity to steal goods. They also carry shopping bags and big purses, so they are in a position to steal without being caught. On the other hand, Mumbai is a crowded city. So, it is

Graph 7.2
Nature of Crime/Offence

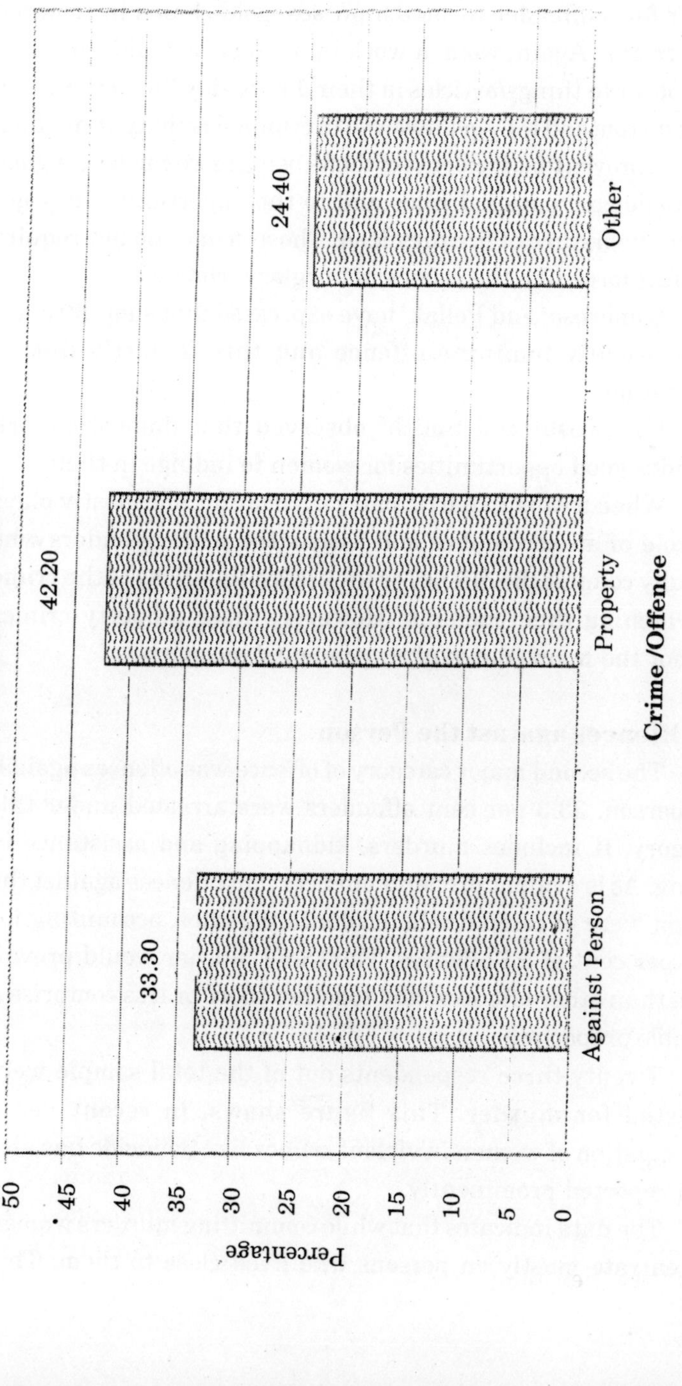

easier for a offender to snatch purses, gold-chains in crowded local trains. Again, women work in a house as maid servants, they observe things/articles in their day-to-day life, temptation plays its role and they get involved in criminal activity of stealing. Thus, it proves that incidents of thefts being more can be assigned to female conventional roles and to the opportunity they get due to the nature of life they lead. These crimes do not require physical force like the crimes of burglary, riots, etc.

Lombroso[2] and Pollak[3] have expressed that shop-lifting is a specifically feminine offence and this is partly due to temptation.

Lombroso[4] and Smith[5] observed that domestic work provides good opportunities for women to indulge in theft.

When a woman participates in cheating, she mostly plays the role of an accomplice and assists the male offenders who actually commit the offence or they learn the tricks of the crime by watching their menfolk. However, these property crimes are not the main source of respondents' income.

7.3 Offences against the Person

The second major category of offence was offences against the person. 33.3 per cent offenders were arrested under this category. It includes murders, kidnapping and assistance in raping. As is evident property offences and offences against the person were of comparable incidence together, accounting for 76.5 per cent of all offences. Theft and murder would prevail more than other offences, and together more or less comprise a sizeable proportion.

Twenty-three respondents out of the total sample were arrested for murder. This figure shows, in recent years participation of women in violent crimes like homicide has also been reported prominently.

The data indicates that while committing murders women concentrate mostly on persons who lived close to them. This

Table 7.2: Respondent's Relation with Victim in the Cases of Murder

Relation with Victim	*Frequency*	*Percentage*
Daughter-in-law	8	8.9
Spouse	2	2.2
Other family member	7	7.8
Neighbour	4	4.4
Any other	2	2.2
Not applicable	67	74.4
Total	90	100.0

finding supports the review findings of Ahuja[6] and Pollak.[7] As Ahuja observed that 92.2 per cent cases were those in which the victim was a member of the female criminal's family. Pollak also observed that female offenders concentrated on victims, such as children, husbands, family members and lovers, who are close to them. Pollak further explained that such a focus on victims is consistent with the various roles women play in society. This proves the validity of the hypothesis of stressful situations within the family which play an important role in female criminality.

The victim-offender relationship is more meaningful in female homicide because the social environment of Indian woman is very limited. She interacts with a very limited number of persons. Therefore, any severe interpersonal conflict or any emotional tension which hampers her life and frustrates her, may ultimately arouse her and lead her to this extreme step. Sometimes, homicide occurs as the only way out of a hopeless situation that a woman is facing.

Out of the 23 murders in table 7.2 very few respondents committed the offence independently. Most of them played the role of accomplice but were actively involved in offence. Some of the respondents were involved in the murder incidentally.

Two respondents out of the total sample were kidnappers. One respondent, who continues to be a prostitute and was also running a brothel, lured a helpless girl into accepting the profession of a prostitute. The other respondent reported that she picked up a child on the road and took him away.

There were 5 cases of women who helped men in committing the offence of rape. They were arrested under the crime of assistance in raping.

7.4 Other Offences

Twenty-two respondents committed crimes under this category. It includes Immoral Traffic Act, NDPS Act and Passport Act offences.

Out of 90 undertrial female criminals only 2 were arrested for Immoral Traffic Act offence. They had confessed to their occupation as prostitutes. They were involved in obscene behaviour at public places. In this type of crime an individual violates the rules of conduct in society. Eleven respondents were arrested for NDPS Act (Narcotic drugs and psychotropic Substances Act, 1985) offence. They were actively involved in this offence. Most of the women accepted this disapproved business as main or subsidiary source of income. They did it either independently or with the assistance of their family members, friends or neighbours or playing the role of accomplice. They carried out the business in their homes or near their residential area. The remaining 9 respondents, who were included in other offences, were arrested for Pass Port Act (Refugees) offence. All of them were citizens of Bangladesh. They had migrated to Mumbai with an economic motive.

7.5 Nature of Involvement

The present study reveals that women indulge in a variety of offences. They are involved in different types of offences either as main culprit or accomplice. The following table shows the involvement of women in offences.

Table 7.3: Involvement of Respondents in Committing Crime

Nature of Involvement	*Frequency*	*Percentage*
Offence committed alone	40	44.4
In association with others	50	55.6
Total	90	100.0

Table 7.3 indicates that, nearly less than half of the respondents committed crime without taking anybody's help and majority have committed crime with the help of others. This data shows the nature of criminal act of the respondents. Majority of them were involved in crime as accomplices.

7.6 Type of Companion

The data on this aspect is presented in Table 7.4.

Table 7.4: Respondents' Distribution according to Type of Companion

Type of Companion	*Frequency*	*Percentage*
Spouse	7	7.8
Family member	23	25.6
Friend	4	4.4
Neighbour	12	13.3
Any other	4	4.4
Not applicable	40	44.4
Total	90	100.0

Majority of the respondents committed an offence by taking help from others or assisting others. Spouse and family member, were accomplices in 30 cases, and in other 20 cases the accomplices were friend, neighbour and outside members (relatives of the accused or gangsters or strangers). Most of the respondents (30 out of 50 respondents) have received help from their close relatives, i.e., from spouse and family members.

Graph 7.3 Nature of Criminality

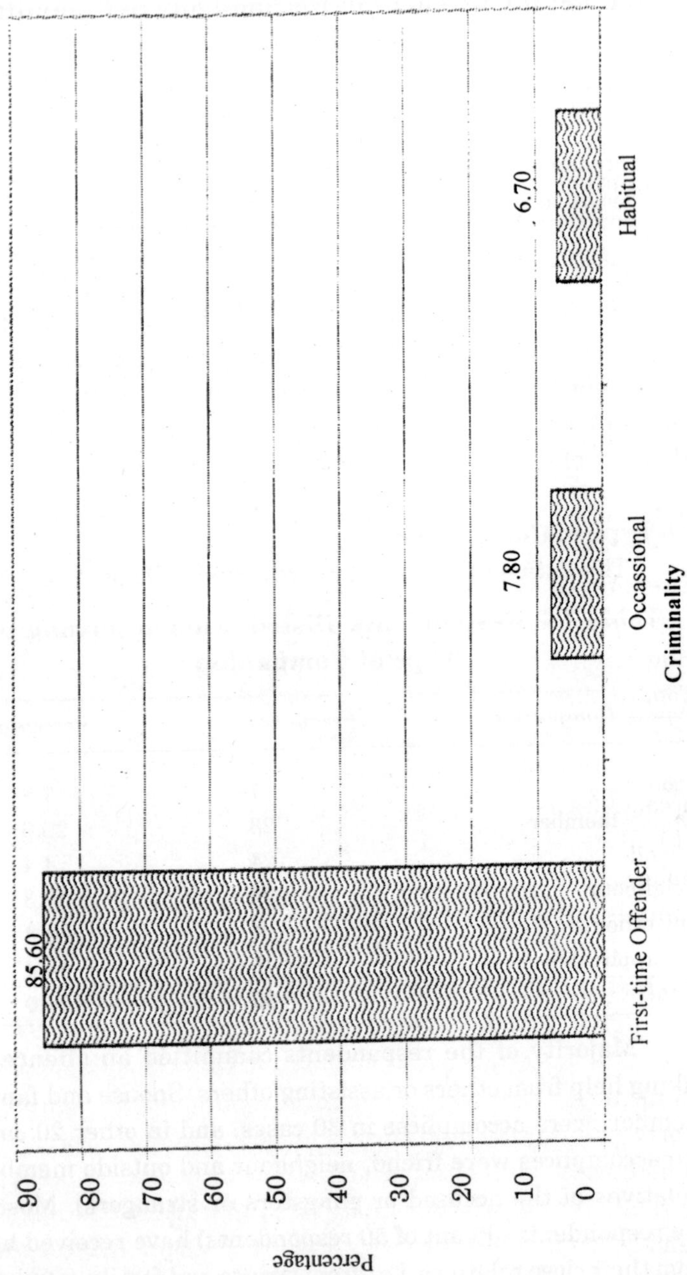

In the present study out of 90 respondents, 83 (92.2 per cent) were arrested for the first time. But that doesn't mean that they have committed the offence for the first time. The official record shows that a few of them have more than one criminal case in their accounts. In other words, they have committed offence in the past but escaped from the eyes of police and law. Seven respondents were arrested more than one time, 6 out of them have committed same type of offence in the past.

7.7 Nature of Criminality

The information on this aspect is presented in table 7.5.

Table 7.5: Nature of Criminality

Nature of Criminality	*Frequency*	*Percentage*
First time offender	77	85.6
Occassional	7	7.8
Habitual	6	6.7
Total	90	100.0

The Table 7.5 shows that, only few respondents were occasional or habitual criminals, while majority were first offenders. It proves that most of the respondents were not habitual criminals. The possibility is that, they might have committed criminal act because of the pressure of situation.

7.8 Nature of Thoughts

The information on this aspect is presented in Table 7.6.

Table 7.6 srows that, majority of the respondents did not think about the results of their action before committing crime. Forty per cent of respondents out of the total sample claim innocence about their action. This is because, the present study is related to undertrial female criminals and not to convicted female criminals. Therefore, these respondents were opposed

Table 7.6: Thoughts of Respondent about the Results of Action

Nature or Thoughts	*Frequency*	*Percentage*
Did not think about it	53	58.9
Fear of getting caught	1	1.1
Claims innocence	36	40.0
Total	90	100.0

to any kind of labeling as criminals since the charges leveled against them were not confirmed by court.

However, as most of the respondents in the present sample are first time offenders and majority of them did not think about the results of their action before they committed crime, proves that either they might have been in tension at the time of criminal act or they did not think it serious and heinous or as harmful to society.

7.9 Causes of Crime

Bonger[8] has classified crimes into four groups on the basis of their motives: economic, sexual, political and vengeance. But it cannot be maintained that all crimes are committed only with one motive. In the present study, motives behind the crime were examined. The following table shows the responses of respondents regarding the motivations to commit crimes.

Table 7.7: Motivations Behind the Criminal Act

Motives Behind Crime	*Frequency*	*Percentage*
Financial causes	49	54.4
Old feuds / disputes	5	5.6
Marital difficulties /Ill-treatment by family members	4	4.4
Other	8	8.9
Claims innocence	24	26.7
Total	90	100.0

Graph 7.4 Motivations Behind the Criminal Act

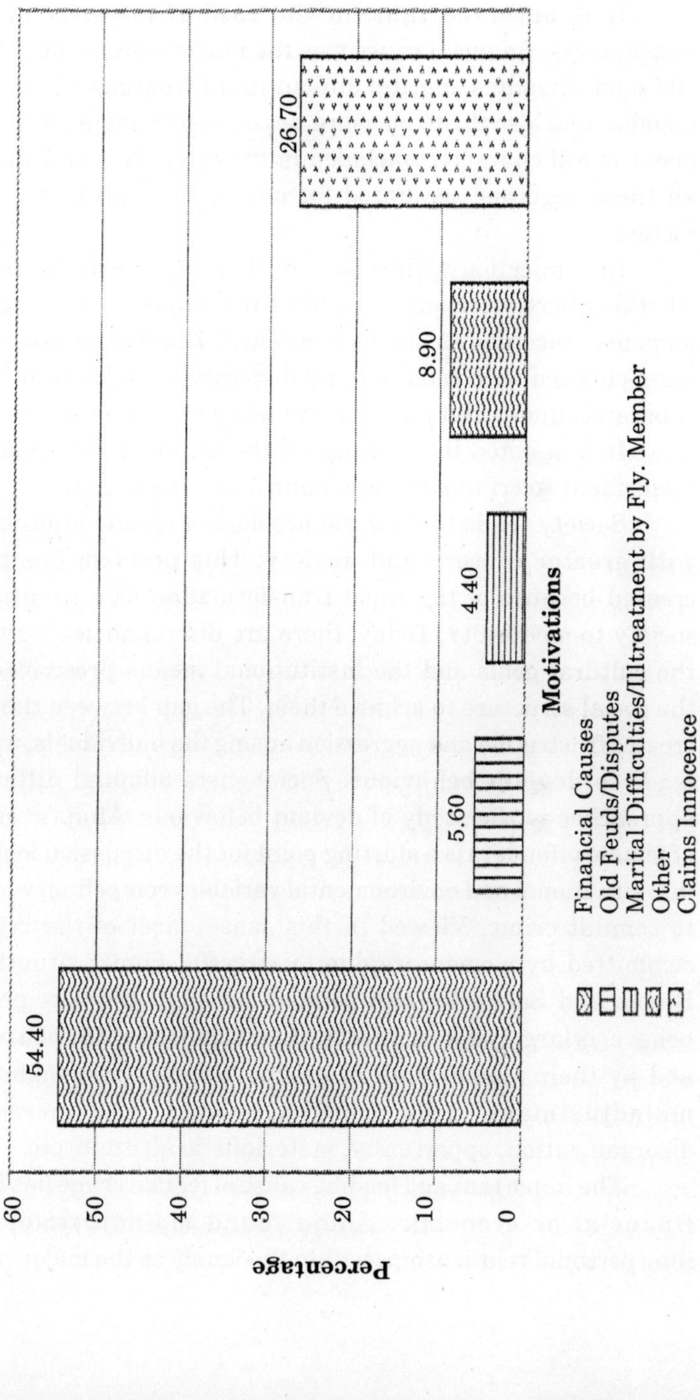

It is observed that, in the case of majority of the respondents, financial cause was the major motivating factor. Old feuds/disputes, marital difficulties/ill-treatment by family member and also thrill/ pleasure, sexual harassment, suspicion about moral character (included in the category - 'any other'), all these together accounted for one-fifths of all motivating factors.

In connection with table 7.6, there was curiosity to see whether there were any disparities in opinions regarding the responses recorded as 'claims innocence'. These responses were cross-checked with table 7.7 and disparity was observed. This is because undertrial female criminals were under stress.

It was noted that among all the factors motivating the respondent to criminality economic factor is prominent.

Society tends to view the problem of female criminality with greater concern and anxiety. This problem has been created because of the rapid transformation of a traditional society to modernity. Today, there are discrepancies between the cultural goals and the institutional means prescribed by the social structure to achieve them. The gap between the two creates frustration and aggression among the individuals, which leads to deviant behaviour. Sociologists adopted different approaches to the study of deviant behaviour. Ahuja's[9] study of female offenders is a starting point for the discussion looking into situational and environmental variables compelling women to commit crime. Viewed in this sense, most of the crimes committed by women are due to stressful family situations. Broom and Selznick[10] also pointed out that, the way people behave, is largely determined by their relations with each other and by their membership in groups. Sociologists emphasize maladjustment, role conflict, social and personal disorganization, opportunity, materialistic attitude, etc.

The important and leading cause of female crime has been financial or economic. Ahuja found maladjustment in interpersonal relationships within the family as the major cause of female criminality. About the crimes like thefts, his contention is that most of the thefts committed by women are the result of family and economic compulsions. Ahuja found that economic compulsion leads women to crime.

As regards theories of deviant behaviour, the most outstanding theories formulated by sociologists - criminologists relate to factors such as social strain, differential opportunity structure, etc. The social strain theory was first propounded by Durkheim and was later developed by Robert Merton. According to this theory, man deviates from norms and expectations of his group only when he experiences some major disjunction between his goals and the legitimate means of attaining these goals, or if the group's expectations themselves become contradictory or meaningless. Cloward and Ohlin[11] explain that deviant behaviour results when legitimate channels to attain goals are blocked. Cohen[12] explains that, deviant behaviour is the result of 'reaction formation' among lower class people. Failing to reach the goals by adhering to middle class precepts, lower class people reject middle class values and participate in anti-social acts as a solution to their inward frustrations.

The present study shows that, 31.1 per cent females were arrested for theft, 25.6 per cent for murder, 12.2 per cent for NDPS offences, 11.1 per cent for cheating, 10 per cent for pass port offences, 5.6 per cent for assistance in raping and 2.2 per cent for kidnapping and immoral traffic offences respectively.

The pattern of crime shows that women are moving out of traditional crimes like sex offences and shop-lifting to thefts, NDPS, and pass port offences and also to crimes of violence like murder. Greater freedom has allowed them to enter new positions and new roles, thereby giving them more opportunities for participation in crime. Maintaining double standards by women also helps create female crime because it leads to frustrations. The present study supports Ram Ahuja's theory of family maladjustment as cause of female crime.

In 17 out of 23 murder cases, the victim was the member of respondent's family, while in other 4 cases victim was respondent's neighbour. This shows that in 21 out of 23 cases, the female criminal had primary relationship with the victim. This proves that the primary group, i.e., family and neighbour plays a very significant role in women's criminality. It is clear that maladjustment in interpersonal relationships is one of the most important cause of criminality amongst women.

Prasad's[13] findings have revealed that, the major areas of conflicts which provoke crime are: (i) Husbands with habits like drinking, gambling, drug-addiction; (ii) Lack of interest in the family and lack of affection; (iii) A forced marriage; (iv) Illegal connection with in-laws or others due to sexual incompatibility and maladjustment with husband; (v) Jealousy due to husband's illegal connection with other women; (vi) Low income and excessive expenditure; (vii) Conflicts over sex and (viii) Sexual jealousy and jealousy over property.

Family was found to be an important factor in female criminality. In crimes like murders, assistance in raping, cheating, NDPS and pass port offences, female criminals play secondary or supportive roles. Therefore, they are not to be treated as sole perpetrators of these crimes. For example, in NDPS offences, when husband was arrested for crime, his wife too was arrested for helping the husband in illegal activities. Since women accompanied men, they too were arrested and penalized. Most of the thefts committed by women are due to family and economic compulsions. Women arrested for minor thefts are those, who usually lack money to be able to buy things which were later stolen. Many female criminals engage in immoral traffic and property offences to earn money to support their families.

In Indian society a woman has to adjust with all members of the family, whatever her marital status may be. This is particularly so in joint families. Lack of adjustment with ever present members of the family either brings about aggression or depression which accumulates and may result in violent outbursts. Family is responsible for producing such adverse situations that ultimately lead to homicidal activity. When the family does not help to adjust to environment, a woman loses the most important means of psychological support and the most effective agent for socialization. Marital disharmony, intra-familial conflict and dowry which arise out of family interactions are major factors that bring about undesirable problematic situations in the Indian families. The situations affect every member's behaviour in the family and a woman's in particular.

Various scholars have attempted to build different criminological theories to explain crime systematically. These theories indeed differ in their explanation of crime, but most of these explanations do not explain crime situation in India. In our country Women's Liberation Movement is taking place. In spite of that, large number of women are unaware of equal rights and there is no breakdown of sexual inequality, as the scope of this movement is limited for certain groups of females in certain areas. It has not spread all over India. Thus, a woman has to perform the basic role of a housewife within the home which subjects her to greater social restrictions. A few criminologists have used 'Role Theory' to explain female crimes. Frances Heidensohn[14] pointed out that, owing to close supervision and social restrictions on women, socialization, development of consciousness and self-perception vary considerably between boys and girls. Girls are usually trained to be passive, domesticated and non-violent and are not allowed to learn how to fight or use weapons. Contrary to this, boys are aggressive, ambitious and out-going. Girls thus shrink from violence and do not possess the necessary technical ability or strength to engage in crimes of violence, armed robberies, gang fights, etc. At worst, they engage in petty or domestic offences. The role theorists highlight the way in which opportunity structures predispose males rather than females to crime but it does not explain the cause of crime by females, it only explains the differential rates of male and female criminality.

As per the data of the present study, factors responsible for female crime are found to be socio-economic conditions. In other words, economic instability and lack of adjustment in family relationships mainly explains crime among women.

7.10 : Version of Complaint

The present study analyses female criminality in Mumbai. Now, it is essential to highlight the initial findings of the study. One major problem in criminological research is that of obtaining accurate information as to the nature of crime and more than that, the determination of causation of crime. Some of the undertrial female criminals did not agree with the nature and degree of their involvement in crimes as recorded in the charge-sheet. The discrepancy between the versions provided by the charge-sheet and those given by the undertrials need to be looked into carefully.

Table 7.8: Respondent's Version of the Complaint

Version of the Complaint	*Frequency*	*Percentage*
False	48	53.3
True	32	33.6
Caught red-handed	10	11.1
Total	90	100.0

It was found that, in 32 cases out of 90 the records in the charge sheet and the versions of the complaints as given by the undertrials were the same. In 10 cases, respondents were caught red-handed, and in 48 cases (53.3 per cent) there was total disagreement. There are number of problems in determining the crime such as, intention behind the criminal act, motivation, circumstances, types of witnesses produced in the court and evidence recorded. Under trials are not in a condition to talk frankly about the nature of their criminal act, because their court cases have begun and since the charges leveled against them were not confirmed by court, they did not agree with the nature and degree of involvement in crime as filed by the police. The findings of the present study have to be judged in the light of these various limitations. On the other hand, one more fact to be taken into consideration in analyzing the incidents of crime is that, the different types of crimes committed by women in the present sample, were not uniformly considered anti-social or criminal by the individual criminals. Passport Act (Refugees) and Immoral Traffic Act offences are not considered anti-social or bad by respondents as they expressed in their responses at the time of data collection. But they are crimes from a legal point of view.

However, today female criminality is coming more and more to the surface as it is being recorded and hence is becoming more visible. In the present study, researcher also examined the co-relation between socio-economic and demographic characteristics and the nature of offences.

7.11 Age and Nature of Offence

The data regarding these aspects are presented in table 7.9.

Table 7.9: Respondent's Age and Nature of Offence

Age (in years)	*Nature of Offence*			
	Offences against the Person	*Property Offences*	*Other Offences*	*Total*
18-29	7 (23.3)	13 (43.3)	10 (33.3)	30
30-39	8 (28.6)	13 (46.4)	7 (25.0)	28

(Contd.)

(Contd. Table 7.9)

Age (in years)	*Nature of Offence*			
	Offences against the Person	*Property Offences*	*Other Offences*	*Total*
40 and above	15 (46.9)	12 (37.5)	5 (15.6)	32
Total	30 (33.3)	38 (42.2)	22 (24.4)	90

Age and offence-wise classification of the figures in the table 7.9 shows that, more women in the age group of 30 to 39 years were involvcd in property offences and the age group of 40 years and above (46.9 per cent) showed a greater involvement in offences against the person. The women in 18-29 years age group were involved more in other offences.

A more detailed picture has been given in the Table 7.10, about the participation of women in criminal offences.

Figures given in Table 7.10 show that, women from the age group of 40 and above years participated mostly in homicide offences (40.7 per cent) and in the crimes of theft, cheating, NDPS offences. They were not found in crimes like kidnapping, immoral traffic and passport act offences. The women from age group 30-39 years indulged largely in thefts, kidnapping, and assistance in raping. Two cases of immoral traffic act offences of the sample were concentrated in the age group of 18-29 years and there were more women in this age group related to passport act offences.

The cause of Passport Act offences and Immoral Traffic Act offences is particularly economic deprivation. Criminality rates among youths are closely co-related to low income. According to Landis[15] there are some important ways in which economic deprivation enters as a risk factor in youth criminality: (a) when material success is highly prized, economic deprivation

Table 7.10: Respondent's Age and Nature of Offence

Age (in years)	*Nature of Offence*								
	Murder	*Thefts/Pick-Pock e tin g*	*Kidnapping*	*Cheating*	*Assistace in Raping*	*Immoral Trafic*	*NDPS Act*	*Passport Act*	*Total*
18-29	6	11	1	2	-	2	3	5	30
	(20.0)	36.7	(3.3)	(6.7)		(6.7)	(10.0)	(16.7)	
30-39	4	11	1	2	3	-	3	4	28
	(14.3)	(39.3)	(3.6)	(7.1)	(10.7)		(10.7)	(14.3)	
40 and above	13	6	-	6	2	-	5	-	32
	(40.7)	(18.8)		(18.8)	(6.3)		(15.6)		
Total	23	28	2	10	5	2	11	9	90
	(25.6)	(31.1)	(2.2)	(11.1)	(5.6)	(2.2)	(12.2)	(10.0)	

breeds demoralization and apathy; (b) economic deprivation hampers integration into society. Those who are unemployed or who receive low wages have no secure place in the community of work and their ties to the larger society are extremely tenuous.

Thus, economic deprivation could be considered a significant factor in youth criminality, which provokes them to get involved in property offences, passport act offences, NDPS offences and immoral traffic act offences.

7.12 Education and Nature of Offence

Education is an indicator of a person's ability and capacity to cope with the function of living. Education plays an important role in improving the quality of life.

Table 7.11: shows the co-relation between educational level and nature of offence

Table 7.11 Respondent's Educational Level and Nature of Offence

Level of Education	*Nature of Offence*			
	Offences against the Person	*Property Offences*	*Other Offences*	*Total*
Illiterate	17 (33.3)	21 (41.2)	13 (25.5)	51
Primary	6 (46.2)	4 (30.8)	3 (23.1)	13
Secondary	7 (33.3)	9 (42.9)	5 (23.8)	21
Graduation	-	4 (80.0)	1 (20.0)	5
Total	30 (33.3)	38 (42.2)	22 (24.4)	90

Education and offence-wise classification in table 7.11 discloses that the variation in the proportion of lliterates and literates of different standards in the commitment of offences is not marked. The women who completed graduation were involved in more proportion in property offences. It should however be noted that the majority of respondents were illiterates. This indicates that illiterate people are least logical and rational and their criminal instincts are not properly socialized.

7.13 Religion and Nature of Offence

Religion is the most influential force in controlling human behaviour. It may also provide clues to the understanding of varying incidence of crime rate among different sections of the community. The following table shows the co-relation between religion and the nature of offences.

Table 7.12: Respondent's Religion and Nature of Offence

Religion	*Nature of Offence*			
	Offences against the Person	*Property Offences*	*Other Offences*	*Total*
Hindu	17 (32.7)	27 (51.9)	8 (15.4)	52
Muslim	8 (30.8)	5 (19.2)	13 (50.0)	26
Others	5 (41.7)	6 (50.0)	1 (8.3)	12
Total	30 (33.3)	38 (42.2)	22 (24.4)	90

Table 7.12 reveals that, Hindus are participating more in property offences, while Muslims are found participating largely in 'other' offences (it includes NDPS, Pass port and Immoral Traffic Act offences). Respondents from religions other than Hindu and Muslim are predominantly found in offences against the person.

7.14 Caste and Nature of Offence:

Caste determines the social status of a person in the society. It is therefore found necessary to study the relation between caste and nature of offences.

Table 7.13: Respondent's Caste and Nature of Offence

Castes	*Nature of Offence*			
	Offences against the Person	*Property Offences*	*Other Offences*	*Total*
Upper Caste	19 (44.2)	16 (37.2)	8 (18.6)	43
SC/ST & NT&DT	7 (25.0)	17 (60.7)	4 (14.3)	28
O.B.C	4 (21.1)	5 (26.3)	10 (52.6)	19
Total	30 (33.3)	38 (42.2)	22 (24.4)	90

Table 7.13 indicates that, upper caste women are more involved in offences against the person. Scheduled Castes, Scheduled Tribes and N.T./D.T. (Nomadic Tribes/Denotified Tlibes) women are more involved in property offences. Other backward classes (O.B.C.) women are more involved in 'other offences'.

7.15 Marital Status and Nature of Offence

Most crimes are related to the marital status of a person. Responsibilities and Socio-cultural expectations are always attached to marital status. If they cannot be fulfilled within the framework of socially and culturally approved ways, a woman tends to participate in criminal activities. The following table shows the co-relation between marital status and nature of offence.

Table 7.14: Respondent's Marital Status and Nature of Offence

Marital Status	*Nature of Offence*			
	Offences against the Person	*Property Offences*	*Other Offences*	*Total*
Unmarried	1 (11.1)	4 (44.4)	4 (44.4)	9
Married	15 (35.7)	18 (42.9)	9 (21.4)	42
Widowed/ Deserted	14 (35.9)	16 (41.0)	9 (23.1)	39
Total	30 (33.3)	38 (42.2)	22 (24.4)	90

Considering the nature of offences with regard to marital status, table 7.14 shows that, married and widowed/deserted respondents are involved mostly in offences against the person. The unmarried respondents showed a greater involvement in property and other offences.

Table 7.15: Respondent's Occupation and Nature of Offence

Occupation	*Nature of Offence*			
	Offences against the Person	*Property Offences*	*Other Offences*	*Total*
Service	3 (30.0)	6 (60.0)	1 (10.0)	10
Domestic Servant	5 (31.3)	8 (50.0)	3 (18.8)	16

(Contd)

(Contd. Table 7.15)

Occupation	*Nature of Offence*			
	Offences against the Person	*Property Offences*	*Other Offences*	*Total*
Business	5	8	6	19
	(26.3)	(42.1)	(31.6)	
Housewife	11	6	2	19
	(57.9)	(31.6)	(10.5)	
Any other	6	10	10	26
	(23.1)	(38.5)	(38.5)	
Total	30	38	22	90
	(33.3)	(42.2)	(24.4)	

7.16 Occupation and Nature of Offence

The data on these aspects are presented in table 7.15.

Table 7.15 shows the relation between occupation and nalure of offcence. It is interesting to note that the housewives were involved predominantly in offences against the person. Those who were in service, business or working as domestic servants got involved considerably in property offences.

7.17 Income and Nature of Offence

Following table shows the co-relation between respondent's income and nature of offence.

Table 7.16 reveals that, a majority of the respondents in the income groups of below Rs. 1000/- are involved in property offences. Those who were in the income group of Rs. 3001-5000 are involved more in other offences. The respondents from the income group of Rs. 5001 and above are more involved in offences against the person. Respondents included in 'don't know' and 'not applicable' category are mostly involved in the offences against the person. Respondents who are housewives are shown in the 'not applicable' category.

Table 7.16: Respondent's Monthly Income and Nature of Offence

Monthly Income (in Rs.)	*Nature of Offence*			
	Offences against the Person	*Property Offences*	*Other Offences*	*Total*
Below 1000	3 (13.6)	15 (68.2)	4 (18.2)	22
1000-3000	7 (25.9)	11 (40.7)	9 (33.3)	27
3001-5000	2 (22.2)	3 (33.3)	4 (44.4)	9
Above 5001	5 (71.4)	2 (28.6)	-	7
Dont know and Not applicable	13 (52.0)	7 (28.0)	5 (20.0)	25
Total	30 (33.3)	38 (42.2)	22 (24.4)	90

It is found that low income provokes the individual to commit property offences. A poor person does not find economic security and fails to satisfy the basic needs. Sometimes poverty operates directly to produce criminal activities. Illness, accident, providing dowry for marriage, etc. may provoke the individual to indulge in thefts, fraud. Cheating, robbery, etc. A woman may steal to supply her children food, clothing and other necessities of life. Thus the great majority of female criminals in the income group of below Rs.1000/- are involved in property offences.

Income gives an insight into the economic status of the family and it is also instrumental in the formation of the behaviour of female criminals in the society. Following table shows the relation between family income and nature of offences:

Table 7.17: Family Income (per month) and Nature of Offence

Family Income (in Rs.)	*Nature of Offence*			
	Offences against the Person	*Property Offences*	*Other Offences*	*Total*
Below 1000	2 (14.3)	10 (71.4)	2 (14.3)	14
1001-3000	8 (25.0)	12 (37.5)	12 (37.5)	32
3001-5000	9 (40.9)	8 (36.4)	5 (22.7)	22
5001 and above	5 (35.7)	7 (50.0)	2 (14.3)	14
Don't know and Not applicable	6 (75.0)	1 (12.5)	1 (12.5)	8
Total	30 (33.3)	38 (42.2)	22 (24.4)	90

The figures given in table 7.16 and table 7.17 are showing the same picture about the correlation between low income and property offences. The women under the family income of Rs.1000-3000 were involved more in other offences.

7.18 Family and Nature of Offence

The data on these aspects are presented in table 7.18.

Out of the 60 respondents, who were living in nuclear families, majority of them are involved in property offences. In the case of respondents in joint families majority wcre involved more in offences against the person.

Family is the most important social group that exists in the society. It is one of the primary agencies of socialization. It is the significant social group that shapes the personality of its

Table 7.18: Type of Family and Nature of Offence

Type of Family	*Nature of Offence*			
	Offences against the Person	*Property Offences*	*Other Offences*	*Total*
Nuclear	17 (28.3)	30 (50.0)	13 (21.7)	60
Joint	11 (44.0)	7 (28.0)	7 (28.0)	25
Not applicable (No family)	2 (40.0)	1 (20.0)	2 (40.0)	5
Total	30 (33.3)	38 (42.2)	22 (24.4)	90

members through its functions of socialization and social control. Thus, family exerts a deep influence on the life of an individual. However, family situations vary from individual to individual. All individuals may not be able to live in normal families and experience socializing in inter-personal relationships. Factors such as lack of control, too strict or lack of discipline, parental neglect or rejection, physical abuse, broken homes, insecure homes and immoral home atmosphere appeared to corroborate the wise notion that family influence in general had an influence on subsequent criminality. It is imperative on the part of the researcher to examine the co-relation between family pattern and nature of involvement of respondents, in committing crime and also to examine the co-relation between family pattern and the type of companion involved with respondent in criminal act.

7.19 Family and Nature of Involvement

The data in these aspects are presented in Table 7.19.

Table 7.19 shows that, majority of the respondents committed crimes in association with others. There were more respondents from nuclear families who committed offence alone and there were more respondents from joint families who committed offences in association with others. These figures emphasize the role of the family behind the criminal act.

Table 7.19: Type of Family and Nature of Involvement in Crime

Type of Family	*Nature of Involvement*		
	Offence Committed Alone	*In Association With Others*	*Total*
Nuclear	*28 (46.66)*	*32 (53.33)*	*60*
Joint	*8 (32.00)*	*17 (68.00)*	*25*
Not Applicable (No Family)	*4 (80.00)*	*1 (20.00)*	*5*
Total	*40*	*50*	*90*

7.20 Family and Companion in Criminal Act:

The data on these aspects are presented in Table 7.20.

Table 7.20 reveals that, 6 out of those 7 cases, where the respondent's companion was spouse, were from nuclear families, while, respondents from joint families mostly received help from the family members other than spouse. In comparison to this, in case of respondents from nuclear families, their accomplices were predominantly their neighbours.

There is no doubt that family is an influential institution. This influence of family on the members is complex and cannot adequately be explained in simple causal terms.

However, financial difficulties is one of the important direct contributory causes. In a country like India this factor hardly needs any detailed explanation. In fact financial cause is the chief factor which gives rise to different situations of stress and strain compelling the individual to think of and take to different types of deviant behaviour. In fact, all types of crimes

Table 7.20: Type of Family and Type of Companion in Criminal Act

Type of Family	*Type of Companion*						
	Spouse	*Family Member*	*Friend*	*Neighbour*	*Any other*	*Not Applicable*	*Total*
Nuclear	6 (10.00)	12 (20.00)	1 (1.66)	10 (16.66)	3 (5.00)	28 (46.66)	60
Joint	1 (4.00)	11 (44.00)	3 (12.00)	1 (4.00)	1 (4.00)	8 (32.00)	25
Not Applicable	-	-	-	1 (20.00)	-	4 (80.00)	5
Total	7 (7.8)	23 (25.6)	4 (4.4)	12 (13.3)	4 (4.4)	40 (44.4)	90

are the result of adjustments, economic needs, social conditions and situation or environment, which turns into anti-social behaviour.

References

1. Dhanagare, D.N. - "Urbanism and Crime", Economic and Political Weekly, p. 1241.
2. Lombroso and Ferrero - "The Female Offender", p. 206.
3. Pollak Otto - "The Criminality of Women", p. 36.
4. Lombroso and Ferrero - "The Female Offender", pp. 207-208.
5. Smith Ann D. - "Women in Prison: A study in Penal Methods", p. 31.
6. Ahuja Ram - "Female Offenders in India", p. 32.
7. Pollak Otto - "The Criminality of Women", pp. 8-14.
8. Bonger - "Criminality and Economic Conditions", pp. 36-37.
9. Ahuja Ram - "Female Offenders in India", pp. 48-54.
10. Broom and Selznick - "Sociology", p.17.
11. Cloward and Ohlin - "Delinquency and Opportunity", p.86.
12. Cohen Albert K. - "Deviance and Control", pp.65-66.
13. Prasad S.K. - "A study of Women Murderers in Tamil Nadu", p.72.
14. Heidensohn Frances - "The Deviance of Women: A critique and an enquiry", *British Journal of Sociology*, Vol. 19, No. 2, p. 170.
15. Landis Paul - "Social Problems", p. 55.

8

Respondents' Attitudes and Feelings Towards Offence, Prison and Society

Introduction

Today, female share in crime has increased considerably all over the world. Poverty, strains of urban life, lack of adequate amenities, are some of the earliest factors to have been identified as having a bearing on female crime and delinquency. However, poverty and other hardships in daily life are presumed to comprise the most commonly accepted scenario for crime generally, whether by men or women. In other words, low economic level among female or male offenders is neither a surprise nor improbable in a country like India. On the other hand, family is considered as the most important factor in the life of female criminals contributing to criminal behaviour. Family structure, lack of adjustment, shortage of money, role conflict within the family, pressures of household work and child rearing cause individuals to resort to non-conformist ways to overcome stresses and strains. Therefore, it is necessary from the researcher's viewpoint to study attitudes and feeling of the respondents towards offence, prison and society. In this connection, Sanober Shekhar's[1] study of "Women Prisoners: The Remand and Undertrial Experience" deals exclusively with unconvicted women prisoners. The object of the study is to throw light on the experiences and perceptions of women prisoners in relation to their arrest and subsequent processing as accused persons in criminal cases. However, the major areas of experience were: police arrest, investigation, police custody, prison custody and the visit to court as prisoner.

There is little doubt that criminal behaviour is human behaviour at its most complex. While exploring attitudes and feelings regarding such behaviour, the researcher has to contend not only with its complexity, but also with the obvious risk of subjectivity, not only in the respondent but also in the researcher, e.g., the criminal views herself as essentially innocent and non-criminal, while the researcher holds the opposite view. The gap between what a respondent is and what she would like to appear to be creates a certain element of self-consciousness in the respondent that can work as a constraint. Thus, what is stated by the respondents may often be what they believe the researcher would like to hear and not necessarily what may have been experienced. There is a thin line between what is reality and what is fantasized that can also affect the authenticity and the quality of response in this type of study. Keeping in mind all these limitations, the researcher has made an analysis of respondent's responses and expressions. These responses are motivated by the attitudes which are generated through their interactions with their environment. These reactions are viewed in terms of their behaviour pattern.

8.1 Feelings about the Offence

The researcher has tried to obtain the respondent's own feeling and attitude towards offence. The 48.9 per cent respondents feel that they have not done any offence, 24.4 per cent showed indifferent attitude towards offence, i.e., they neither felt it to be right as it had spoilt their lives nor did they feel guilty. The 24.4 percent respondents expressed the view that, they have done wrong. Only 2.2 per cent respondents were of the opinion that they have done right. They felt that there was no other way to survive. The nearly half of the respondents felt that they had not done any offence mostly because present study consists of undertrial female criminals and some of them were of the opinion that, if fair means for existence are not possible then the only option is to get what you want without bothering about the means.

8.2 Response to Arrest and Custody

Out of the total sample, 92.2 per cent respondents felt that decision about their arrest and custody was unjustified. Only 6.7 per cent respondents felt that it was justified, while one respondent showed indifferent attitude about her arrest and custody. Some were of the opinion that the charges against them are unjustified because from their point of view crime committed out of necessity is no crime. They should be released on probation and allowed to live in their homes, because arrest and custody affects their family life.

It is true that the imprisonment of a woman is dysfunctional to her family and particularly to her children in the sense that the family has to face a dual crisis. The crisis of absence of a member due to imprisonment and on the other hand, the social stigma of the family due to its member's criminality, both cause her family to suffer social and psychological deprivations. But society demands changes in the way of maintaining social order. In changing society, no system of social control works perfectly and the individuals often deviate from social and legal norms. Prisons are concerned simply with holding prisoners while they waited for trial. The places for detention of lawbreakers are known as prisons. It is interesting to know how much time is spent by respondents in prison.

The Central Prison at Arthur Road in Mumbai has authorized accommodation for 23 females and for that, prison has 3 barracks. Only Arthur Road, Central Prison in Mumbai has a female yard. Undertrial female criminals are a floating population. On an average 100 prisoners are accommodated at a time in this prison. Therefore, it is found necessary to study attitudes of the respondents towards stay in prison.

Table 8.1: Period in Jail

Period (in months)	*Frequency*	*Percentage*
Less than one	17	18.9
1 to 6	48	63.3
6 to 12	11	12.2
More than one year	14	15.6
Total	90	100.0

Table 8.1 shows that, majority of the respondents were in prison for a period of less than six months.

Nursing women prisoners are allowed to keep children upto the age of 4 years along with them in the prison. In 8 cases out of the total sample their children live with them in prison. So the time of life in which these children ought to be socialized is spent in prison environment.

8.3 Feelings about Prison Custody

Imprisonment cannot be pleasing to anyone. The respondent's stay in prison and her perceptions concerning that experience, were considered an essential part of the study. Majority of the respondents (55.6 per cent) stated that, It is forced separation from their family. The remaining (8.8 per cent) felt that it was rejection by society or restriction on their freedom (12.2 per cent) or felt that they had lost their livelihood (20.0 per cent). However, forced separation from family was the overwhelming factor. This gives an insight into respondents'

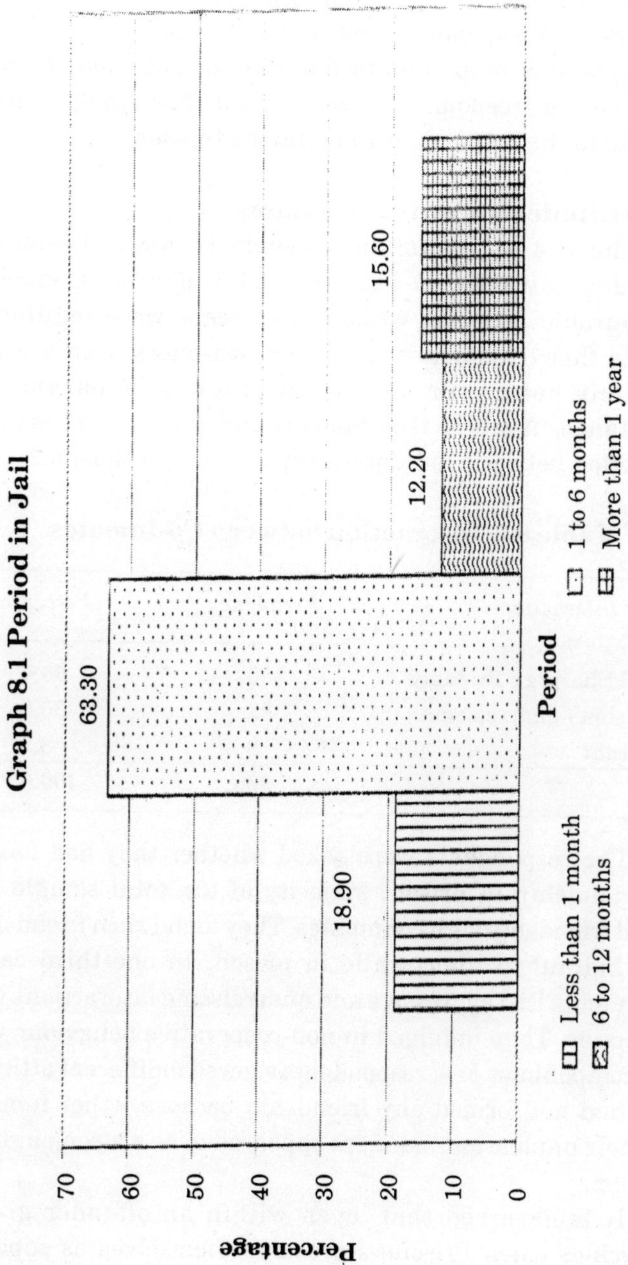

Graph 8.1 Period in Jail

psychological and emotional background and also shows the attachment of respondents towards their family.

Very few respondents felt that prison custody puts restriction on freedom. It is pointed out that family is more valuable to the respondent than having freedom.

8.3.1 Attitudes towards Co-inmates

The 64.4 per cent of the respondents showed favourable attitudes towards co-inmates, 31.1 per cent showed unfavourable attitude, while 4.4 per cent were indifferent towards their co-inmates. In prison, prisoners from a group and their behaviour with each other is of paramount importance. Against this background the data regarding interaction between co-inmates is presented in table 8.2.

Table 8.2: Interaction between Co-Inmates

Type of Interactions	*Frequency*	*Percentage*
Helpful/Sharing / Friendly	50	55.6
Aggression / quarrelsome	32	35.6
Indifferent	8	8.9
Total	90	100.0

The respondents were asked whether they had formed any friendship in prison. Majority of the total sample had formed friendship with co-inmates. They found such friendships to be helpful to them while in prison. In one-third cases, respondents had aggressive and quarrelsome interactions with co-inmates. They indulged in non-cooperative behaviour with their companions. Few respondents showed indifferent attitude. They had not formed any friendship because, other inmates and their unpleasant manners appeared to be a strong irritant for them.

It is observed that, even within an offender group, hierarchies exist. Prisoners presume themselves as superior or inferior to others. It has also been observed that, quarreling and fighting among inmates and use of abusive language are a common feature of prison life.

8.3.2 Attitudes towards Prison Authorities:

In the present study an attempt has been made to observe the attitude of the respondents towards prison authorities, viz., Jailor, Mahila Rakshak and Mahila Hawaldar. There is no direct contact between respondents and the superintendent. The 36.7 per cent respondents had cordial relations with the prison authorities, where as few (14.4 per cent) were reluctant. They expressed their opinion that, prison authorities should behave properly and humanely, 48.9 per cent respondents were found to be indifferent.

Among 90 respondents 87 (96.7 per cent) felt that, they did not find any difference in treatment by prison authorities, while 3 respondents replied negatively. These three respondents felt that money can purchase everything. From their point of View, prison authorities paid more attention to those prisoners who are willing to pay for more facilities. One respondent replied that, "If you are rich the whole world is with you, but if you are poor no one will come forward to help you".

8.3.3 Daily Routine of the Prisoner

Life in prison cannot be pleasing to anyone. There was curiosity therefore to know how the respondents spent their time in prison atmosphere.

Table 8.3 shows that, majority of the total sample did nothing in the prison except their personal routine. They are not assigned any duty (according to Maharashtra Prison Manual unless undertrial so desires, no undertrial prisoner shall be allotted any work except that it shall be her duty to keep her bedding, clothing and yard clean). Therefore, undertrials are busy with their daily routine according to family

Graph 8.2 Daily Routine of the Prisoner

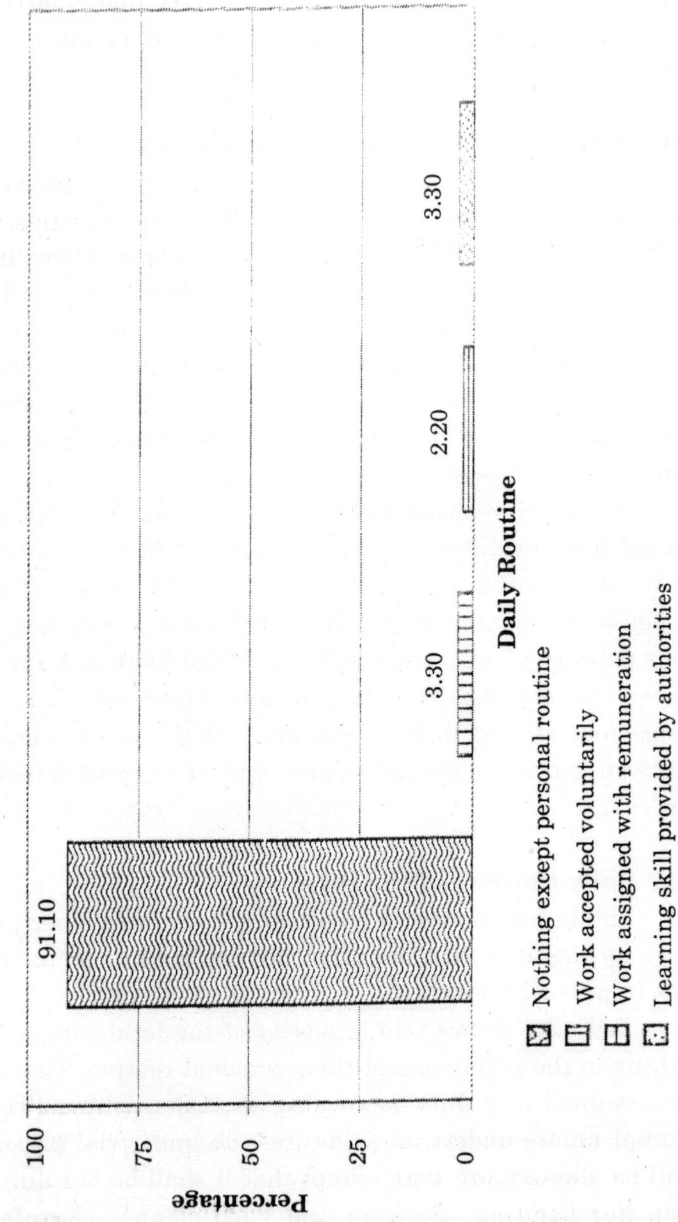

Table 8.3: Daily Routine of the Prisoner

Daily Routine	*Frequency*	*Percentage*
Nothing except personal routine	82	91.1
Work accepted voluntarily	3	3.3
Work assigned with remuneration	2	2.2
Learning skills provided by authorities	3	3.3
Total	90	100.0

lifestyle. During remaining hours of the day they spent their time either in gossiping or in sleeping or attending to their children. Out of the total sample very few were working voluntarily or had remuneration. In rare cases they engaged themselves in learning skills, provided by authorities. Vocational programme facilities are very rare for undertrial female prisoners. Literacy and tailoring facilities were available but most of the respondents did not find them interesting. One respondent replied that, 'prison authorities should provide some kind of work which would help them after their release, otherwise prison life amounted to a waste of time and it would have no impact at all'. Here, the interest was also to seek the respondent's opinions about the activities available inside the prison.

Table 8.4: Useful Activities Available Inside the Prison

Opinions about the Activities	*Frequency*	*Percentage*
Adequate	44	48.9
Inadequate	46	51.1
Total	90	100.0

Table 8.4 shows that, nearly half of the respondents were of the opinion that they have adequate learning facilities

available in the prison, while majority did not find them adequate. Even those who found them adequate did not take advantage of them or did not use them (as indicated in Table 8.3 that only 3.3 per cent respondents learn the skills provided by authorities). Majority of them were of the opinion that prison must have proper recreational facilities. The undertrial female prisoner suffering from insecurity may also tend to possess a negative attitude towards the activities provided in prison.

8.3.4 Responses about the Problems Faced in Prison

It was considered desirable to get the respondents' assessment of how they reacted about the prison life, its amenities and prison programmes.

Table 8.5: Problems Faced in Prison

Problems	*Frequency*	*Percentage*
All facilities inadequate	43	47.8
No problems	33	36.7
Any other	14	15.5
Total	90	100.0

Table 8.5 reveals that nearly half of the respondents were not satisfied with the facilities available for them in prison. More than one-third stated that they did not have any problems in prison. 'Any other' responses consisted of: (i) absence of recreation; (ii) not taken to court on given dates; (iii) did not get bail; (iv) no freedom; (v) no work and remuneration facility; (vi) poor medical facilities; (vii) corruption inside the prison; (viii) low quality of prison amenities; (ix) dullness of prison routine; (x) absence of comfort; and (xi) lack of religious teaching or daily prayers.

In this context, Dr. Sudha Kaldate[2] has pointed out that, in India, all types of women inmates are crowded into small narrow cells and unhygienic atmosphere. They have no access to any of the amenities clothing, work, education or even medical examination.

8.3.5 Researcher's Observations on Prison Environment

Society adopts a variety of means to control the crime. Imprisonment is one of the most commonly used means of handling the crime. It provides protection to offenders so that they cannot commit crime for a specified period of time and others would not hurt or attack them out of vengeance. Thus prison is expected to put a check on the rising rate of crime by incapacitating the offender on the one hand and by deterring the public on the other. To adjust in prison environment under deprived conditions, for uncertain periods, is a thing noteworthy.

It is found that, all categories of female inmates are huddled together in the same wards barracks. There is no segregation of habituals from first offenders. Only foreign women who have been arrested under the NDPS Act are detained in a separate barrack, and are constantly confined to their cells. This is particularly noticeable when a foreign woman is imprisoned for NDPS Act, for them security is tightened.

Most of the women kept in prison are uneducated and unaware of their legal rights. They are unable to defend themselves and are totally ignorant about the ways and means of securing legal help. They are unaware of the rules of remission or premature release and are at the mercy of the officials.

Lack of vocational training and leisure time leads to indiscipline. Lack of work for the inmates causes quarrels and fights among themselves. Use of abusive language is a common feature of prison environment. Some undertrial female prisoners are found to be mentally disturbed. The custodial staff are unable to deal with these mentally disturbed individuals.

Some respondents are able to obtain tobacco, lipstick, perfume, etc. (contraband). It may lead to jealousy among other prisoners who are unable to obtain all these things. However, since the co-inmates live in the same set up and share the same problems, they may have positive attitudes towards co-inmates. Except for a few prisoners who always stay aloof from others, majority have a sympathetic attitude towards the prisoner who is experiencing a depressive mood for some personal reasons.

Assaults take place rarely but when they go to extremes, the women are confined in isolation cells.

Majority of respondents indicated their negative opinion towards recreational activities available in the prison. It is observed that inmates are deprived of their basic needs, especially clothing and medical treatment.

The possibility of criminals being submissive and dependent on the authorities for their personal needs, may be an underlying cause for criminals to give positively oriented responses towards authorities. Even the attitude of the inmates towards authorities though generally favourable is filled with distrust and jealousy due to favouritism by the prison staff. In a prison, the jailor is an important figure. He conducts the total functioning of the prison. Therefore, he is the focus of attention of the prisoners, who may have fear or regard for him on one hand and open hostility on the other.

Prison community has its own independent identity. In prison, a female undertrial is constantly affected by acceptance and rejection of other co-inmates. Even if she wishes to remain aloof from other criminals, she fails to do so because in a limited space where so many prisoners confined, there is a total absence of privacy. Thus, an inmate is more close to her co-inmates.

8.4 Attitudes towards Family and Society

It is essential to get the information about the responses of the respondents as to whether after their release family members will treat them as before or not from their point of view.

Table 8.6: Treatment to be Received after Release

To be treated as before	*Frequency*	*Percentage*
Yes	70	77.8
No	10	11.1
Can't say	5	5.6
Not applicable	5	5.6
Total	90	100.0

Table 8.6 indicates that, majority of the respondents have the belief that after release, they would be treated by the family members as before or felt that they would be accepted. This feeling either might be based on belief in their innocence or the respondent's value to family members as an earning member. There is also a possibility that, in some cases family members are co-accused. The undertrial perceives herself as innocent and on that basis also, anticipates no change in the relationship with family members. Some respondents felt that they would not be treated as before because of the stigma attached to them of being criminals. One respondent replied that, "I don't know whether my family is going to accept me or not." Another respondent commented, "my family is not going to accept me and I have no alternate plan in my mind". Another respondent stated that she would not be accepted by in-laws, even though she would go back to their house for the well-being of her children.

It was significant to get respondent's evaluation of how their relatives reacted to their arrest and imprisonrnent.

Table 8.7 reveals that, one-fourth of the total sample accounted for helpful reactions, while 8.9 per cent accounted for indifferent reactions. 14.4 per cent respondents did not react on the query, 5.6 per cent did not have family (shown as 'Not applicable'). The remaining nearly half of the respondents (combining unable to help, not helpful, felt necessary, stopped talking) reported hostile reactions of relatives. These reactions

Table 8.7: Reactions of Relatives to Respondent's Arrest and Imprisonment

Reactions	*Frequency*	*Percentage*
Helpful/Sympathetic	23	25.6
Unable to help	34	37.8
Not helpful	5	5.6
Felt it was necessary	1	1.1
Stopped talking	1	1.1
Indifferent	8	8.9
No reactions	13	14.4
Not applicable	5	5.6
Total	90	100.0

may act as obstacles in providing bail support to the respondent. On the contrary, N.K. Sohoni's[3] findings revealed that over one-half of the sample (58.4 per cent) accounted for helpful reactions of relatives to respondent's arrest and conviction.

8.4.1 Receiving Support from Family

Majority of the respondents (55.6 per cent) replied that they did not receive support from their families, while 38.9 per cent had given positive reply. 5.6 per cent respondents fall under the 'not applicable' category.

There was curiosity to know what type of support respondent rercived from family. Table 8.8 shows the replies of the respondents to this query.

Table 8.8: Support Received from Family

Type of Support	*Frequency*	*Percentage*
Financial and emotional	18	20.0
Emotional	17	18.9
Not applicable	55	61.1
Total	90	100.0

Out of 35 respondents who received support, 18 got financial and emotional support and 17 respondents received emotional support from their families. It shows a worsening situation in that only 20.0 per cent of the total sample were able to get financial support. The remaining majority of respondents were not able to get any type of bail support, legal aid, or witness in favour of their case and basic necessities because of lack of financial support.

8.4.2 Respondents' Interactions with Family Members

The respondents were asked about visits from their family members. Table 8.9 shows the frequency of visits by family members.

Table 8.9: Visits by Family Members to the Prison

Visits	*Frequency*	*Percentage*
Frequent	16	17.8
Infrequent	16	17.8
No visits	53	58.9
Not applicable	5	5.6
Total	90	100.0

It is evident from table 8.9, that only about one-fifth of the respondents had frequent visits by family members, nearly one-fifth of respondents had infrequent visits and majority of the respondents had never had any visits by family members. Five respondents did not have family, so they had no visitors. Following table shows the reasons for infrequent visits or no visits to prison by family members.

Table 8.10 indicates that, the major reason for infrequent or no visits by family members was the distance and expense entailed in visiting. In case of 15 respondents, their family members were not aware about prisoners' custodial

Graph 8.3

Visits by Family Members to Prison

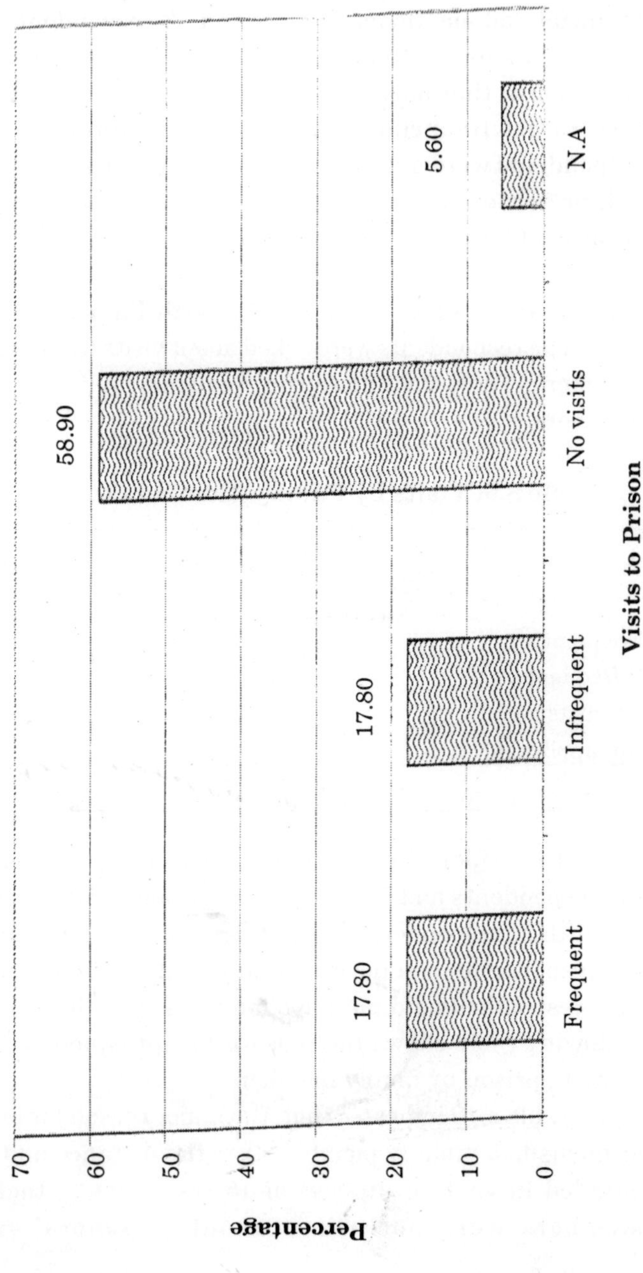

Table 8.10 : Reason for Infrequent Visits or No Visit to Prison

Reasons	*Frequency*	*Percentage*
Distance from prison and expense involved in visiting	17	18.9
Prisoner's where abouts not known	15	16.7
Lack of interest in prisoner	10	11.7
Just arrived in jail (less than 15 days)	11	12.2
Other	16	17.8
Not applicable	21	23.3
Total	90	100.0

arrangements. The family members of 10 respondents showed lack of interest in prisoner. Eleven respondents had arrived in jail just within two weeks. Other reasons referred to: relatives are too young or too old to travel, it is possible to meet in court, all family members were in jail, respondents did not know the reason, family members were not aware about visiting arrangements, scared by police, did not like to come to jail.

It is observed that prisoners were continuously anxious till someone came to visit them or release them on bail. But there were complaints about the visiting arrangements. The visitors waited for hours outside before they were allowed to meet the prisoners for just five minutes. Also constraints and restrictions are placed on the persons visiting the inmates and the time and place of visit. Moreover, the relatives are permitted to visit only in the presence of an official so that free conversation or close physical contact is not possible. Some prisoners did not want to inform anyone at home about their arrest or custody. There were a few who were not too keen on having their families visit them. On the other hand, since imprisonment is a social stigma, relatives too are reluctant to visit the prisoner.

The reactions of the prisoners to personal contact with their family members were studied. Responses of 32

Graph 8.4

Reasons for Infrequent Visit or No Visit to Prison

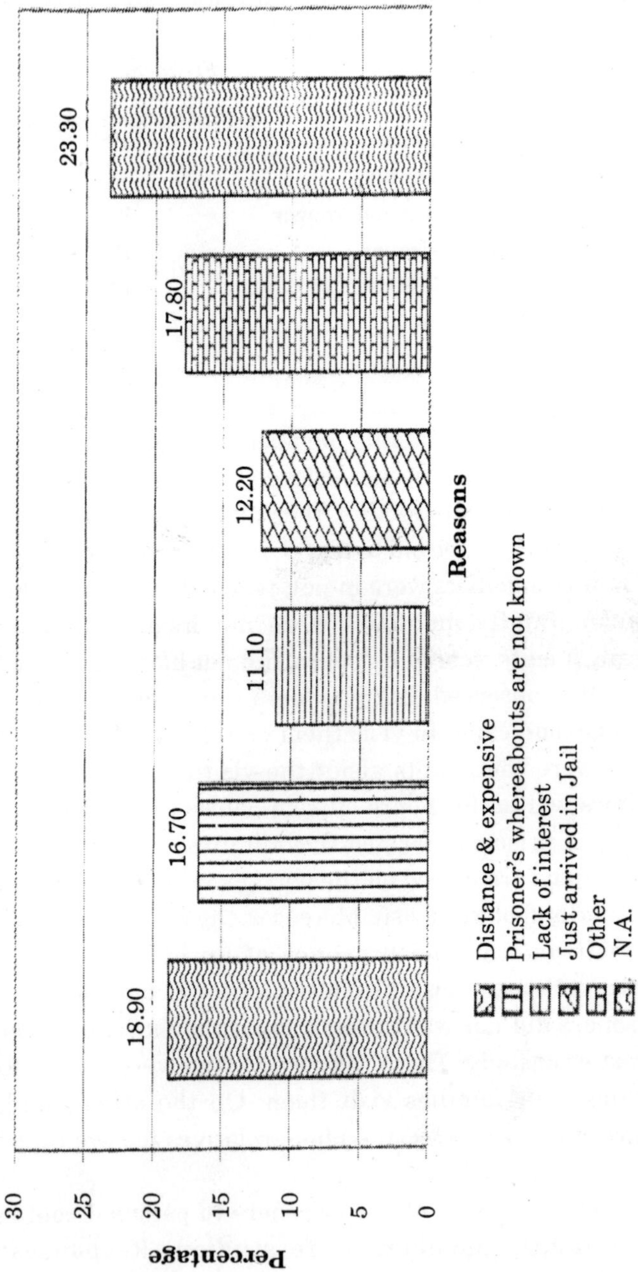

respondents, whose family members visit them, are included in Table 8.11.

Table 8.11: Reactions to Personal Contact with Family Members

Reactions	*Frequency*	*Percentage*
Very fulfilling	7	7.8
Satisfactory	17	18.9
Disturbing	8	8.9
No visits	53	58.9
Not applicable	5	5.6
Total	90	100.0

Table 8.11 shows that, 17 out of 32 respondents described it as satisfactory, while 7 felt it 'very fulfilling'. Eight respondents responded with negative reaction, in terms of 'disturbing'. This is because after the meeting most of them felt depressed and sad. One respondent replied, "we stay here in distress and family members come here with their own problems".

8.4.3 Visits by Friends to the Prison

Out of 90 respondents, 57 had no friends. The remaining 33 respondents had friends but not a single respondent was visited by their friend. Therefore, all 33 respondents' replies were included in the category of 'No visits'.

There may be a possibility that respondents did not want to inform their friends about their arrest and custody. Or, some of them might have been arrested along with their friends.

Letters are another mode of interaction with family members. Out of 90 respondents only 3 received or sent letters. 'No letters' reply referred to: either respondent was illiterate or family members were illiterate, all were illiterate, visits were regular, family members did not know respondent's whereabouts, possibility to meet in court, lack of interest in prisoner, all family members were in jail, respondent did not know the reason, no money to send letters, arrived in jail recently and did not have faith in postal services of the prison.

According to prison regulations, undertrials may write post-cards both at their own and government cost. But all letters must be censored. Taking letters for posting outside or sending them through another is strictly prohibited. It appeared that some prisoners did not have faith in the prison mail box. This was either because the letters were read or they were posted late. It was found that prisoners really did not know what happened to letters posted through the office.

The researcher noticed that the frequency of visitors in prison was very low. In most of the cases, the undertrials have not received even a post card from their family members. Thus, they have feelings of insecurity and loneliness. It was also observed that the undertrials are found waiting either for visits or letters. But there was no response and sympathy for them. Therefore, efforts should be made to help continue their relationship with family members which would help them to have sound family life after their release.

8.4.4 Respondent's Attitude toward Society/Outside World

Table 8. 12 : Respondent's Attitude towards Society / outside world

Attitudes	*Frequency*	*Percentage*
Positive	78	86.7
Negative	12	13.3
Total	90	100.0

Table 8.12 shows that, majority of the respondents have a positive attitude towards the people in the society outside the prison. Very few respondents have negative attitude. The cause behind the negative attitude may be society's criticism of their

offences and rejection. It is observed that they have lost faith in everyone. The prisoners who have shown negative attitude have described the people in the society as bad and cruel. They also have negative opinion about the society, and they hold society responsible for their present condition. One respondent remarked, "in this society, you cannot live the way you want. You have to always live as per the wishes of others". This remark indicates the status of Indian woman and also the situations existing in the family. Respondents who possess negative attitude towards society might have faced stress and adjustment problems in family and society and now they must be living under stress in prison. The positive attitude indicates their desire to affiliate with their family and society outside the prison after release.

It was considered essential to enquire whether the respondent felt the need to take revenge on the people responsible for getting them arrested. 83 out of 90 respondents have expressed negative responses. Only 7 respondents gave a positive reply to the query. The positive response to this query may also indicate the prisoner's wish to retaliate towards people living in the free world outside the prison.

8.5 Feelings of the Respondents:

Undertrial female criminals continue to suffer from emotional disturbances. Emotional unstability is a uniform feature seen in the prisoners. The suffering from feelings as follows:

Table 8.13: Respondent's Feelings

Feelings	*Frequency*	*Percentage*
Insecurity / fears	23	25.6
Anxiety	21	23.3
Loneliness	7	7.8
Depression / mental fatigue	7	7.8

(Contd.)

(Contd. Table 8.13)

Feelings	*Frequency*	*Percentage*
Frustration	11	12.2
Insecurity and anxiety	7	7.8
Insecurity and frustration	6	6.7
Anxiety and frustration	8	8.9
Total	90	100.0

Table 8.13 indicates that, insecurity / fears and anxiety are highly significant in criminals. Inside the prison, female undertrial criminals continue to suffer from emotional disturbances which in turn obstruct their adjustment to the prison. The socially deprived conditions in which these women live, is responsible for further weakening their emotional stability. Even though prisoners within the four walls of the prison are confined with co-inmates, yet isolation from the outside world creates tension and stress for them. It is assumed that, female undertrials being placed in situations of social isolation and extreme deprivation may exhibit emotional disturbances. In other words, alienation from the society may result in increase in insecurity and anxiety. These feelings may increase when the inmates are deprived of their autonomy and are confined in the prison and also because the individual's ability to cope with such problems may be in jeopardy.

Fear of consequences has become the additional content of these feelings. After the commission of the crime, a female criminal may remain in fear of the consequences that she would confront, foremost among which is deprivation of family members, by being separated from them and placed in prison.

It is observed that, sometimes female undertrials justify their actions and obtain relief from these feelings, by making another individual responsible for the offence. Most of them, when interviewed, tried to express their innocence. Those who were suffering from anxiety, frustrations and insecurity they may tend to affiliate more with others who were in a situation similar to their own. However, it should not be assumed that this is the case with all criminals. There are many women who are attracted towards a particular group of co-inmates with the desire to affiliate. Only they are prone to be selective in choosing their friends.

In the case of a few women, there is no hope of quick release or they doubt that family members will fight the case in court or not, those undertrials became extremely depressed and felt loneliness.

Sanyal and Agarwal[4] studied a sample of 69 female convicts and found that about 75 per cent criminals had a feeling of insecurity. In the present study the attitudes of the female undertrial criminals are studied in relation to offence, prison authorities, co-inmates, society comprising of family members and friends. Since female criminals generally come from broken homes where they have been deprived of parental affection, there is a tendency for them to have a hostile and an indifferent attitude towards the authorities and a negative attitude towards the prison and its activities. However, since the co-inmates live in the same set up and share the same problems, the chances of a favourable relationship with the co-inmates, are greater than with others.

A female undertrial suffering from extreme insecurity may also tend to posess a negative attitude towards her prison programmes. The separation from the outside world, fear of the loss of support by family members and a dark future, all combine, to keep her emotionally disturbed and hinder her acceptance of the prison activities.

8.6 Respondent's Expectations from Children

Children are the most important assets, especially to mothers and they are more attached to children. So, it is imperative to know the expectations of female criminals from their children. The following table shows their expectations from children.

Table 8.14: Expectations of Respondents from Children

Expectations	*Frequency*	*Percentage*
Live happily	6	6.7
Get educated	27	30.0
Get employed	3	3.3
Stand on their own feet	16	17.8
Any other	20	22.2
Not applicable	18	20.0
Total	90	100.0

Table 8.14 shows that, majority of the respondents spoke in favour of children, and also thought about children's betterment. They did not expect anything from children. In prison, many of the respondents are deprived of the love, affection and respect of their children. Hence, they are found to be more sensitive towards them. 'Any other' referred to: well settled, children should stay with their mother, children should understand their mothers and no expectations. In brief, respondents have different expectations from their children. Generally, they want that their children should not suffer and they should lead a good life.

8.7 Feelings of Respondents regarding Happiness and Anger

The respondent's views were sought on certain feelings concluding an individual's conduct in society.

Table 8.15 shows that, children are more closer to the respondent. The response of happiness of children was supported by more than one-third respondents. Children are a very important component of the family. The mother-child relationship is of great importance and plays a vital role in behavioural patterns. Nearly one-fourth of the respondents were found so dejected that nothing can make them happy. More

Table 8.15: Things making Respondent Feel Happy

Feelings	*Frequency*	*Percentage*
Happiness of children	32	35.6
If husband treats well	3	3.3
Nothing much	21	23.3
Any other	34	37.8
Total	90	100.0

than one-third of the respondents gave 'other' responses. 'Any other' referred to: someone talking to them affectionately, somebody supports them, during festivals, receipt of gifts, on someone's release from the jail, worshipping god, husband's happy mood and good literature.

To know the actual personality of the individual, it is found essential to get the infonnation about this particular query.

Table 8.16: Things making Respondent Feel Angry

Feelings	*Frequency*	*Percentage*
Telling lies	20	22.2
Back answering	7	7.8
Children disobeying elders	6	6.7
Nothing much/do not get angry	27	30.0
Any other	30	33.3
Total	90	100.0

The responses are justified by moral standards. Most of the respondent's feelings were found in favour of social values. Nearly one-fourth of the respondents replied that, 'telling lies' is one of the major reasons which makes them feel angry. In their view, one must be honest and should not tell lies. 'Back answering' and 'children disobeying elders' accounted for 7.8 per cent and 6.7 per cent responses respectively. 30.0 per cent respondents did not get much angry. 'Any other' responses (33.3 per cent) consisted of: deception, treachery, disgusting behaviour, not taken to court on given dates, respondent frequently gets angry because of her peevish nature, constant nagging by relatives about respondent's mistake and not allowed to roam-freely.

The responses of table 8.16 and 8.17 indicate indirectly the concepts of respondents' about 'good' and 'bad'. The respondent's standards of behavioural pattern and perceptions are reflected in their notions of happiness and anger.

The involvement of women in crime indicates the perversion in value orientation in them. So it is better to know the values of the prisoners regarding idols.

Table 8.17: Respondent's Idols

Idols	*Frequency*	*Percentage*
God	72	80.0
Parents	8	8.9
None	3	3.3
Other	7	7.8
Total	90	100.0

Table 8.17 reveals that, majority of the respondents of the total sample mentioned 'god' as their idol. 'Other' referred to: husband, elder brother, daughter/children and astrology. Most of the respondents have faith in god, while very few did not believe in anything. Parents would be the main objects of respect in the Indian milieunce, 8.9 per cent replied that parents are their idols. God fearing women also committed crimes, though most of them were not habitual offenders. Their committing crime, indicates their compulsive state of criminality. No doubt religion is an important agency of social control. However, it is assumed that their situations and circumstances, frustrations, ignorance, socio-cultural

obligations, etc., are the chief culprits which dragged them to crime. Now, the future appeared dark and gloomy for them. So faith in god gives them the little strength they still possess. It is understood that confinement in a deprived condition makes the individual extremely paralyzed both physically and mentally. Therefore, belief in God preserves hope for their future.

The respondents were asked whether they have a desire to go out: All of them (100 per cent) have given positive reply. In their opinion, no one could be reformed in jail.

8.8 Other Information provided by Respondents

The respondents were asked to express their views openly about any other information not included in interview schedule. This information included (i) prison must have congenial atmosphere; (ii) prison authorities should behave properly and humanely; (iii) prison should have provisions of such vocational training which can be useful to earn money in the prison and also when they are released; (iv) there should be a speedy disposal of the cases; (v) there is corruption inside the prison; and (vi) justice should be less expensive.

A major problem which undertrial female criminals face is delayed trial period. It is not only criminal justice system which is partial and silent about women but even outside its circle, society, family, religion are equally responsible for the present miserable conditions of women prisoners, e.g., if family members are arrested for the same offence, the family spends money and also provides more legal support to defend male relatives rather than female. In that case, female members stay in prison for long periods.

Finally, criminal processes beginning with arrests and ending in release and readjustment with society involves a lot of deprivation including the deprivation of contacts with family members and the inevitable disruption of management and care of children. Emotional imbalance, lack of freedom, loss of security, a feeling of isolation, forced separation from family were largely felt by prisoners. They had fears if family members would accept them or not. They were anxious about the care of children. They were also worried about their future due to the stigma of imprisonment.

8.9 Researcher's Observations

(1) The women's barrack has a capacity of 23 as against more than 100 women undertrials forced to live a cramped existence.

(2) Cleanliness in the barracks was good.

(3) Those suffering from contagious diseases have no separate arrangements and are mixed with the other co-inmates. There was no segregation of murderers and prostitutes from others.

(4) The quality of food given to the undertrials in the prison was not good (e.g., Dal and Vegetable was watery). There is discrimination in the food given to Indian women undertrials and the foreign women inmates. 'The latter are provided with bread, eggs, more milk, and other essentials. On the other hand, the locals have no such privilege because rules regarding food provisions prior to the pre-independence era are still in vogue.

(5) Most of the respondents were unhappy with the food and the meal timings (lunch would be given at 11.00 a.m. and dinner at 4.00 p.m.).

(6) Canteen facilities of the prison were good but not all the respondents availed of this facility as they had no money.

(7) The undertrials were not satisfied with the medical facilities. They reported that medicines were also not very effective.

(8) Some of the respondents had admitted being beaten up during interrogation by the police when they had been first detained in police lock-ups.

(9) Most of the respondents had found the prison to be a terrible place.

(10) Undertrials could meet their family members or relatives. They also could meet their family members detained in the male section of the prison.

References

1. Shekhar Sanober - 'Women Prisoners: The Remand and Undertrial Experiences'.
2. Kaldate Sudha - 'Convicted Female Offenders in Indian Prisons', Female Criminals and Female Victims, p. 229.
3. Sohoni, N.K. - 'Women behind Bars', p. 157.
4. Sanyal S. and Agarwal V. - 'Women Convicts in Nari Bandi Niketan', Indian Journal of Criminoloty, Vo1. 9, No. 2, July 1981, p. 128.

9

Undertrial Female Criminals Some Case Studies

Introduction

The following case studies are analyzed, highlighting the contributory causes and the important situations which gave rise to different kinds of criminal behaviour. Tnese undertrial female criminals represent different types of offences like robbery, theft, counterfeiting, cheating, murder, attempt to murder, kidnapping, assistance in raping, NDPS Act offence and passport act offence.

The names mentioned in the case studies are fictitious in order to protect the privacy of the accused.

9.1 Sonabai: Needed Money for Husband's Second Marriage

Sonabai is a fifty year old, illiterate woman, belongs to Hindu- Vadar community. Her parents got her married at an early age. After attaining puberty, she went and resided with her husband in a village in Maharashtra. Her husband was a labourer, earned Rs.1000/- per month. She gave birth to three sons and four daughters. Her husband had to work very hard to maintain the family. So she also started working as a road-construction labourer and assisted her husband in maintaining the family. But after few years her health was affected and she could not do any more work as a labourer. As a result the whole burden of the family fell on her husband. This gave rise to ill-feelings between Sonabai and her husband, Her husband was a drunkard. There were frequent quarrels between Sonabai and her husband, and these were followed by beatings by the husband. Her husband wanted to remarry.

Sonabai's nature was submissive and she did not have much power in the family. She felt that she was a great burden on the whole family. This made Sonabai decide to come to Mumbai. She also admitted that, she had begun resorting to crime in order to finance her husband's future second marriage. In the 'vadar' community, to which Sonabai belongs, the groom has to pay dowry to the bride. To finance this, Sonabai put together a gang of fellow criminals and came to Mumbai.

Sonabai was arrested the first time by the Government Railway Police. According to Railway Police officials, she was involved in at least 60 cases of robbery and chain snatching. The Sonabai gang operated for over two years between Kurla and Kalyan railway stations. They robbed women commuters in local trains. They used to cut or open women's handbags and steal their money and other valuables. They were experts in opening the zips of handbags and cutting them from the base without the victims suspecting. All of them were arrested along with Sonabai. One of her accomplices was Sunita, twenty years old. Her marriage was almost finalized when the groom demanded that she should start earning. Sunita, a resident of the same village as Sonabai, joined because she liked the boy and decided she would do everything that was needed to make the marriage a reality.

Sonabai chose the profession in order to marry off her husband to another girl end Sunita joined the profession as the groom demanded that she should earn. In this case, it can be specifically stated that the money needed for mariage drove them to crime. Sonabai was almost at the verge of being abandoned as her husband had decided to go in for another marriage. For no fault of hers she was threatened. Her criminality was more a sacrifice for the sake of her husband and her family. Sonabai is an offender in the eyes of the law, but socially she sacrificed a great deal.

This case, especially Sunita's case is a manifestation of Sutherland's theory of "differential association". This theory states that criminal behaviour is learnt in a process of communication with other persons, principally in small intimate groups. This learning includes the techniques of committing the crime. The specific direction of motives, drives, rationalizations and attitudes is learned from definitions of the legal codes as favourable or unfavourable.

9.2 Leena: A Sociopath and a Case of Personality Disorder

Leena, a twenty-five year old, fair and smart unmarried Christian girl arrested for counterfeiting. She has studied upto HSC. Her father works as a auto-rickshaw driver and her mother is a housewife. Her father earned Rs. 3000/- per month. Leena worked as a receptionist in a private firm and earned Rs.4000/- per month. There she entered into a love affair with a Muslim boy. She spent most of her time outside her house in his company. Her boy-friend was a deviant person.Her mother found her friend's behaviour doubtful and warned her several times, and also tried to change her mind but could not succeed. One day Leena ran away from-home and sought shelter with one of the friends of her boy-friend. There she was influenced by other friends who took an active part in gang activities. Leena got involved with them and made some extra money out of it. When she refused to do so, she was asked to leave the house. After a while, she too got used to easy earnings and gained acceptance in the group. When her mother came to know about her involvement in smuggling, she warned her to stop but Leena could not quit the profession. Once, when she was passing over counterfeit currency in a mobile show-room with her male companion, she got arrested. The customs personnel also raided their residence. Eleven of her co-workers were also arested. All these people produced counterfeit notes and passed them off. It is suspected that their activities were connected with Mumbai's most dreaded gangsters.

Leena's offence is non-bailable. She spent fourteen months in jail. At the time of arrest she was in early stages of pregnancy. In prison she delivered an illegitimate child.

When asked about her plans after her release from jail, she replied, 'my family is not going to accept me', and she has no alternate plan in mind. In prison, she is suffering from the feelings of insecurity, rejection by society and loss of livelihood.

Leena's father refuses to communicate with her.Her mother contacts her sometimes without his knowledge. Leena says, "My mother goes on asking me why I did this. She comes to me with her own problems, as if I don't have enough poblems already. This makes meeting her disturbing rather than giving me any satisfaction".

According to Leena, "I made a mistake but I admitted it - so I should be pardoned. After all everyone makes mistakes, sometime or the other."

The researcher had the impression that Leena did not necessarily become a criminal because of her family. She became a criminal of her own volition, or it may be said that her own demoralization and lack of self discipline appear to be more decisive factors in her criminality. In the beginning the researcher felt that this case was a manifestation of Lombroso's theory of 'born criminal' but at the same time, another point of view also emerged that it was the environment in which she was entangled which was responsible. While, sub-culture theory explains the influence of unfavourable environmental conditions on the person and how it forced him/her to crime.

9.3 Fatima: Paranoid, Suspicious and Dominant Nature

Fatima is a sixty-five year old, married Muslim woman and her.daughter Saida, a thirty-one year old married woman were involved in a crime of attempted murder. Fatima lived with her husband, son and daughter-in-law in a suburb of Mumbai. Her family income was Rs.2000/- per month. Daughter Saida stayed very close to Fatima's house.

Fatima's relations with her husband and son, except for her daughter-in-law, were cordial. She was not happy with the daughter-in-Iaw's behaviour. She wanted her to wear a 'burkha' and did not allow her to come out of the house without burkha. But the daughter-in-law refused to start wearing one. Fatima felt that a daughter-in-law should obey her in-law's.

During the interview, Fatima and Saida complained about how the daughter-in-law refused to behave properly. They reported that, she frequently visited her parental house. Both of them were extremely suspicious about these visits and thought that, she must be having an affair. Fatima's son also became suspicious of his wife character and began ill-treating her.

Matters became worse and in a fit of anger Fatima and her daughter administered poison to the daughter-in-law through her food. She began to have convulsive fits and was taken to a nearby hospital and her life was saved. The doctor discovered the attempt of murder and a case was filed against Fatima and her daughter.

Fatima and her daughter claimed innocence. According to them, the daughter-in-law was beaten up severely by her husband for not listening to him and frequently visiting her parent's house and so, in her husband's absence the frustrated victim attempted suicide.

Saida claimed that, when this incident happened, her mother called her for help, so she was present there.

Fatima has been in jail for only two months - however, she said everyday seemed like a year. Fatima's son and husband come to visit her. She has been suffering from feelings of insecurity. She does not take interest in her srroundings not even in talking to her co-inmates. All she wishes is to escape from this place as soon as possible.

The researcher had the strong impression that although both mother and daugtlter feigned innocence they were not telling the truth. When asked what made her the most angry, Fatima said that if anybody went against her wishes, especially those younger in age, that infuriated her.

9.4 Shabana: Influence of Multiple Factors in Crime

Shabana, a Muslim woman of thirty-one years, lived with her husband, mother-in- law and four children. She was married at the age of fifteen to a thirty-five year old man. Her husband was a taxi-driver and the only bread-winner in the family. He had illicit relations with another woman.

Shabana was arrested under the charge of kidnapping of her neighbour's son aged three years. Her version of events was that, she did not have any intention of kidnapping the boy. She had taken away the boy to feed him, but when she heard that the parents were searching for the boy, she panicked and instead of returning the boy to the parent hid him in her house.The neighbour filed a case and the police arrested her for kidnapping the boy. Shabana maintained that she never intended to kidnap him.

Throughout the interview, tears were rolling down from her eyes. She seemed to be very concerned about her children. She has spent six months in the prison. She has breast-cancer and suffers from severe pain. Nobody from her family came to visit her or sent letters. In prison, Shabana suffers from feelings of insecurity and frustration and also felt forced separation from family.

9.5 Sudha: Desertion by Husband and Social, Economic and Emotional Deprivation

Sudha is a Hindu-Gauda caste woman aged thirty years. She lost her mother in her childhood. She has two sisters and one brother. She was brought up by her father. The family supported itself by working as agricultural labourers in

Bangalore. Their earnings were too meager to maintain themselves. In her seventeenth year, she was married to an agricultural labourer. After a year, her husband deserted her. Then she developed illicit relations with one of the villagers.

It so happened that, the man migrated to Mumbai with Sudha and abandoned her in a brothel pretending that the house belonged to a relative and went away. Slowly, Sudha got acquainted with the brothel inmates, and was persuaded by them to take up prostitution. After a few years, Sudha opened her own brothel and did good business. She earned upto Rs.3000/- per month.

One day Sudha came across a young girl, whom she lured with visions of providing a good job, and brought her to the brothel. Later, she tried to force the girl into prostitution. It was only after a few days, that the young girl escaped from the brothel and filed a complaint of rape against Sudha. Police raided Sudha's brothel and arrested her.

According to Sudha, she had no intention of misleading the girl, the girl came into the brothel of her own accord.

Sudha has spent seven months in prison. She has neither children nor family ties. After her release, she wants to continue her life as a prostitute.

There is no rehabilitation strategy available after their release. A woman who is socially boycotted and destitute, what other option will she have other than indulging in the same profession again.

The researcher felt that unfavourable environmental conditions influcnced sudha and forced her to crime. What she appears to be today is a natural product of her circumstances.

9.6 Rama: Ill-treatment by Family Members and Enviroment influence

Rama is a widowed woman of forty years, belongs to Hindu-Shetty caste. She lost her mother in her childhood. Her father who worked as an agricultural labouer in Karnataka, got her married in her fifteenth year. The age difference between Rama and her husband was ten years. After marriage, she resided in her husband's house consisting of her widowed mother-in-law and a deserted sister-in-law. She gave birth to two sons and a daughter. After the death of her mother-in-law, Rama's sister-in-law took charge of managing the house. Rama used to assist her husband financially by doing building construction work.

Meanwhile, Rama's husband died of alcoholism. After that she started quarreling with her sister-in-law on financial and domestic matters and migrated to Mumbai with her children. She rented a thatched house in the city and started working as a maidservant. She strove hard to maintain the house with her meager earnings.

One day her neighbour informed her about the availability of a new job as a domestic servant with an ex-film actress who lived in a bungalow at Juhu, Mumbai. Rama accepted the job and shifted to Juhu. She resided in the servant's quarters and erned Rs.2000/- per month. She had to do all the domestic work in the bunglow including preparation of food for the aged actress who lived alone. At this stage, Rama was living happily with her children.

After a few years, the relatives of the actress's friend conspired with Rama to murder her in order to acquire her property.

One day with the assistance of these relatives Rama managed to mix poison in the cooked food. The lady ate the food and died. Rama and three other male members were arrested for the crime of murder.

A close acquaintance (whom she treats like a brother) used to come to prison bringing her kids. But these visits were very disturbing for her. Now his visits have stopped. So Rama does not know the whereabouts of her children. She said may be her community people are taking care of them. She expects her children to stay away from bad things and become good human beings. She said, "But now that I have been in jail, I cannot advise my children. They might answer back and question my authority to teach them what is right and wrong".

(Recently, news came in the daily newspaper that Rama and her accomplice have been sentenced to life imprisonment.)

9.7 Asha: Financial Difficulties and Desire to Assist Spouse

Asha, a forty year old married woman, belongs lo Hindu-Bania caste . She was married at the age of fifteen. She had four children. She was a migrant from Delhi. She came to Mumbai with her husband to earn a living. In the beginning she and her husband maintained their family with great difficulty. Her husband worked as a labourer in a jute mill. To supplement their income Asha stitched clothes at home. But even then it was difficult to manage with the money they earned. They earned Rs.3000/- per month.

Then they were attracted to their neighbour's drug business and now they earned extra money. So they maintained it as a side occupation and continued it for eight years prior to the day of their arrest. To look after this new business better, they sent their children to their native place.

Asha and her husband assisted their neighbour in selling the drugs. One day in a sudden raid on the 'neighbour's house Asha and her husband being on the spot were arrested by the excise personnel. Excise authorities collected 30 kg. marijuana (ganja) from the neighbour's house.

Asha spent two and a half years in the prison. She has been arrested for the first time, but was familiar with the procedures of police, courts and prison because of her neighbour who had been constantly arrested in the past.

In this case, financial difficulties drove Asha to crime and environmental influences also played a major role.

Asha said, "Both of us being in jail, the children's education must have been discontinued. We cannot face the in-laws of my married daughter since they know about this." Asha has been suffering from the feelings of insecurity, fear and anxiety.

9.8 Salma: Economic Crisis in the Family Compelled to Adopt Illegal Means

Salma, a thirty year old Muslim woman, lost her parents during childhood. She was brought up by her paternal aunt. She experienced an unhappy childhood because of poor family background. Salma was illiterate and came from Bangladesh. She and her husband were arrested under the Passport Act at Chhatrapati Shivaji Terminus, Mumbai.

At the age of fifteen Salma married a man of twenty and gave birth to two daughters. Her husband was a labourer and earned Rs.1500/- per month. To maintain the family Salma too started working as a domestic servant. But their jobs were casual in nature, therefore, their income was uncertain. Salma started that there are no job opportunities except agricultural work and rearing of sheep. Besides, that there are no proper wages for labour work and majority of people live in poverty.

With no good job and severe financial crisis in the family Salma and her husband decided to migrate to India to earn a livelihood, leaving behind their two daughters with Salma's sister.

Salma had never thought about the consequences of her action before coming India. She was aware that many people come from Bangladesh to India with the hope of getting a job. So she also decided to come to India.

She had no relatives or acquaintances in Mumbai. She was caught on the first day of her arrival in Mumbai by the police and was put into the jail along with her husband. Since then, they have been unable to contact their relatives in Bangaladesh. Salma has already spent six months in jail. She has been suffering from feelings of insecurity and fear.

9.9 Vanita: Torture and Sexual Abuse by Husband

Vanita, a thirty-four years old, Hindu-Mahar caste woman was arrested under the charge of murder of her husband. She had two daughters and a son.

Vanita's relations with her husband were not satisfactory. She said her husbamd was a drunkard, gambler and a perverted person. Very often he avoided work and spent most of his time at home. He wanted to have sex night and day. During her pregnancy and after delivery also he continued to demand sex every day and beat her if she refused. Every day, after 8.00 p.m. he used to wander in the house naked. Whenever Vanita tried to dissuade him from this, he became angry and beat her. All that her husband was interested in, was sex and that sex was violent and without any love or tenderness. After the third child was born, her husband's behaviour grew worse. Vanita denied his sexual demands from time to time. Her husband kept telling her to leave the house since she was not giving him enough sex. He used obscene and abusive language with his own daughters. A few times he forced Vanita to have sex with him in front of the daughters.

Once her husband took off her clothes and threw her out of the house in that condition. Vanita made three attempts to kill herself by pouring kerosene over herself and by poisoning. But each time she was rescued.

Vanita told her story to her parents and complained to them saying she was unable to bear sexual harassment by her husband. But there was no response from her parents.

One day, Vanita discovered that her husband had undressed her fourteen year old daughter. She became furious. This incident made her lose control and she decided to teach him a lesson. So she took the assistance of neighbourhood boys and told them to beat him up. After this beating, he fell down and died on the spot. Vanita claimed that she never had any intention to murder him.

During police interrogation, these boys confessed that Vanita told them to beat him up. Today, Vanita feels insecure in prison and worried about her children's future. She said, "My children had no happiness in life. If I am kept here, who will make them happy?"

Nobody understands the mental trauma she has experienced. The question is whether she should be looked at as a criminal or a victim of circumstances. Perhaps, this is the worst example of female victimization. This is not just the story of Vanita alone. Even in the 21st Century in India we have thousands of Vanitas who are being exploited and humiliated for no fault of their own.

9.10 Neeta: Unhappy Married Life and Economic Compulsion

Neeta is twenty-nine years of age, a Gujarati woman, belonging to Patel community. She completed her graduation in Gujarat. Her father had passed away when she was very young. She had a elder brother. Mother was the sole earning member in the family, but she was not able to give much attention to her children.

Neeta's mother tried her best to satisfy the needs of her children by giving them enough money for their expenses. Neeta was a truant girl since childhood. During her college days, Neeta got acquainted with a boy of different caste and got married to him at the age of twenty years, against her mother's wish. He was a mechanic. Since the very beginning of her marital life she developed a hatred for her husband. Neeta's relations with her husband and mother-in-law were not satisfactory. In the meantime she gave birth to four sons.

Neeta's husband was always busy with his work and never took interest in her. She also heard about his illicit contacts with another woman. This created unhappy feelings in her and she experienced frustration and absconded from home. In a moment of desperation, she migrated to Mumbai with her children and mother.

In Mumbai, she lived in an open space, with her mother and children. Her mother started working as a domestic servant and earned Rs.1000/- per month. Neeta was doing a part-time survey job as a sales girl and earned Rs.500/- per month. She underwent stress and strain to manage the family with their meager earnings. In order to overcome their economic difficulties, she started pilfering articles from shops. After some time, she became a habitual shop-lifter. The only way to meet expenses was by way of shop-lifting. One day she was caught red-handed by the jewellery shop owner and later was imprisoned. In this case "financial difficulties" play a major predisposing and direct role in theft.

Neeta spent one and a half year in prison and suffered from feelings of anxiety and forced separation from family. In prison, she assists the jailor and the matron to maintain discipline.

Says Neeta, "My being in jail affects my children. The life of my mother and my children is being destroyed because of my absence. I committed this crime because I could not bear to see my children go hungry - the court should have considered this before passing its judgment". She further says, "I can hardly swallow my food in jail. Everyone should be given some responsibility here. Tailoring is taught here but it is not compulsory. Bag-making or candle making should be taught so that the women can be occupied in work and also get to earn some money".

Neeta's mother brings her children to the jail to visit her - these visits are a source of happiness for her.

9.11 Indu: Initiation into Offensive Acts by Family Member

Indu, a Hindu-Maratha caste widow, seventy years of age, mother of three children, resides in Mumbai.

Indu owned five garages. Ten years ago, her eldest son absconded from home and joined a criminal gang. He never came back. He has been arrested many times in gang-war cases. As there was no one to look after her business, she rented out all motor garages. She made an income of Rs.15 ,000/- per month.

Out of her two daughters, one got married and the unmarried daughter lived with her. Indu was associated with different political parties and she used to take active part in their activities. Some times political actions by the party gave rise to severe conflict and often resulted in severe violence and sabotage.

Currently, Indu has been arrested under the charge of murder. A case was filed against her that she had paid money to finish off a person from the opposing political party. This is her second arrest. The first time, she was arrested for demanding a ransom of Rs.25 lacs and provoking a gang-war.

Indu looks very simple and homely. According to her, it was not a planned crime but simply the result of a dispute which happened accidentally. In prison, lndu has been suffering from feelings of depression and mental fatigue. Her daughters come to visit her here.

9.12 Uma: Desire to Earn More Money

Uma, fifty-seven years of age, a Hindu-Brahmin woman was arrested under the charge of cheating. She has two children. She is from a middle-class family and has a good family background. She has completed M.Com. Her husband and son are Chartered Accountants and her daughter is a practicing advocate. The family did not have any financial problems. Her family income was above Rs.25 ,000/- per month.

Uma's family resides in Mumbai. She started her own investment agency. She was the proprietor. Many people invested their money with her and later on, she was unable to deliver on her promises. Therefore, people started withdrawing their money. She was in a financial crisis. She started issuing cheques to various investors. Due to insufficient balance in her accounts, the cheques bounced. A few of the investors filed cheating cases against her. One of her clients pursued the case in court. She was found guilty and sent to prison.

Some of her former employees come to visit her in prison. Uma has to return total of Rs.12 lacs owed to various investors. Her family members are unable to help her. One reason for this could be that she had started this business against the wishes of her family.

Uma has a strong desire to see her daughter become one of the leading advocates. When Uma came for the interview she looked very disturbed, unable to adjust herself to prison atmosphere. She has been suffering from feelings of anxiety and forced separation from family. However, she felt that her arrest was justified. She agreed that she had committed an offence.

Uma says, "Basic necessities are not provided in prison. Prison administration is not good. Canteen coupons are given only on the 1st and 15th of each month to purchase retail items which are available in prison canteen. This is not correct-if the prisoners are paying for the coupons, why these restrictions?"

Uma has faith in astrology. She gets joy from reading good literature.

9.13 Mala: Inappropriate Upbringing and Unhappy Married Life

Mala, a thirty-two year old woman hails from Punjab. She is illiterate, married and has three children. Mala was a habitual criminal and was committing thefts ever since childhood. Her parents died in an accident in her infancy. She spent an unhappy childhood in her maternal aunt's house.

At the age of fifteen Mala married a man aged nineteen years. It was love marriage. She lived in a joint family and her husband was jobless. Mala tried to lead a good life by working as a domestic servant but was unsuccessful. The money was insufficient and also she did not like the work. So, to run the household, she had to continue with her old occupation i.e., pilfering and theft. She committed acts of thefts as and when she found the opportunity. Her husband spent most of her earnings on his vices. Mala started nagging him. Tried beyond endurance, she deserted him and started living separately with her children. Her married life lasted only for four years.

Later, failing to pay the house rent, she vacated the house and was forced to live on temple premises with her children. She faced difficulties in providing for her children. Then she turned into a habitual thief and managed her livelihood with these illegitimate earnings. She could not give much care and attention to her children because of her activities.

During her interview, she claimed that all she did was to visit Mumbai's Chorbazaar (an area known for second hand goods and black-marketing) and took back garments to Punjab, where she sold them for a profit. She earned Rs.2000/- per month. Mala has 16 cases of robbery and theft registered against her. Once, as she snatched a gold chain from a young girl, in a Delhi bound train, she was caught red-handed and was prosecuted.

During her arrest, Mala had gone through many police interrogations and third degree methods. Being in prison has not made much of a difference to her, but she had been badly beaten up by the police which she could not bear. She said that now she was fed up of leading such a life i.e., thefts, lock-ups, prison, courts, etc.

When asked about her kids she said that the neighbours might have left them in an ashram. She added that if nobody took care of the children, they too would become thieves one day. 'Government is making three thieves by arresting one' - she said. This is because she has three children.

It is true that just to punish one person, it is wrong to deprive the family of their means of survival. It is a tragedy of law that in order to provide justice to one, it commits injustice towards many. There is no remedy for innocent victims in the process of law.

In this case, the circumstances which prompted Mala to enter into crime seem to be a lack of affection and care in her childhood. She was a neglected child and no proper attention was paid by her aunt towards her well-being and socialization. She appears to be a victim of her circumstances.

10

Conclusions and Suggestions

Introduction

This is a study of under-trial female criminal prisoners. This study has been conducted on the total population of female undertrials of Arthur Road, Central Prison, Mumbai, in the state of Maharashtra.

Since each chapter carries its own findings, only a broad overview of the major impressions on the basis of analysis and interpretation of facts and the observations of the researcher have been presented here:

10.1 Findings

10.1.1 Demographic Profile

The demographic profile of 90 undertrial female criminals from a women's prison in Mumbai was examined. It was noted that undertrial female criminals were found in all age groups, majority of them were illiterate residents of Mumbai and its suburbs, slum/chawl dwellers, Hindus, Marathi speaking population, belonged to upper, S.C./*S.T.* and O.B.C. castes in descending order, married and widowed / deserted, married before 18 years of age, earning and earned below Rs.3000/- per month.

10.1.2 Socio-Economic Background

The socio-economic characteristics of 90 undertrial female criminals were analyzed. It was found that majority of respondents were from nuclear families, illiterate family background, belonged to the families of which the monthly income was less than Rs.3000/- per month.

Economic condition of the family does not necessarily indicate the role of poverty in female crime, yet, it is significant, in the sense that low income is an important contributory factor to family tensions; and a combination of unsatisfactory social relationships and poverty is conducive to criminal behaviour.

It was also noticed that these women were preponderantly breadwinners of their families. Most of the respondents have less than three children. Majority of them had come from emotionally integrated family background and have cordial interpersonal relationships within the family (most of the respondents lived alone with their children). A majority of respondents did not have friends before their arrest and had friendly good relations with their neighbours. In majority of the cases the income status of neighbours was found either higher or lower to the income status of respondents.

Majority were unable to decide on any matter without their husband's consent and did not have decision making powers. Most of the respondents did not live in criminal surroundings.

10.1.3 Nature and Causes of Female Crimes

The offence profile of 90 undertrial female criminals was examined. It revealed that majority of respondents had been arrested for thefts and murders. In most of the murder cases, the victim was a member of the respondent's family. Majority had committed offence with the help of others, indulged in offence for the first time, did not think about the results of their action before committing crime, claimed innocence about their crime and committed crime predominantly for financial causes.

Majority of the women in the age group of 18 to 29 and 30 to 39 years were more involved in property offences. Illiterate and graduate undertrials were also more involved in property offences. Majority of Hindus were found participating in property offences while, Muslims were more involved in 'other offences' i.e., NDPS Act., Passport Act and Immoral Traffic Act offences.

Upper caste women were more involved in offences against the person. Majority of S.C. / S.T. and N.T./D.T. caste women were involved in property offences while, O.B.C. caste women were more involved in 'other offences'. Married and widowed / deserted women category showed their involvement in property offences, while, unmarried women were equally involved in property offences and 'other offences'. Majority of housewives had been arrested for offences against the person. Those who were engaged in some occupation were involved in property offences predominantly. Majority of the respondents in the income group of below Rs.3000/- per month were seen to be involved in property offences.

Respondents belonging to nuclear families were more involved in property offences, while respondents belonged to joint families were more involved in offence against the person. Respondents who themselves were breadwinners in the family were involved mostly in property offences. In most of the cases, those who belonged to nuclear families, had their spouses as companions in criminal act, while respondents from joint families mostly received help from family members other than spouse.

10.1.4 Attitude and Feelings of Respondents

It was noted that majority of the respondents felt that decisions about their arrest and custody were unjustified. They showed perception of themselves as innocent, found prison custody as forced separation from family, showed favourable attitudes towards co-inmates, did not find any difference in treatment by prison authorities. It was also observed that majority of the respondents have the belief that after their release they would be treated by their family members as before. However, most of them neither received support from their families nor did their family members come to visit them. Most of them did not receive or send letters to family members.

Undertrial female criminals possess positive attitudes towards people in the society outside the prison and have expressed negative responses about the query as to whether they feel like taking revenge on the people responsible for getting them arrested. Majority of respondents spoke in favour of their children and expressed that the happiness of their children is the main factor which makes them feel happy. They have faith in God and have a desire to go out. On the other hand, they have acute feelings of insecurity and anxiety.

10.2 Researcher's Observations

This study of 90 undertrial female criminals shows the changing forms of female criminality. The findings of this study indicate that, today women of all age groups are equally involved in crime. Illiteracy and low level of education dominate the crime scenario. Higher percentages of criminals are seen to be emanating from urban areas. In urban areas, checks imposed on women both by the community and the authorities operate less effectively. This relative freedom lies behind the exposure to the evil effects of city life. In the city, the influence of relatives and community has weakened. Moreover, urbanization has led to the breaking up of the joint family.

The findings of the study also show that dwelling in slums produces more criminals in the city. Slums and unauthorized structures are an outcome of irresistable inflow of population into the city and subsequent pressures on land and resources. It reflects inhuman living conditions coupled with hardships in life and have a far reaching impact on the quality of life.

In any case, no significant association with 'low caste' was established in the present study. Caste-wise distribution shows that upper-caste women are more involved in crime. Hence, this study presents a slightly different picture of female crime than the earlier studies on female criminality conducted in 1980s and 1990s.

The earlier studies highlighted the involvement of married women as prominent in crime, while this study shows an almost equal proportion of married and widowed / deserted women involved in crime.

Most of the empirical studies in India showed that offences against the person were dominant offences. However, the present study shows that property offences are higher than offences against the person. The majority of female criminals were found to belong to poor sections of society, with either very low or no stable source of monthly income. Economic deprivations are the main cause for criminal activities. Fluctuation in crimes seemed to be clearly tied to economic conditions and to two factors in particular: prices of consumer goods, especially food and availability of work.

Although, women still represent only a small fraction of those arrested for NDPS Act offences, their involvement may be increasing. It is also found that women committed Passport Act offences. The motivation behind it was the chance of getting a job in a city like Mumbai.

The general point made in almost all the studies is that the impact of socio-economic status on trends in crime is revealed most strongly.

Most of the respondents came from nuclear families and in many cases respondents were playing the role of breadwinner of the family. Hence, the respondents must have experienced strain and pressures as a result of economic conditions.

Majority of the married women were unable to decide on any matter without their husband's consent. In a male dominated society, decision making power also indicates family culture and understanding in the family. The processes of modernisation and industrialization transformed the socio-economic environment. More and more women started working outside and supplementing the income of their families. The increasing rate of family breakdown, widowhood and desertion, home responsibilities, rearing children and financial difficulties all contribute to the incidents of female criminality.

In the present study, poverty was found to be a significant factor in provoking *a* woman to crime and it may be the root of marital or other frustrations. Poverty creates severe economic strain on women; search for altemative sources of livelihood and it may be a stimulus to crime. In a city like Mumbai, there are great opportunities for theft. The findings indicated that, these females are mostly from lower income backgrounds. The rising prices have forced women to seek jobs in cities.As urbanization increases, property offences in cities also increase.

However, low socio-economic status of the family and family circumstancs or stressful situations within the family may be at the root of female criminality.

The socio-economic analysis emphasizes poverty and financial crisis as the primary causes of crime. Female crime rates have increased mainly in economic crimes. This can be explained in terms of 'Opportunity theory'. Cloward and Ohlin contended that some people in society have limited access to achieve goals by legitimate ways or means so, they may turn to illegitimate opportunities. This theory explains why a particular class of society turns to particular kind of crime patterns. Today, women are more involved in property offences because they have more opportunities to commit such crimes.

On the basis of review findings, it may be viewed that the main causes of female criminality are economic insecurity and family circumstances. The people of lower socio-economic status face more deprivations throughout their life. It is difficult for them to satisfy their economic needs, therefore, they are tempted to commit crimes.

It was found that majority of the respondents were of the opinion that decision about their arrest and custody was unjustified. They claimed innocence. This is because, they were undertrials and being in stress and tension, opposed to any kind of labeling as criminals. They found prison custody as forced separation from family. However, they showed positive attitude towards society and had desire to go out of prison. Insecurity and anxiety feelings are found more among the inmates.

Very often women are themselves responsible for becoming criminals. Since, a large number of crimes committed by women are due to their adjustment problems or circumstances and are not due to their criminal tendencies, and also, most of them are first offenders. There is a great need for a flexible policy for female criminals.

10.3 Conclusions

The present study covers a variety of aspects related to female criminality.However, as the study deals with a limited sample size, the findings should be accepted with some caution. Certain conclusions can be drawn based on the findings of the present study about the nature and trends of female criminality. The analysis of the variables helps in hypothesizing the role of low socio-economic status and stressful situations within the family caused by illiteracy, early marriage and poverty, in female crime.

For this study, the researcher adopted three hypotheses as follows:

(1) Low socio-economic status of the family is an important factor in female crime.

(2) Stressful situations within the family play an important role in the life of female criminals.

(3) Undertrial female prisoners are prone to certain feelings and attitudes.

The analysis detects low socio-economic level to be more influential.As far as women are concerned, their inferior status, both within the family and society can put unusual stress on them leading them to deviance in reaction to such stress. In the case of females in India this stress is enormous because of cultural norms. A woman is not supposed to leave her husband's house no matter how many hardships she may suffer. If the Indian woman seeks freedom at home and asserts her rights, it creates further stresses and strains in the marital relationship.

The present study reveals that the female criminality was more prevalent among illiterate women and poverty was predominantly at the root of marital or other frustrations. Majority of the female criminals were found to have an income below Rs.3000/- per month. This is significant in the sense that low income is an important contributory factor to family tensions and a combination of unsatisfactory social relationships and poverty leads to criminal behaviour. For example, most of the thefts committed by women are not the result of social deviation but are due to family and economic compulsions. Hence, the hypothesis - low socio-economic status of the family is an important factor in female crime, is found valid.

The findings of the present study reveal that majority of the respondents were married at a young age (below 18 years) and therefore were open to stress and strain of an early marriage. Economic instability and lack of adjustment in family also explains crime among women. There is no doubt that family is an influential institution. The influence of family on women is complex and cannot adequately be explained in simple causal terms. So, family's role appeared as one of the most significant factor pushing most of the women towards criminal behaviour. In fact, financial cause is the chief factor which gives rise to different situations of stress and strain compelling the individual to think of and take to different types of deviant behaviour. Frustration is associated more closely with lower socio-economic status. This status creates additional problems and results in frustrations.

The present study reveals that in most murder cases, the victim was a member of the respondent's family. This shows that the respondent had primary relationship with the victim. Not only in murders but also in other crimes, family was found to be an important factor in criminality. This supports the hypothesis that stressful situation within the family plays an important role in the life of female criminals. B.R. Sharma also observed that strained interpersonal relations with husbaad and other family members, husband's extra-marital relations, deprivation and denial of basic needs of life, like - affection, security, etc., were the main causes of frustrations and ultimately of crime.

The researcher found that Dr. Ram Ahuja's 'Social Bond' theory is more relevent in explaining female crime scenario in India. Rani Bilmoria has also supported Ram Ahuja's theory of family maladjustment as cause of female crime. But apart from low socio-economic status of the family and stressful situations within the family, researcher observed that personality disorder and desire to earn more money or easy money are also important causes of crime.

The findings of the study prove that, undertrial female prisoners possess certain feelings and attitudes. The present study focuses on the experiences of undertrial female criminals. Most of the respondents felt that decisions about their arrest and custody were unjustified, since the charges levelled against them were not confirmed by court. Majority of the respondents found imprisonment as forced separation from the family. Most of them showed favourable attitude towards co-inmates and unfavourable attitude towards prison authorities.

According to Maharashtra Prison Manual, no undertrial shall be allotted any work in the prison. Hence, they spent their time in gossiping and in sleeping. Nearly half of the respondents were not satisfied with the facilities available in the prison. Majority of the respondents had never had any visits or contact through letters from their family members. However, majority of them have the belief that after their release, they would be treated by family members as before.

Most of the respondents have a positive attitude towards people in society outside the prison and they did not feel the need to take revenge on people responsible for getting them arrested.

It is observed that insecurity, anxiety and frustrations are highly significant in the undertrials. They were also anxious about the care and happiness of their children. On the other hand, they were worried about their future due to the stigma of imprisonment and mentioned that they have faith in 'God'.

In the present study, the above findings are obtained regarding the emotionality of the undertrial female criminals. This proves the validity of the hypothesis that the undertrial female prisoners are prone to certain feelings and attitudes.

10.4 Suggestions

A criminal is not a born criminal, efforts can and should be made to correct and re-socialize the individual. Those who commit crime as a matter of choice or as a means of livelihood are few indeed. A large number of criminals are victims of situations or criminals by accident.

One of the prison system's greatest failings may be treating all insiders similarly, because not everyone in prison is a criminal. A woman going in for one or two weeks out of her whole life, who may never offend again, is not a criminal although a jail sentence usually means that to the community. As soon as such a woman is released, friends and neighbours shy away from her as though she was contaminated. At this point, chances are high that such a woman might offend again because of community attitudes.

There is no doubt about the fact that removal of the criminal from the family has a very serious and disabling impact on her family. In fact, her family may be as much affected as that of the victim, or even more so because of the stigma involved in it. Further, the prevalent conditions may force the children of the criminal to take to anti-social modes of behaviour. When the criminal has committed a crime, she has to be punished. Whether her children or other family members who have not been involved in the crime should also suffer for it, is an important issue that needs to be looked into. The most important reason for this is that, efforts have not been made to evaluate or even to understand the impact of policies and practices in the criminal justice system on family life. A family is very greatly affected by the sentence passed on its member. It has to be understood and dealt with. This is by no means an easy task. But, it is an important, which has to be performed.

Women prisoners are hardly a bunch of dangerous criminals. Less than a handful might need to be locked up for public safety. There is also the possibilitly of female criminals being psychologically disturbed rather than criminal.

Keeping all this in view, the following steps are found necessary at different levels to improve conditions of female criminals:

10.4.1 Prison Facilities

- Conditions of living in the prison should be humane and sensible. It is also necessary to create hygienic conditions.
- Improvement in daily facilities, cleanliness and hygiene education should be introduced and carried out with seriousness.
- The quality of food should be improved and the meal timings be made more suitable.
- Proper clothing should be provided for needy undertrial female prisoners.
- Proper medical facilities and medical examinations of women inmates should be ensured in prisons. Lady doctor should behave humanely and sympathetically.
- Enough soap should be provided to the undertrials as a preventive measure against the spread of skin diseases and also for cleanlines.

10.4.2 Legal Aid

- All women in custody must be informed of their rights in custody including their right to demand legal aid if needed. Efforts should be made to provide legal aid.

- If the family of the prisoner has problems and is not able to arrange legal assistance, then legal assistance may be made available to prisoners in jails.

10.4.3 Voluntary Organizations / NGO's

- There is a need to involve more voluntary organizations while dealing with female criminals. NGO's and activists should be allowed to study their situations.
- Legal assistance may be provided by NGO's to undertrial prisoners to help them with problems for which they are being detained. This would not entail any extra financial expenditure.

10.4.4 Criminal Justice Procedure

- More family courts should be established for the smooth and flexible administration of justice and for speedy disposal of the cases.
- Justice needs to be less expensive. As early as possible, undertrials should be brought into the judicial procedure and cases should be settled.
- There should be female judges to deal with the cases of female offenders, which might ensure better understanding of the situation which led these women to crime.
- Imprisonment stigmatizes persons. Most female criminals can easily be released on probation. This will also reduce over-crowding in prisons.
- During the training period police should be properly sensitized over issues relaled to women.
- The whole judicial system needs to be sensitized towards women's issues. The judges, magistrates and advocates require a thorough sensitization and orientation for a more sensitive handling of judicial and legal procedures affecting women.

10.4.5 Recreational and Educational Facilities:

- More recreational and cultural activities should be generated for women undertrials to reduce the monotony of life in prison.
- Education and literacy programme should be made available. For literate prisoners, books and reading materials should be provided.
- Spiritual programmes, yoga or meditation practices should be made available for improving the atmosphere of the prison. It will also help to stimulate prisoner's sensitivity.

10.4.6 Other Facilities:

- Prison must appoint counsellors, social workers and also a qualified person with some knowledge of psychiatry.
- A female social worker must be appointed at the prison who can look into the problems of the undertrials, specially to ease their worries about their families.

10.5 Suggestions For Further Study

Social unrest is increasing almost in all sections of our society. It develops frustrations and strains which lead to violation of legal and social norms.Thus, considering these facts, further research has to be undertaken (i) to point out the factors weakening conformity to social norms and the disruption of social bonds. Also (ii) an attempt should be made to emphasize social implications of female crime.

11

Feminist Perspectives in Criminology

Feminism: Criminological Aspects

Feminist perspectives in criminology developed in reaction to silences and gaps in mainstream criminology. According to the critique that feminists began to mount in the late 1960s and early 1970s, mainstream or traditional criminology was inadequate in five key respects: (1) it focused almost exclusively on male offenders; (2) it was androcentric in its understandings and interpretations of crime; (3) it paid little attention to crime victims; (4) it ignored sex differences in criminal justice processing; and (5) it disregarded the dynamics of gender and power. Although criminology claimed to be an objective social science, the field itself (feminists charged) was deeply biased and implicated in the maintenance of male domination. Feminist criminologists have aimed at including women in analyses of crime, taking power differentials into account, and contributing toward the elimination of inequalities based on gender and other personal characteristics.

The Critique

Feminist critics of the late 1960s and early 1970s found criminology lacking in five major respects; many of them would repeat these same criticisms today.

(1) Mainstream criminology has focused almost exclusively on male offenders. It was perhaps natural for mainstream criminologists to focus primarily on male subjects, given that males have comprised the great majority of offenders across time and place. Nonetheless, feminist critics argued, much might be learned about the causes of crime from studying low-rate as well as high-rate offenders. Why should criminologists not also investigate why females are less likely than males to break the law?

Feminists further argued that the use of all male samples had led to theories of offending that in fact applied only to males, even though most advertised themselves as general explanations of crime. For example, Travis Hirschi, in formulating his well-known control theory of delinquency, deliberately excluded the female subjects on whom data were available in his original sample (p. 35,). "Since girls have been neglected for too long by students of delinquency, the exclusion of them is difficult to justify," Hirschi admitted, expressing a "hope to return to them soon" (pp. 35-36,). However, he has not. Titled *Causes of Delinquency,* Hirschi's book is in fact a study of the causes of male delinquency. Most other criminologists, too, assumed a male norm, placing boys and men at the center of their discussions and making women "invisible" (Belknap).

(2) Mainstream criminology is androcentric in its understandings and interpretations of crime. Feminists found little to admire even in the work of those few criminologists who had focused on female crime; this work, the critics maintained, analyzed female lawbreaking from a patriarchal point of view. Relying on cultural stereotypes, Cesare Lombroso, W. I. Thomas, Otto Pollak, and others who in the past had discussed female crime tended to sort women into two opposing categories, good woman or bad woman, madonna or whore (Feinman), leaving little room for ordinary mortals in between. Criminologists defined the law-abiding woman as passive, obedient, chaste, and childlike while describing the criminal woman as aggressive, defiant, sexually impure, and unbecomingly adult, even masculine in nature. These stereotypes had little to do with actual women, feminists objected; they sexualized and condemned women criminals instead of treating them objectively; they reinforced the paternalistic view that good women are those who are submissive and docile; and they bolstered the double standard of sexual morality that accords men but not women sexual autonomy.

Feminists used prostitution to exemplify how criminologists sexualized female crime while remaining silent about the economic pressures that force some women into crime. Some criminologists had attributed prostitution to nymphomania, others to a hatred of men stemming from underlying lesbian tendencies, but few had recognized that disadvantaged women often lack economic alternatives. The Gluecks and other criminologists went so far as to condemn prostitutes as carriers of sexually transmitted diseases. Before the late 1960s, one could search the criminological literature in vain for recognition that prostitution usually involves two parties, a man as well as a woman, and that diseases are more likely to be transmitted by the clients than the service providers, who routinely take measures against infection. In the case of prostitution as in that of other crimes, the effect of criminological commentaries was to make women offenders seem sexually abnormal and even evil while exonerating whatever males were involved. One of the most egregious failures of traditional criminology in the feminist view was its insistence on interpreting crimes against women from a male perspective. To exemplify this point, critics pointed to

Menachem Amir's 1971 study, *Patterns in Forcible Rape.* Nineteen percent of the victims in his sample had arrest records, Amir reported, assuming that negative information on victims was relevant; many had been arrested for sexual misconduct, and 20 percent had a "bad" reputation.Some rapists had used "temptation" to overcome their victims while others used "verbal coercion"; in only 13 percent of the cases had the offender used "physical aggression"-a fmding that implied most victims had actually been "asking for it." Moreover, in 19 percent of the cases, the victim had "precipitated" her own rape, a conclusion Amir based on rapists' own accounts. In studies of incest and domestic violence, too, mainstream criminologists interpreted crimes against women from the vantage point of the male offender, suggesting that men are more credible than women and likely to be falsely accused.

(3) Mainstream criminology has paid little attention to crime victims. One of the chief feminist complaints against traditional criminology was its relative disinterest in victimization and its tendency, when discussing crimes in which women were the primary victims, to blame the victim. Domestic homicide was said to be victim-precipitated in many cases, as was wife battering. Incest was a problem of seductive teenage step-daughters, not of power imbalances within the family or male views of women as sexual property, while stranger violence might be provoked by women who wore tight sweaters and drank alone in bars. Home was the safest place for women to be, mainstream criminologists concluded, ignoring the huge volume of domestic violence against women.

(4) Mainstream criminology has ignored sex differences in criminal justice processing. Feminists also faulted mainstream criminologists with either ignoring or underestimating the impact of gender on criminal justice processing. Taking a male norm for granted, conventional criminologists assumed that justice officials treated women the same as men or more leniently. They did not investigate the system reacts differently to male and female defendants or to different types of female defendants. They did no research on whether women are punished more harshly than men for sex offenses and public order crimes. Even though criminologists had no empirical evidence for assuming that women fared the same as men or better in the criminal justice system, they were not interested in testing the assumption.

(5) Mainstream criminologists have disregarded the dynamics of gender and power. Feminists further charged that traditional criminologists had failed to investigate the interplay of male power, female economic dependency, and abusive male-female dynamics. While mainstream criminology presented itself as an objective social science concerned with all crime, it was in fact masculinist, deeply biased against women, and riddled with hidden agendas for perpetuating male power. Thus criminology itself served to reinforce the status quo and ensure continuance of female subordination.

Development of Feminist Perspectives

Over the thirty years of their development, feminist perspectives in criminology have evolved through three stages, each lasting roughly a decade: a mobilization stage, 1968-1977; a maturation stage, 1978-1987; and a stage of differentiation that began around 1988 and continues into the present.

Stage 1: mobilization. During the decade 1968-1977, feminists mobilized for criminological reforms on two fronts, in grassroots organizations and within the academy. The grassroots movement began with nonacademic women organizing at the grassroots level to help the victims of rape, spouse abuse, and incest by setting up hotlines, establishing shelters to which battered women could flee with their children, and raising public awareness through marches and rallies. They also worked with lawyers and legislators to achieve rape law reform. These grassroots organizers called for nonhierarchical relationships, consciousness raising, and victim empowerment.

A literature began to accrete around their work, some of it produced by professional authors such as Susan Brownmiller (*Against Our Will,* 1975), some published by activists themselves (e.g., Martin, 1976); this literature led to reforms in mainstream criminology, especially in its treatment of female victims. Many of these activists perceived a radical, hostile divide between men and women, a perception that persists in the work of so-called radical feminists such as Andrea Dworkin, Catharine MacKinnon, and members of the group Women Against Pornography.

The second front on which the feminizers of criminology mobilized during this first stage was within the academy. Three academic criminologists, working independently and indeed in ignorance of one another's efforts, issued the first in-house challenges to traditional criminology. Canadian Marie-Andree Bertrand exposed the myth of sexual equality before the law. Britisher Frances Heidensohn asked why female crime rates are lower than those of males and why conventional criminologists showed so little interest in this issue. And Dorie Klein, an American, revealed the sexist biases of the literature on female crime. The first stage ended with the publication of the first book-length critique of mainstream criminology, Carol Smart's *Women, Crime, and Criminology: A Feminist Critique* (1976).

In a related development, feminists in law schools produced legal theory that helped frame and validate the reform efforts of grassroots activists and academic criminologists. Feminist legal theorists of this period concentrated on exposing ways in which the law operates to perpetuate women's economic, political, and social disadvantages (Smart, 1990/1998). Although there was little direct interaction between the two sets of academic feminists, the legal theorists created an intellectual context for the criminologists and to some extent authenticated their enterprise.

During this first developmental stage, the concepts of *sex, sexism,* and *equality* were central to feminist work in criminology. Arguments tended to be framed in terms of a struggle between the sexes, male and female; critiques were posed in terms of sexism, or male bias against women; and demands were based on the idea of equality. What feminists sought was to be treated the same as men. Few noticed that this ideal involved the internalization and promotion of male standards. Moreover, feminists assumed and fostered solidarity among women, paying little attention to divisions created by age, race, sexual orientation, or social class.

Stage 2: maturation. During the decade 1978-1987, the feminist enterprise came to maturity by developing its agendas, establishing footholds within the academic world, and producing a substantial body of literature. Whereas first-stage feminists had usually worked in isolation, the graduation of a significant number of feminists with doctoral degrees in criminology and related areas now created opportunities for alliances and collaborations. When these feminists assumed editorial positions on journals, reviewed manuscripts for publishers, or were invited by book editors or conference organizers to contribute a chapter or deliver a talk, feminist work received a hearing.

In the early 1980s, feminists established the Division on Women and Crime, the first section within the American Society of Criminology, thus creating another forum for feminist work and offering members routes to professional office. Researchers laid the groundwork for studies of women in policing (Martin), in the courts (Kruttschnitt), in prisons (Rafter) and prison reform (Freedman), and as victims (Dobash and Dobash). Textbooks began to appear, opening up the possibility of courses in women and crime and of training a new generation of feminist criminologists. Toward the end of this period, Meda Chesney-Lind published an important review of the literature on women and crime, one sign of its maturity.

Sex, a concept that had figured prominently in the first stage, was replaced in the second stage by the concept of gender.

Although variously defmed, "gender" was generally used to denote socially constructed differences between males and females. Whereas first-stage theorists had been concerned about sexism, a problem that could be fixed by achieving the ideal of equality, secondstage theorists were concerned about gender inequality, a more intractable problem that included the very nature of law and organizations, which now appeared to be gendered and masculine institutions. Doubts emerged about the wisdom of pursuing equality, the first-stage ideal, because it now became clear that to be equal meant to adopt masculine standards and values.

Stage 3: differentiation. The third stage, kicked off in 1988 with a major review of accomplishments to date (Daly and Chesney-Lind), has been characterized in part by highly specific research projects built on the groundwork established in the second stage. The new work includes sophisticated empirical studies of court processing (e.g., Albonetti); victimization studies assessing violence against women (Bachman, forthcoming; Koss); reconceptualizations of the implications of criminal justice policy (e.g., Miller, ed.); and research on particular prison issues (Human Rights Watch; Morash, Bynum, and Koons). One result of third-stage activity has been documentation of previously unrecognized differences between women and men, among groups of women, and in the practices of various courts and prisons (e.g., Kruttschnitt, Gartner, and Miller, forthcoming). Another result has been the opening up of new territory for theorizing about difference and its criminal-justice effects. Also characteristic of this third stage is an internationalization of feminist work in criminology, starting formally with a 1991 conference in Quebec (Bertrand, Daly, and Klein, eds.) and continuing through smaller conferences and individual initiatives (Rafter and Heidensohn, eds.).

This cross-fertilization has sensitized feminists to national differences and to some extent refocused them on global problems such as female circumcision and child prostitution.

During this third stage, the concept of gender evolved even further from its roots in biological sex differences as feminists became concerned with intersectionalities or the ways in which gender is cross-cut by such variables as age, class, race, and sexual preference, creating a multiplicity of ways of being masculine, feminine, something in between, or something entirely different. As the concept of gender fragmented, it gave rise to work on masculinities and crime (e.g., Messerschmidt). Definitions of the key criminological problems also splintered into issues of "multiple inequalities" (Daly and Maher, eds., p. 11). Feminists concentrated more on crime and crime control, less on problems presented by mainstream criminology, which despite some accommodations to the feminist critique has remained remarkably impervious to change. In fact, by the end of the third decade, some feminists had turned away from criminology itself (Daly and Maher, eds.; Rafter and Heidensohn, eds.), refusing to let mainstream criminologists set their political or research agendas.

A Feminist Perspective on Women and Crime: Freda Adler

Until recently, criminology has been primarily focused on men and crime with little reference to women. Feminist criminology developed in the late 1960s and into the 1970s, and was closely associated with the emergence of the Second Wave of feminism at this time. This movement helped to project many issues into the public domain, one of which was women and crime. Like most feminist issues, women and crime was mostly discussed from a male perspective and has been about men, for men and by men. The women's liberation movement having developed almost alongside feminist criminology appears to have blurred some feminist writer's perspectives about women and crime, perhaps none more so than Freda

Adler (1975) and her theory of 'Sisters in Crime' . Although the field of criminology comprises of offenders, victims and those who work within the criminal justice system such as the police, judges and various institutions, the following will concentrate on women as offenders

Why is there a need for a feminist criminology?

Criminology refers to any kind of study concerned with crime and criminal justice. It is a term used to include a multitude of topics and approaches. Feminist perspectives, over the past thirty years have not only put some new topics under the criminological cover, they have challenged the theories, concepts, methods and assumptions of most of the people already involved in the study of crime. Criminology, has for most feminist writers and researchers been a constraining rather than a constructive and creative influence. Theories of criminality have been developed from male subjects and validated on male subjects. Whilst there is nothing wrong with this, the problem is that these theories have been extended generally to include all criminals, defendants and prisoners. It was assumed that the theories would apply to women; most do not appear to do so (Gelsthorpe and Morris, 1990: xii-8).

Usually feminism is included in chapters about 'Gender and Crime' and woman as offenders are more likely to be discussed within the boundaries of sexual and petty offences such as prostitution and shop lifting (Naffine, 1997: 1). Voigt et al, in their recent book called *Criminology and Justice,* make particular mention of the inadequacies of criminology texts suggesting that 'criminology is nothing more than specialised theories of male delinquency and crime' (1994: 238-249). In other words, the facts about crime tend to be based on the sex of the offender and not the crime itself. This 'sexism' in criminology is more in keeping with Gelsthorpe's critique of 'accumulated wisdom' about female offenders. She proposes that women are discriminated against in areas such as crime because of their sex and this sexism influences the sentencing, punishment and incarceration of women (1986: 138-149). She accuses many police, welfare institutions and judges among others as assuming 'sweeping generalisations' about crime as something *men* are expected to do, because they are men' (Gelsthorpe, 1986: 149). Women are not expected to be criminals and if they are, they may be described as '*mad* not *bad*' (Lloyd, 1995: xvii).

The perception that women may be *mad* because they 'dared to go against their natural biological givens such as 'passivity' and a 'weakness of compliance', appears to originate from the view that women who conform as pure, obedient daughters, wives and mothers benefit society and men (Feinman, 1994: 16). Women became 'doubly damned' that is, they are seen as weak and in need of protection while being judged as having 'uncontrollable sexuality' (prostitutes and delinquent girls) (Bottoms, 1996: 1). Results from studies conducted by Gelsthorpe showed how sexual promiscuity amongst girls resulted in them being institutionalised and treated for 'abnormal' behaviour. On the other hand male's sexual permissiveness was encouraged and thought to be 'natural' to the male persona (1989: 34). According to Cain, these equity studies were 'androcentric' as 'women and girls appeared to exist as Other'. Men were used as the 'yardsticks' against which actions and treatment were measured (1990: 2).

Such androcentric studies urged many feminist writers to develop theories that engaged in negative and/or reactive projects and/or criticised social, theoretical, and political relations, thereby challenging theories that currently existed. Critique and construct were important creative alternatives for the production of feminist, not simply anti-sexist theory, and without them according to Grosz, problems of the past, especially patriarchal assumptions, could have been repeated (1990: 59). According to Spelman, feminist theory has not changed all that much and has neglected to include the 'problem of difference'. She suggests that 'feminists have extrapolated the condition of the most privileged type of woman - the white, middle-class, heterosexual - to all women' and the 'conflation of women in feminist theory has not produced a melting pot of different ages, colours and classes' (1988: 4). She also suggests that white feminist criminologists, although objecting to the 'stereotypical representations of female offenders', have had little to say about indigenous women or those from developing countries. To fail to see differences in racial groups is to 'reinstate the white woman's assumption that the problem is always first one of gender, never one of difference' (Spelman, 1988: 57-58). This apparent absence of race and other factors such as employment are mentioned in the following discussion.

'Sisters in Crime'

Could women's emancipation account for the apparent increases in crime? If not. what has?

The word 'feminism' today remains entrenched in some people's minds as the 'cause of most of societies problems'. Chesney-Lind suggests that 'the invention of the liberated woman' has forced women to bear the brunt of the hostility towards the women's movement (1980: 15). Prominent feminist theorists such as Freda Adler (1975) and her 'Sisters in Crime' seems to have done little to alleviate these negative assumptions. Real problems within the criminal justice system appear to have been obscured and such deflection may have provided those opposed to the women's movement with scientific evidence of the 'dark side of liberation' (Chesney-Lind, 1980: 16-17) as is discussed below.

Freda Adler believed that the arrival of the Second Wave of Feminism during the 1970s consequently coincided with a 'dramatic' upsurge in women's criminal activity. She claimed while 'women have demanded equal opportunity in the fields of legitimate endeavours, a similar number of determined women have forced their way into the world of major crime such as white collar crime, murder and robbery' (Adler, 1975: 3). That women criminals today represent a 'new breed' can be demonstrated, according to Adler, by evidence of the changing nature of female involvement in a wide variety of crimes. The emergence of this 'new female criminal' engaged in predatory crimes of violence and corporate fraud has broken into a man's world (Brown, 1986: 373). For example, female white-collar crime has increased since the 'liberation' of women. Adler suggests that as women are 'climbing up the corporate business ladder', they are making use of their 'vocational liberation' to pursue careers in white-collar crime (1975: 83-84).

Adler's theory has invited much criticism from other feminist writers such as Brown. She describes it as an 'embarrassment to feminism' and argues instead that feminism has made female crime more visible through increased reporting, policing and sentencing of female offenders. She mentions that the degree of sentencing (more severe penalties) would be a more acceptable index of increases in offences among women rather than statistical measures as adopted by Adler (1986: 374). Carol Smart argues that Adler's theory is based on 'statistical illusions caused by a smallness ofthe base' (1979: 53). Carlen argues that Adler's 'new female criminal' is cast as the 'biological female' who is essentially masculine. The 'new female' criminal turns out to be the 'old maladjusted masculinist female' of traditional criminology, rejecting her proper feminine role (1983: 376-377) such as institutionalising rather than incarcerating women who commit 'male' offences such as robbery. In other words, Adler's 'sisters in crime' appears to work within the frameworks of traditional criminology rather than a feminist one.

Her perspective also seems to exclude factors such as race, ethnicity, age and class. Many feminist writers see these factors as very important. For example, Jane Chapman's (1980) studies of the connection between labour force participation and female crime revealed an increase in criminal activity during times of economic hardship. The smallest increases in arrests coincided with periods of the greatest increase in economic activity with the most common offence being that of shop lifting. These findings would seem to support a theory of a relationship between employment and crime (economic perspective) rather than that offered by the 'women's liberation thesis'. When times are good, the offending woman appears to stabilise rather than escalate. An absence rather than availability of employment opportunities (liberation thesis) would seem a more plausible explanation for increases in female crime. Naffine believes the criminal woman's motive appears more rational and straight forward than manifesting her gender-role concerns or seeking to compete with the criminal male (1987: 99).

Giordano and Cerkovich conducted studies in 1979 involving women between the ages of 17 and 29. Their findings suggested that the 'more liberated' the response to questions, the less delinquent participants were. For example, they found that women who believed women should enter the workforce and a woman's role was not necessarily that of housewife and mother, were the least delinquent (1979: 477). James and Thornton revealed from studies involving women prisoners that those incarcerated were primarily from impoverished and uneducated backgrounds. When asked why they offended, responses did not appear to be 'liberation' motivated (1980: 240). In other words, contrary to Adler's theory of emancipation, feminism appeared to be a positive force for conformity when there was opportunity to offend.

Conclusion

When a woman is seen to be physically, sexually or psychologically dominant, even violently aggressive, she tends to be treated as unusual, a freak of female nature or as mentioned previously, 'mad'. Many women appear to be encouraged to fear men and to circumscribe their public behaviour. The customary association of men with the use of force and power is not confmed to the criminal population. Female vulnerability is often invoked to strengthen both the senses of male power and the need for its considered use, that is, to protect women.

The agenda for feminist criminology is to demonstrate to the more traditional members of the discipline that the conventional view of women is inaccurate. Women are to be observed behaving in ways that do not fit the theories. It tends to be the theories not the women that have been found to be deficient. Results from studies suggest that women are not thinking nor acting in ways which criminologists have normally assumed. Such discoveries do much to contradict the idea of the passive and compliant female contained in many standard accounts of crime. For example, the complex hypothesis that white-collar female crime is expanding because of improved occupational opportunities for women is undermined by crime statistics which show that women are still principally shop-lifters.

Some feminists such as Freda Adler, have not helped the female fight for equality and individual circumstance; instead they appear to have entrenched existing views of women and the women's movement. The women's movement has born the brunt of much criticism as causing an increase in crime amongst women, especially those of a more serious nature. Contradictory to Adler's theory of female emancipation as the cause, it appears from other studies to be a case whereby women are forced to commit offences as a result of impoverished and oppressed conditions due to unemployment, a lack of educational opportunities, domestic violence, and divorce or separation. This may explain the apparent increase in petty theft, robbery and homicide.

Bibliography

Albonetti, Celesta A. (1997): "Sentencing Under The Federal Sentencing Guidelines: Effects Of Defendant Characteristics, Guilty Pleas, And Departures On Sentence Outcomes For Drug Offenses, 1991-1992." *Law & Society Review* 31, No.4: 789-822. Amir, Menachem. *Patterns Of Forcible Rape.* Chicago: University Of Chicago Press, 1971.

Bachman, Ronet. (2000)"Estimates Of Violence Against Women: A Comparison Of The National Crime Victimization Survey And The National Violence Against Women Survey." *Violence Against Women..*

Belknap, J. *(1996)The Invisible Woman: Gender, Crime, And Justice.* Belmont, Calif.: Wadsworth,.

Bertrand, Marie-Andree. (1967)"The Myth Of Sexual Equality Before The Law." In *Proceedings Of The Fifth Research Conference On Delinquency And Criminality.* Montreal: Quebec Society Of Criminology,.

Bertrand, Marie-Andree; Daly, Kathleen; And Klein, Dorie. (1991): Eds. *Proceedings Of The International Feminist Conference On Women, Law And Social Control.* Vancouver, B.C.: International Centre For The Reform Of Criminal Law And Criminal Justice Policy, 1992.

Brownmiller, Susan. *(1975)Against Our Will: Men, Women And Rape.* New York: Bantam.

Chesney-Lind, Meda. (1986): "Women And Crime: The Female Offender." *Signs* 12, No. 1, 78-96.

Daly, Kathleen; And Chesney-Lind, Meda. (1988): "Feminism And Criminology." *Justice Quarterly* 5, No.4, 498-538.

Daly, Kathleen; And Maher, Lisa, (1998): Eds. *Criminology At The Crossroads: Feminist Readings In Crime And Justice.* New York: Oxford University Press.

Dobash, R. W.; And Dobash, R. P. (1979): *Violence Against Women: A Case Against Patriarchy.* New York: The Free Press.

Feinman, Clarice(1980): *Women In The Criminal Justice System.* New York: Praeger.

Freedman, Estelle B. (1981): *Their Sisters' Keepers: Women's Prison Reform In America, 1830-1930.* Ann Arbor: University Of Michigan Press.

Glueck, Eleanor; And Glueck, Sheldon. (1934): *Five Hundred Delinquent Women.* New York: Knopf.

Heidensohn, Frances M. (1968): "The Deviance Of Women: A Critique And An Enquiry." *British Journal Of Sociology* 19, No.2, 160-175.

Hirschi, Travis. (1969): *Causes Of Delinquency.* Berkeley: University Of California Press.

Human Rights Watch Women's Rights Project (1996): *All Too Familiar: Sexual Abuse Of Women In Us. State Prisons.* New York: Human Rights Watch.

Klein, Dorie. (1973): "The Etiology Of Female Crime: A Review Of The Literature." *Issues In Criminology* 8, No.2, 3-30.

Koss, Mary P. (1992): "The Measurement Of Rape Victimization In Crime Surveys." *Criminal Justice And Behavior* 23, No.1, 55-69.

Kruttschnitt, Candace. (1980-1981): "Social Status And Sentences Of Female Offenders." *Law & Society Review* 15,247-265.

Kruttschnitt, Candace; Gartner, Rosemary; And Miller, Amy. (August 2000): "Doing Her Own Time? Examining The Impact Of Life Experiences In The Context Of The Old And The New Penology." In The Journal *Criminology.*

Martin, Del. (1976): *Battered Wives.* New York: Pocket Books.

Martin, Susan. *(1980):"Brealdng And Entering": Police-Women On Patrol.* Berkeley: University Of California Press.

Messerschmidt, James W. (1993): *Masculinities And Crime: Critique And Reconceptualization Of Theory.* Lanham, Md.: Rowman & Littlefield.

Miller, Susan L. Ed. (1998): *Crime Control And Women.* Thousand Oaks, Calif.: Sage.

Morash, Merry; Bynum, Tim S.; And Koons, Barbara A. (1998): *Women Offenders: Programming Needs And Promising Approaches.* National Institute Of Justice Publication No. 171668. Washington, D.C.: National Institute Of Justice.

Rafter, Nicole H. *Partial Justice: Women In State Prisons, 1800-1935.* Boston: Northeastern University fress, 1985. Published In 2d Ed. *Partial Justice :: Women, Prisons, And Social Control.* New Brunswick: Transaction Publishers, 1990.

Rafter, Nicole H.; And Heidensohn, Frances, Eds. (1995) *International Feminist Perspectives In Criminology: Engendering A Discipline. Buckingham* U.K.: Open University Press.

Smart, Carol. (1976): *Women, Crime And Criminology.* London: Routledge Kegan Paul.

-. "Feminist Approaches To Criminology, Or Post-Modem Woman Meets Atavistic Man." In *Feminist Perspectives In Criminology.* Edited By Loraine Gelsthorpe And Allison Morris. Buckingham, U.K.: Open University Press, 1990. Reprinted In *Criminology At The Crossroads: Feminist Readings In Crime And Justice.* Edited By Kathleen Daly And Lisa Maher. New York: Oxford University Press, 1998. Pages 21-36.

Spohn, Cassia; Gruhl, John; And Welch, Susan. (1987): "The Impact Of The Ethnicity And Gender Of Defendants On The Decision To Reject Or Dismiss Felony Charges." *Criminology* 25, 175-191.

12

Gender Differences in Crime

Both males and females have low rates of arrest for serious crimes like homicide or robbery; and high rates of arrest for petty property crimes like larceny-theft, or public order offenses such as alcohol and drug offenses or disorderly conduct. In general, women tend to have relatively high arrest rates in most of the same crime categories for which men have high arrest rates. For example, rates of homicide are small for both sexes, as compared to larceny rates.

Male and female arrest trends over time or across groups or geographic regions are similar. That is, decades or groups or regions that have high (or low) rates of male crime tend to also have high (or low) rates of female crime. For example, in the second half of the twentieth century, the rates of arrest for larceny-theft increased dramatically for both men and women; and declined even more dramatically for both men and women in the category of public drunkenness. Similarly, states or cities or countries that have higher than average arrest rates for men also have higher arrest rates for women (Steffensmeier, 1993; Steffensmeier, Allan, and Streifel).

Male and female offenders have similar age-crime distributions, although male levels of offending are always higher than female levels at every age and for virtually all offenses.

Female offenders, like male offenders, tend to come from backgrounds marked by poverty, discrimination, poor schooling, and other disadvantages. However, women who commit crime are somewhat more likely than men to have been abused physically, psychologically, or sexually, both in childhood and as adults.

Gender Differences in Offending Patterns

Females have lower arrest rates than males for virtually all crime categories except prostitution. This is true in all countries for which data are available. It is true for all racial and ethnic groups, and for every historical period. In the United States, women constitute less than 20 percent of arrests for most crime categories. Females have even lower representation than males do in serious crime categories. Since the 1960s in the United States, the extent of female arrests has generally been less than 15 percent for homicide and aggravated assault, and less than 10 percent for the serious property crimes of burglary and robbery.

Aside from prostitution, female representation has been greatest for minor property crimes such as larceny-theft, fraud, forgery, and embezzlement. Female arrests for these crime categories has been as high as 30 to 40 percent, especially since the mid-1970s. The thefts and frauds committed by women typically involve shoplifting (larceny-theft), "bad checks" (forgery or fraud), and welfare and credit fraud-all compatible with traditional female consumer/domestic roles.

Trends in female crime relative to male crime are more complex. Some writers claim that female crime has been increasing faster than male crime, as measured by the percentage of female arrests. This has clearly been true in the case of minor property crimes, where the percentage of female arrests had about doubled between 1960 and 1975 (from around 15 to 30 percent or more), with slight additional increases since then. Smaller but fairly consistent increases are also found for substance abuse categories, but they remain less than 20 percent for all categories. The same can be said of major property crimes (which remain less than 10 to 15%). However, the percentage of female arrests has declined for other categories like homicide and prostitution; and it has fluctuated for still other categories such as aggravated assault and druglaw violations (see Steffensmeier, 1993, for a review of trends and explanations).

The patterns just described are corroborated by other sources of data. the National Crime Victimization Survey asks victims about the gender of offenders in crimes where the offender is seen. The percentage of female offenders reported by victims is very similar to (or lower than) the female percentage of arrests for comparable categories. Self-report studies also confirm the UCR patterns of relatively low female involvement in serious offenses and greater involvement in the less serious categories.

From a variety of sources, it is clear that females are less involved in serious offense categories, and they commit less harm. Women's acts of violence, compared to those of men, result in fewer injuries and less serious injuries. Their property crimes usually involve less monetary loss or less property damage.

Females are far less likely than males to become repeat offenders. Long-term careers in crime are very rare among women. Some pursue relatively brief careers (in relation to male criminal careers) in prostitution, drug offenses, or minor property crimes like shoplifting or check forging.

Female offenders, more often than males, operate solo. When women do become involved with others in offenses, the group is likely to be small and relatively nonpermanent. Furthermore, women in group operations are generally accomplices to males (see Steffensmeier, 1983, for a review). And males are overwhelmingly dominant in the more organized and highly lucrative crimes, whether based in the underworld or the "upperworld."

Females are far less likely than males to become involved in delinquent gangs. This distinction is consistent with the tendency for females to operate alone and for males to dominate gangs and criminal subcultures. At the onset of the twenty-first century, female gang involvement was described as a sort of "auxiliary" to a male gang. By the 1980s and 1990s, gang studies found somewhat increased involvement on the part of girls (perhaps 15%), including some allfemale gangs. Regardless, female gang violence has remained far less common than male gang violence.

The criminal justice system's greater "leniency" and "chivalry" toward females may explain a portion of the lower official offending rates of women in comparison to men. Likewise, the justice system's tendency to be relatively less lenient and chivalrous toward females today may help explain recent increases in levels of female arrests. Although there appear to be relatively small differences between adult women and men in likelihood of arrest or conviction, women defendants do appear to have a lower probability of being jailed or imprisoned. This difference appears to be related to a variety of factors: pregnancy, responsibilities for small children, the greater likelihood to demonstrate remorse, as well as perceptions that women are less dangerous and more amenable to rehabilitation (Daly; Steffensmeier, Ulmer, and Kramer).

Explanations for Patterns of Crime

Opportunities for criminal behaviour	*	Female involvement in criminal activity is not restricted to a few areas. While females do not tend to commit crimes of violence (violence by females tends to occur within the family, mainly as a final response to male violence), they are involved in a wide cross-section of crime.
	*	Therefore, while, in theory, women have similar opportunities as men to

commit crime these may be limited by other factors...

* In terms of the ratio of conviction between females and males, where women have similar opportunities for criminal behaviour in relation to males, their respective patterns of crimes appear to be broadly similar:

  For example, where female crime most-closely approximates to male crime is in relation to shop-lifting and it's no coincidence that in this area of their social lives women have similar opportunities for crime to men.

* Marsh ("Sociology in Focus: Crime", 1986): "In areas where females have similar opportunities to men they appear as likely to break laws"

Opportunity Structures

* Where opportunity structures differ, so too does the pattern of crime: For example, burglary is predominantly a male crime and one way of explaining the difference is that this type of crime tends to be a relatively solitary pursuit that takes place late at night. A female alone late at night is both more-likely to: Attract attention and / or Involve some degree of personal danger.

* Employment related crime: Fewer women than men work, therefore, less opportunity exists.

  Women tend to occupy less powerful positions within an organisation. They are more-likely to be subject to close supervision, have less opportunity for acting on their own initiative, unsupervised and so forth. Hence, they generally have less opportunity for committing "white- collar" crimes such as fraud, embezzlement, etc.

* Women are more-likely than men to have primary responsibility for child-care, which restricts opportunities for various types of criminal behaviour.

Primary/Secondary Socialisation

* Male gender socialization prompts men to be more aggressive and more-likely to solve p[problems using violence.
* Female gender socialization prompts women to be less aggressive and more-likely to seek non-violent solutions to problems.
* Peer pressure: Different influences for males (eg. gang / street-corner behaviour).
* Male socialisation stresses active, individualistic, behaviour.
* Media emphasises male role as "breadwinner" / "family provider" may increase pressure on men.
* Media emphasises female role as "carer" decreases pressure on women to act as family provider.
* Marsh ("Sociology in Focus: Crime", 1986): "In the world of organised, professional, crime, sex-segregation is the norm. Women are likely to be viewed in terms of traditional sex-role stereotypes, as unreliable, emotional, illogical and so on. Moreover, males tend to see the crimes they commit as

too dangerous for women, or too difficult, or their masculine pride may not be willing to accept women as organisers of crime, as 'bosses'".

Social Control Agencies

* Much female crime involves "sexual delinquency" (especially "status offences" - running away from home, being in "moral danger" and so forth). It involves behaviour which, in the adult world is not classified as criminal/ delinquent. This may account for a great deal of young female "crime" and also explains why older females do not appear to commit as much crime as older males.
* This form of explanation focuses upon the idea that females in our society are socialised and controlled differently to males. Female socialisation stresses passivity as a feminine characteristic (which might help to explain something about the relative lack of female violence) . Abbott and Wallace ("An Introduction to Sociology: Feminist Perspectives", 1990) note female behaviour is more closely watched / strictly controlled within the family.
* Female sexuality is more heavily "policed" than young male sexual behaviour.
* As females are given more freedom we would expect them to become involved in various forms of criminal behaviour. Police and judicial expectations may be significant, since if the police start to

see females differently, the likely development is greater levels of arrest and criminalisation. This appears to be happening, insofar as more females are being subjected to a process of criminalisation.

* Men have greater freedom within the family than women, giving more opportunity to commit crimes. Eg: Young women: parents restrict who they associate with / control times they can associate with friends etc. Adult women: freedom may be limited by family responsibilities.

Judicial behaviour
Labelling
Stereotypes
Medical models

* Courts may deal more-leniently with females: sometimes called the "Chivalry factor". However, when women commit crimes that go against male stereotypes of femininity (violence, for example) women tend to be more harshly punished than men.
* Much female crime is petty, non-violent etc. (the two most popular tending to be shop-lifting and prostitution - the latter being an interesting example of a double-standard, whereby women can be criminalised for selling sex whilst men can't be criminalised for buying it...), therefore, women not imprisoned as often as men.
* In relation to shop-lifting, there has been a recent tendency, by the courts, social workers and so forth, to see this type of female behaviour more of a "cry for help" than outright criminal behaviour. Again,

this may simply represent sexist attitudes towards female behaviour, whereby criminal behaviour is seen to be a symptom of some form of psychological malaise.

* Most prostitutes end-up in prison because they could not afford to pay the fine levied on them (which suggests that large numbers of female prostitutes may make very little money from their activities).

Social Visibility Of crime and criminals

* Female forms of crime may be "less visible" to the police etc. This is especially true in relation to crimes of violence, where women tend to be the victims rather than the perpetrators (especially in relation to domestic violence).
* Much male crime (e.g. crimes of violence, petty theft) involves clear victims and is likely to be witnessed.
* Police have an ideological conception of both crime and criminals, which they use as a guide-line in their work. The more the idea of an association between males and crime becomes established, the more the process of criminalisation begins to resemble a self-fulfilling prophecy. Police are more-likely to closely-watch behaviour of men.
* Crimes such as child abuse / family violence largely invisible to the police - rely on victims to complain.

Lifestyle Factors

* Men more-likely to go out at night, in clubs, pubs, etc. where alcohol/illegal

drugs are used. May lead to "loss of control" and relatively minor forms of crime as well as violence.

* Older women (and men) less likely to be in public areas at night. Any crimes will be committed in privacy of the home.

Explaining Female Offending:

Social, biological, economic, and psychological explanations have been used to develop theories to explain why women commit crime, as well as why they commit less crime than men. The number and complexity of these theories has expanded greatly in recent years as part of the growing body of work on gender both in criminology and in the social sciences more generally.

Early social science views. Early explanations of female crime reflected prevailing views regarding crime and human behavior more generally. During the late 1800s and early 1900s, theories of human behavior tended to be deterministic. In criminology this perspective was apparent in theories attributing crime to either biological or social factors beyond the control of individuals. Psychological explanations of crime emerged as psychological theories gained prominence. At the same time, major sociological explanations of crime (differential association, anomie, social disorganization) were emphasizing social and cultural factors that could account for female as well as male criminality .

During the first half of the twentieth century, most explanations of female crime were ancillary to explanations of male criminality. Lombroso, for example, linked both male and female crime to biological predisposition. Early sociological explanations generally rejected biological determinism and offered sociocultural interpretations of both male and female crime as well as of gender differences in crime. Sociocultural views were manifest in criminology textbooks published between

1920 and 1960 (see the review in Steffensmeier and Clark). Whatever the orientation, biological or sociocultural, most criminologists focused primarily on male criminality. Female offending was largely ignored.

Theorists emphasizing the causal role of biological and psychological factors in female crime typically postulated that criminal women exhibited masculine biological or psychological orientations. Lombroso viewed female criminals as having an excess of male characteristics. He argued that, biologically, criminal females more closely resembled males (both criminal and normal) than females.

While some theorists linked female crime to "masculinity," others saw it as distinctly feminine. Eleanor and Sheldon Glueck's studies of adult and juvenile delinquents suggested that female crime reflected the inability of certain women-especially those from disadvantaged neighborhood and family contexts-to control their sexual impulses. The Gluecks also subscribed to the theme of the woman offender as a pathetic creature, a view that characterized much of criminological writings in the 1930s.

Otto Pollak's *The Criminality of Women* is the most important work on female crime prior to the modern period. The book summarized previous work on women and crime, and it challenged basic assumptions concerning the extent and quality of women's involvement in criminal behavior. Pollak himself explained female crime and the gender gap with reference to a mix of biological, psychological, and sociological factors.

Pollak is the first writer to insist that women's participation in crime approaches that of men and is commensurate with their representation in the population. He argues that the types of crimes women commit-shoplifting, domestic thefts, thefts by prostitutes, abortions, perjury-are underrepresented in crime statistics for a variety of reasons: easy concealment, underreporting, embarrassment on the part of male victims, and male chivalry in the justice system.

Pollak consistently emphasizes the importance of social and environmental factors, including poverty, crowded living conditions, broken homes, delinquent companions, and the adverse effects of serving time in reform schools or penitentiaries. Pollak also noted that there is considerable overlap in causative factors for delinquency among girls and boys, and women and men.

Yet another fundamental theme of Pollak's work is the attribution of a biological and physiological basis to female criminality. Pollak stresses the inherently deceitful nature of females, rooted particularly in the passive role assumed by women during sexual intercourse. Also significant are the influences of hormonal and generative phases (e.g., menstruation, pregnancy, and menopause) on female criminality.

In sum, in comparison to explanations for male offending, some early explanations of female crime placed greater emphasis on biological and psychological factors. Nevertheless, early sociological explanations of female crime, stressing sociocultural factors, were also commonplace. Criminology textbooks, in particular, offered an interpretation of female offending and the gender gap that took into account gender differences in role expectations, socialization patterns and application of social control, opportunities to commit particular offenses, and access to criminally oriented subcultures-all themes that have been further developed in more recent accounts.

Recent Developments:

A rich and complex literature on female criminality has emerged over the past few decades. One view received an extraordinary amount of media attention during the late 1960s and the 1970s. This was the argument that "women's liberation" could help explain the apparent narrowing of the disparity between female and male arrest rates. This was a revival of a view long current in criminology, that gender differences in crime could be explained by differences in male and female social positions. This plausible notion gave rise to the "gender equality hypothesis": as social differences between men and women disappear under the influence of the women's movement, so should the differences in crime disappear.

This interpretation of the "dark side" of female liberation was welcomed enthusiastically by the media. However, other criminologists have pointed to the peculiarity of the view that improving girls' and women's economic conditions would lead to disproportionate increases in female crime when almost all the existing criminological literature stresses the role played by poverty, joblessness, and discrimination in the creation of crime (Chesney-Lind, 1997). This and other weaknesses in the gender equality hypothesis have been discussed at length elsewhere, as have more plausible explanations for the narrowing of differences for specific categories of crime. (Recall that gender differences in arrest rates have by no means narrowed for all categories, actually increasing for some and remaining the same for others.)

Another issue receiving much attention is whether traditional theories of crime, developed by male criminologists to explain male crime, are equally useful in explaining female crime, or whether female crime can only be explained by gender-specific theories. Causal factors identified by traditional theories of crime such as anomie, social control, and differential association-social leaming appear equally applicable to female and male offending (Steffensmeier and Allan, 1996).

For both males and females, the likelihood of criminal behavior is increased by weak social bonds and parental controls, low perceptions of risk, delinquent associations, chances to learn criminal motives and techniques, and other access to criminal opportunities. In this sense, traditional criminological theories are as useful in understanding overall female crime as they are in understanding overall male crime. They can also help explain why female crime rates are so much lower than male rates: for example, females develop stronger bonds and are subject to stricter parental control, but have less access to criminal opportunity.

On the other hand, many of the subtle and profound differences between female and male offending patterns may be better understood by a gendered approach. Recent theoretical efforts, often drawing from the expanding literature on gender roles and feminism, typically involve "middle-range" approaches aimed at explaining this or that dimension of female criminality by linking it to specific aspects of the "organization of gender" (a term used here to denote identities, arrangements, and other areas of social life that differ markedly by gender). These approaches are reviewed briefly next, after which we discuss a broader gendered paradigm that offers a general theoretical framework for understanding female criminality and sex differences in offending.

Cloward and Piven, for example, argue that the persistence of gender segregation in the society at large differentially shapes the form and frequency of male and female deviance. Limits on women's opportunities in the paid workforce, in conjunction with their more extensive domestic responsibilities, constrain the deviant adaptations available to women. As a result, "the only models of female deviance which our society encourages or permits women to imagine, emulate and act out are essentially privatized modes of self destruction" (p. 660).

Harris makes a comparable point when he argues that societies are structured such that all behaviors are "type-scripted." These "typescripts" specify acceptable and unacceptable forms of deviance for various categories of social actors including men and women. As a result of these type scripts, "it is unlikely or impossible for women to attempt assassination, robbery, or rape" (p. 12). Instead, consistent with gendered type scripts and roles (e.g., consumer, domestic), women are much more heavily involved in minor thefts and hustles such as shoplifting, theft of services, falsification of identification, passing bad checks, credit card forgery, welfare fraud, and employee pilferage.

Steffensmeier argues that underworld sex segregation adds further structural constraints on female levels of offending, particularly in the more lucrative venues. Compared to their male counterparts, potential female offenders are at a disadvantage in selection and recruitment into criminal groups, in the range of career paths, and access to them, opened by way of participation in these groups, and in opportunities for tutelage, increased skills, and rewards. It is hardly surprising, therefore, that female involvement in professional and organized crime continues to lag far behind male involvement. Women are hugely underrepresented in traditionally male-dominated networks that engage in large-scale burglary, fencing operations, gambling enterprises, and racketeering (Commonwealth of Pennsylvania; Steffensmeier, 1986).

Broidy and Agnew have speculated that the dynamics of gender shape both the types of strains males and females are exposed to and the emotional and behavioral responses available to them, thus leading to distinctly different outcomes. Aggressive, externalizing behavioral responses are acceptable for males in various environments, whereas such responses are less commonly available to females. Thus, female responses to strain are more likely to be nonaggressive and/or self-destructive.

Chesney-Lind (1997) further clarifies the different strains faced by females in her depiction of the differential impact of gender dynamics on the lives and experiences of boys and girls growing up in similar neighborhood and school environments. Specifically, gender-based socialization patterns set the stage for the sexual victimization and harassment of girls. It is this victimization that often triggers girls' entry into delinquency as they try to escape abusive environments. Girls attempting to run away from abuse often end up in the streets with few legitimate survival options, so they gravitate toward crime, drug-use and -dealing, and sexual exchange transactions. Thus, the role of interpersonal victimization in female paths to crime often involves a circular dynamic in which victimization places some females at high risk for offending, which in turn puts them at risk for further victimization (Daly; Gilfus). This dynamic is especially problematic for minority and low income women whose risks for both crime and victimization are already heightened by limited access to resources (Arnold; Richie).

A Gender Paradigm of Female Offending and The Gender Gap:

Steffensmeier and Allan (1996, 2000) provide another attempt to build a unified theoretical framework for explaining female criminality and gender differences in crime. This perspective incorporates factors suggested by other theorists. Their framework recognizes that (1) causal patterns for female crime often overlap those for male crime, but also (2) that continued profound differences between the lives of women and men produce varying patterns of female and male offending.

At least five areas of life tend not only to inhibit female crime and encourage male crime, but also to shape the patterns of female offending that do occur: gender norms, moral development and affiliative concerns, social control, physical strength and aggression, and sexuality. These five areas overlap and mutually reinforce one another and, in turn, condition gender differences in criminal opportunities, motives, and contexts of offending. Key points are summarized here.

Gender norms. Female criminality is both inhibited and molded by two powerful focal concerns ascribed to women: (1) role obligations (daughter, wife, mother) and the presumption of female nurturance; (2) expectations of female beauty and sexual virtue. Such focal concerns pose constraints on female opportunities for illicit endeavors. The constraints posed by child-rearing responsibilities and other nurturant obligations are obvious. Moreover, the frequency of derivative identities restrains deviance on the part of women affiliated with conventional males; however, wives or girlfriends of criminals may be pushed into the roles of accomplices.

Femininity stereotypes are the antitheses of those qualities valued in the criminal subculture (Steffensmeier, 1986); therefore, crime is almost always more destructive of life chances for females than for males. In contrast, the dividing line between what is considered masculine and what is criminal is often thin.

Finally, expectations of female sexuality may restrict the deviant roles available to women to those of sexual media or service roles. Female fear of sexual victimization reduces female exposure to criminal opportunity through the avoidance of bars, nighttime streets, and other crime-likely locations.

Moral development and affiliative concerns: Compared to men, women are more likely to refrain from crime due to concern for others. This may result from gender differences in moral development and from socialization toward greater empathy, sensitivity to the needs of others, and fear of separation from loved ones. This predisposition toward an "ethic of care" restrains women from violence and other behavior that may injure others or cause emotional hurt to those they love. Men, on the other hand, are more socialized toward status-seeking behavior and may therefore develop an amoral ethic when they feel those efforts are blocked.

Social control: The ability and willingness of women to commit crime is powerfully constrained by social control. Particularly during their formative years, females are more closely supervised and discouraged from misbehavior. Risk-taking behavior is rewarded among boys but censured among girls. Careful monitoring of girls' associates reduces the potential for influence by delinquent peers. Even as adults, women find their freedom to explore worldly temptations constricted.

Physical strength and aggression. The weakness of women relative to men-whether real or perceived—puts them at a disadvantage in a criminal underworld that puts a premium on physical power and violence. Muscle and physical prowess are functional not only for committing crimes, but also for protection, contract enforcement, and recruitment and management of reliable associates.

Sexuality. Reproductive-sexual differences, coupled with the traditional "double standard," contribute to higher male rates of sexual deviance and infidelity. On the other hand, the demand for illicit sex creates opportunities for women for criminal gain through prostitution. This in turn may reduce the need for women to seek financial returns through serious property crimes. Nevertheless, although prostitution is a money-making opportunity that women may exploit, it is a criminal enterprise still largely controlled by men: pimps, clients, police and businessmen.

Collectively, the above aspects of the organization of gender serve to condition and shape additional features of female offending, including criminal opportunity, criminal motives, and contexts of crime.

Access to criminal opportunity. Limits on female access to legitimate opportunities put further constraints on their criminal opportunities, since women are less likely to hold jobs such as driver, dockworker, or carpenter, that would provide opportunities for theft, drug dealing, fencing, and other illegal activities. In contrast, abundant opportunities exist for women to commit and/or to be caught and arrested for petty forms of theft and fraud, for low-level drug dealing, and for sex-for-sale offenses.

The scarcity of women in the top ranks of business and politics limits their chance for involvement in price-fixing conspiracies, financial fraud, and corruption.

Motivation. The subjective willingness of women to engage in crime is limited by factors of the organization of gender, but amplified by criminal opportunity. Being able tends to make one more willing. Female as well as male offenders tend to be drawn to criminal activities that are easy and within their skill repertoire, and that have a good payoff and low risk. Women's risk-taking preferences differ from those of men (Steffensmeier and Allan, 1996). Men will take risks in order to build status or gain competitive advantage, while women may take greater risks to protect loved ones or to sustain relationships. Criminal motivation is suppressed in women by their greater ability to foresee threats to life chances and by the relative unavailability of female criminal type scripts that could channel their behavior.

Context of offending. The organization of gender also impacts on the often profound differences in the contexts of female and male offenses. Even when the same offense is charged, there may be dramatic differences in contexts, such as the setting, presence of other offenders, the relationship between offender and victim, the offender's role in initiating and committing the offense, weapon (if any), the level of injury or property loss/destruction, and purpose of the offense. Moreover, female/male contextual differences increase with the seriousness of the offense.

J. Miller's qualitative study of male and female robbery clarifies how gender shapes the context of robbery, even when motives are the same. Males typically target other males, and their robberies often involve direct confrontation, physical violence, and guns. Females most often target other females and seldom use guns. When women do rob men, they may carry a gun, but they are more likely to soften the target with sex than with actual violence. Miller concludes that male and female robbery may be triggered by similar social and cultural factors, but that gender shapes the actual manner in which those robberies are enacted.

Spousal murders also illustrate striking male-female differences in context. Wives are far more likely to have been victims, and they turn to murder only when in mortal fear, after exhausting alternatives. Husbands who murder wives, however, are more likely to be motivated by rage at suspected infidelity, and the murder often culminates a period of prolonged abuse of their wives. Some patterns of wife-killing are almost never found when wives kill husbands: murder-suicides, family massacres, and stalking.

The various aspects of the organization of gender discussed here—gender norms, moral and relational concerns, social control, lack of strength, and sexual identity-all contribute to gender differences in criminal opportunity, motivation, and context. These factors also help explain why women are far less likely than men to be involved in serious crime, regardless of data source, level of involvement, or measure of participation.

Summary

The majority of girls and women involved in the criminal justice system have committed ordinary crimes-mostly minor thefts and frauds, low-level drug dealing, prostitution, and misdemeanor assaults against their mates or children. Some of them commit crime over several years and serve multiple jailor prison terms in the process. But they are not career criminals, and women are far less likely than men to be involved in serious crime. These generalizations hold true regardless of data source, level of involvement, or measure of participation.

The gender gap for criminal offending is remarkably persistent across countries, population subgroups within a given country, and historical periods. This persistence can be explained in part by historical durability of the organization of gender and by underlying physical/sexual differences (whether actual or perceived). Human groups, for all their cultural variation, follow basic human forms.

Recent theory and research on female offending have added greatly to our understanding of how the lives of delinquent girls and women continue to be powerfully influenced by gender-related conditions of life. Profound sensitivity to these conditions is essential for understanding gender differences in crime.

Bibliography

Adler, Freda. (1975): *Sisters in Crime: The Rise of the New Female Criminal.* New York: McGraw-Hill.

Arnold, Regina. (1995): "The Processes ofCriminalization of Black Women." In *The Criminal Justice System and Women.* Edited by B. Price and N. Sokoloff. New York: McGraw-Hill, pp. 136-146.

Austin, Roy L. (1993): "Recent Trends in Official Male and Female Crime Rates: The Convergence Controversy." *Journal of Criminal Justice* 21, 447-466.

Bowker, Lee H. (1978): *Women, Crime and the Criminal Justice System.* Lexington, Mass.: Heath.

Broidy, Lisa, And Agnew, Robert. (1997): "Gender and Crime: A General Strain Theory Perspective." *Journal of Research in Crime and Delinquency* 34, 275-306.

Bureau of Justice Statistics. *National Crime Victimization Survey.* Washington, D.C.: U.S. Department of Justice, 1980-1998.

Campbell, Ann. (1984): *The Girls in the Gang.* Oxford, U.K.: Basil Blackwell.

Chesney-Lind, M. (1997): "Women and Crime: The Female Offender." *Signs* 12, 78-96.-. *The Female. Offender.* Thousand Oaks, Calif.: Sage, 1997.

Cloward, Richard, And Piven Francis. (1979): "Hidden Protest: The Channeling of Female Protest and Resistance." *Signs* 4,651-669.

Commonwealth of Pennsylvania. (1991): *Organized Crime in Pennsylvania: The 1990 Report.* Conshohocken, Pa.: Pennsylvania Crime Commission.

Daly, Kathleen. (1994): *Gender, Crime, and Punishment.* New Haven, Conn.: Yale University Press.

Denno, Deborah. (1994): "Gender, Crime and the Criminal Law Defenses." *Journal of Criminal Law and Criminology* 85, no. 1, 80-180.

Elliot, Delbert, And Ageton, Suzanne. (1980): "Reconciling Race and Class Differences in Self-Reported and Official Estimates of Delinquency." *American Sociological Review* 45,95-110.

Federal Bureau of Investigation. *Uniform Crime Reports: Crime in the United States.* Washington, D.C.: Department of Justice, 1980-1998.

Gilfus, Mary. (1992): "From Victims to Survivors to Offenders: Women's Routes to Entry and Immersion into Street Crime." *Women and Criminal Justice* 4, 63-89.

Glueck, Sheldon, And Glueck, Eleanor. (1934): *Five Hundred Delinquent Women.* New York: Knopf.

Hagan, John. (1989): *Structural Criminology.* New Brunswick, N.J.: Rutgers University Press.

Hagan, John; Simpson, John; And Gillis, A. R. (1987): "Class In The Household: A Power Control Theory Of Gender And Delinquency." *American Journal Of Sociology* 92, 788-816.

Harris, Anthony. (1977): "Sex And Theories Of Deviance: Toward A Functional Theory Of Deviant Type-Scripts." *American Sociological Review* 42,3-16.

James, Jennifer. (1977): "Prostitutes And Prostitution." In *Deviants: Voluntary Action In A Hostile World* Edited By E. Sagarin And F. Montanino. New York: Scott, Foresman.

Lombroso, Ceasar, And Ferraro, William. (1895): *The Female Offender.* London: Fisher Unwin.

Miller, Eleanor. (1986): *Street Women.* Philadelphia: Temple University Press.

Miller, Jo. (1998): "Up It Up: Gender And The Accomplishment Of Street Robbery." *Criminology* 36,37-65.

Morash, Merry, And Chesney-Lind, Meda. (1991): "A Reformulation And Partial Test Of The Power Control Theory Of Delinquency." *Justice Quarterly* 8, 347-377.

Pollak, Otto. (1950): *The Criminality Of Women.* Philadelphia: University Of Pennsylvania Press.

Richie, Beth. (1996): *The Gendered Entrapment Of Battered, Black Women.* London: Routledge.

Simon, Rita. (1975): *The Contemporary Woman And Crime.* Rockville, Md.: National Institute Of Mental Health.

Simpson, Sally, And Ellis, Lisa. (1975): "Doing Gender: Sorting Out The Caste And Crime Conundrum." *Criminology* 33,47-81.

Steffensmeier, Darrell, And Allan, Emilie. (1996): "Gender And Crime: Toward A Gendered Theory Of Female Offending." *Annual Review Of Sociology* 22,459-487.

"Gender, Age, And Crime." In *Handbook Of Contemporary Criminology*, 3rd Ed. Edited By J. Sheley. New York: Wadsworth, 2000.

Steffensmeier, Darrell; Allan, Emilie; And Streifel, Cathy. (1989): "Development And Female Crime: A Cross-National Test Of Alternative Explanations." *Social Forces* 68, 262-283.

Steffensmeier, Darrell, And Terry, Robert. (1986): "Institutional Sexism In The Underworld: A View From The Inside." *Sociological Inquiry* 56,304—323.

Steffensmeier, Darrell; Ulmer, Jeffrey; And Kramer, John. (1998): "The Interaction Of Race, Gender, And Age In Criminal Sentencing: The Punishment Cost Of Being Young, Black, And Male." *Criminology* 36, 763-798.

13

Women in Prison

Historical Background

Understanding the contemporary prison for women requires an examination of the historical development of this system of social control and the critical issues relating to the imprisonment of women in the modem era. These issues include the development of distinct subcultures within these institutions, the enormous rise in the numbers of women in prison beginning in the late 1980s, the characteristics of women prisoners, and the gender-specific concerns such as physical and sexual abuse, separation from children, substance abuse, and unmet programme needs.

Throughout history, the female criminal has been cast as a "double-deviant"; first, because she violated the criminal or moral law and, second, perhaps more importantly, because she has violated the narrow moral strictures of the female role within society. In almost every society, women have been cast as second-class citizens, subservient to the will and wishes of men. Women who violated the law, then, also violated their subservient position and were seen as morally suspect as well as criminal. Prior to the development of prisons in the seventeenth and eighteenth centuries, punishment for women and men took a variety of forms: Serious offenders were put to death by hanging or burning, or banished from their community or sold as slaves. Belknap notes that in the Middle Ages, for example, women who committed adultery or killed their spouses were commonly burned to death. Less serious offenders were subjected to physical punishments such as whippings, stocks and pillories, or branding; and social punishments including public humiliation and shame. For women, mask-like devices, called the brank or bridle, were used in England up until the 1800s and were designed to punish and control outspoken women who gossiped or disobeyed their husbands.

Although death and physical torture remained in use, Western society began to consider alternatives to them in the nineteenth century. Houses of correction, workhouses, and transportation to colonies were precursors of modern confinement and served to bridge the gap between the death penalty and the contemporary prison. The house of correction and the workhouse were designed to address the moral failings of the underclass. In their various forms, these institutions were used to confine less serious offenders, including penniless women and prostitutes. Women could also be sent to bride-wells, poorhouses, or nunneries by fathers or husbands who wanted to punish the unruly, disobedient, or unchaste woman. These early modes of imprisonment attempted to combine punishment for past wrongdoing with attempts at reforming future behavior. Transportation developed in western Europe, most notably in England, as another alternative to the death penalty. In the 1700s, England transported over 60 percent of the convicted offenders to work as indentured servants in the colonies in America and Australia. Historians estimate that between 12 and 20 percent of those transported were women, who were typically convicted of crimes relating to poverty or sexual behavior. Ironically, women were transported to the colonies were often used as prostitutes or mistresses to meet the demand for sexual partners-willing or not-in these rough new worlds.

Those escaping forced prostitution were indentured servants to the managerial class.

The penitentiary was the next step in the evolution of the prison. Dungeons, castles, and the like had been used for centuries to confine wrongdoers until physical punishment could be delivered. The penitentiary, however, was the first attempt to use confinement as the punishment itself. In England, one of the first models for the modern prison was intended to provide a place of penance for prostitutes. This radical experiment was based on principles of separation from the moral contagion of their former lives, religious contemplation, and rigid structure. Up until the late 1800s, women, men, and children were confined together in these attempts at correction, often with no provision for food, clothing, or bedding. Those without families or other means of support lived in brutal and unsanitary conditions. Women often resorted to prostitution with more propertied inmates or officials to survive. However noble in principle, most of these attempts at correction failed. Overcrowding, lack of adequate funding, a corrupt and untrained guard force, and little real commitment to the ideal of reforming the underclass contributed to this failure.

The history of prisons took a new turn in the American colonies. At the end of the American Revolution, incarceration was relatively uncommon. The crimes committed by women were and continue to be-fewer and less serious than those committed by men. For the female minor offender, public humiliations, such as the ducking stool, the stocks, and the "Scarlet Letter," were delivered to those behaving outside the authority of men as well as those breaking the law. Corporal and capital punishment continued to be the primary forms of punishment for serious crimes but new ideas about punishment and reform gained a foothold in the American colonies. By the 1820s, the American solution to crime was the American penitentiary. Based on the principles articulated in England, the American Penitentiary flowered during the Jacksonian era. Two similar models took root between 1820 and 1840-the silent and the congregate systems. Both models used work, discipline, religious contemplation, and separation from the free world to attempt change in the convicted criminal.

Few women were confined in the emerging penitentiary system. While only about 4 percent of the U.S. prison population was female by 1950, most scholars agree that these few imprisoned women did not benefit from this experiment in reform. Robert Johnson states that women and minorities were "barely considered human" (p. 32), and thus not fit candidates for the penitentiary's regime. The few women imprisoned in the early 1880s were confined to traditional prisons that offered no plan for reform. Pollock-Byrne (1986) describes these places of confinement as having little regard for the safety and health of the woman prisoner. Like the first houses of correction, prisons for women in America were dirty, crowded, unsupervised, and without adequate bedding, food, and other provisions. Women were often locked away in rooms above the guardhouse or mess hall of the male prison with little access to workshops and exercise yards. Often left without supervision, women were vulnerable to attacks by one another and the male guards. Male staff and prisoners alike sexually abused women in these early prisons. Freedman argued that women were subjected to the "worst debasement at the hands of prison officials and guards" (p. 60) and that sadistic beatings, rape, and illegitimate births combined to make the prison experience even more terrifying. Dobash, Dobash, and Gutteridge conclude that, "From the very beginning, women in prison were treated very differently from men, considered more morally depraved and in need of special, closer forms of control and confinement" (p. 1).

The reformatory movement in the United States developed later in the mid-nineteenth century. Prisons for women then diverged into two directions, custodial institutions and the reformatory. The custodial model was the traditional prison, adopting the retributive purpose, high-security architecture, male-dominated authority and harsh discipline of the male prison (Rafter, 1985, p. 21). Many women remained confined to the male prison, with little regard to their gendered needs. The reformatory, in contrast, was a new form of punishment designed specifically to house women in entirely separate institutions, with female matrons and programs planned to reform women by promoting appropriate gender roles. Training in cooking, sewing, laundry, and other domestic arts were designed to return the woman prisoner to free society as either a well-trained wife or a domestic servant. The unwalled reformatories were built on large parcels of land, usually in rural areas with small cottages instead of cellblock structures. Rafter (1985) offers evidence that minority women were more likely to be sent to the more brutal custodial prison, whereas white women, particularly young, white women who had committed minor offenses, were more likely to be seen as ideal candidates for redemption in the reformatory. Alderson Federal Prison in West Virginia and the California Institute for Women represent the reformatory model and were still in use at the end of the 1990s.

Ending in the 1930s, the reformatory movement established separate women's facilities with some recognition of the gendered needs of women. After the 1930s, the custodial and reform models merged, combining elements of their two styles with differing results throughout the United States. The legacy of these movements continues to shape prisons for women. First, with the exception of a relatively few "cocorrections" experiments that housed women and men together with common programming, most prisons in the 1990s were single sex. Second, vocational programming tends to reinforce gender stereotypes, although some innovative programs that offer training in welding, woodworking, and ether male-identified trades are found in the contemporary prison.

Third, women in prison continue to be subjected to the neglect that characterizes their history from the early houses of correction to the modem prison.

By the 1940s and 1950s, the medical model of corrections emerged as a new philosophy of punishment. Called "correctional institutions," these prisons moved away from the harsh discipline and work orientation of the custodial prison and instead attempted to introduce treatment to a newly defined inmate-rather than convict-population. "Correctional officers" replaced prison guards, and the inmates were introduced to a treatment regime that attempted to diagnose, classify, and treat the inmate prior to release. An indeterminate sentencing system rewarded those who appeared to conform to this treatment by release on parole. There is little evidence that this approach had any more success in rehabilitating women or men than other prior forms of punishment.

During this time, the social sciences "discovered" the prison and began investigating the way prisoners adjusted to and lived their lives in prison. While most of these studies of the prison focused on men, some of the classic work on the subcultures of women's prisons was conducted in the 1960s and early 1970s (Owen; Ward and Kassebaum; Giallombardo; and Heffernan).

The Contemporary Prison:

Beginning in the 1970s, prison systems began to return to a custodial or "warehouse" model, with few prisons offering rehabilitative programs. This trend continued into the 1980s and 1990s. In this period, the numbers of women in prison began to skyrocket, due primarily to enhanced and punitive sanctions against drug offenders. Prisons for women then became increasingly crowded as women were hard hit by this national trend. The female prison population increased disproportionately to the increase in women's involvement in serious crime. Some states began to build new prisons for women, again using designs based on male prisons. Many of the reformatory prisons remain in use, but the majority of modern prisons for women are now run as custodial rather than as rehabilitative institutions.

Most states have a relatively small number of prisons for women and thus house women prisoners at one or two geographically isolated locations. California, with the largest prison population in the United States, is the exception with five prisons for women. Women are often housed far from home, friends, and their families and are distant from services more available in urban communities. While male prisoners are assigned to the more numerous facilities with a wider range of security levels, the majority of women in the United States are confined to prisons that encompass all classification and security levels in one facility. In the contemporary prison, security procedures often interfere with privacy. While privacy is eroded by crowded conditions, shared housing units, and the need for surveillance, the presence of male staff undennines a woman's ability to attend to personal hygiene and grooming without the scrutiny of men. In most prisons, between 50 and 80 percent of the custody staff is male. Male staff supervise housing units, monitoring women in showers, toilets, and in the rooms or cells where they dress. Most prison systems prohibit male staff from performing strip searches.

With the exception of newly arrived prisoners and the small number held in the more restrictive special housing units (such as administrative segregation or security housing units), most women prisoners remain in the general population. Most women prisoners work, attend school, and participate in other programs with all prisoners, whose classification may range from minimum to maximum custody. A very small number of women are housed in administrative segregation or security housing units. Movement within the institution, programme participation, and other privileges are severely restricted in these housing units. Women in these units are confined to their cells an average of 23 hours a day, eat their meals in their cells, and are allowed very limited recreation and visiting privileges (Owens, 1998). Only a small percentage of all the women in prison are confined to special housing units but these conditions are often severe.

Prison Subcultures

The study of prison subcultures investigates the way prisoners adjust to prison, the way they learn to "do their time," and the resulting prison social structure. By the 1960s and 1970s, scholars began to study the subculture of women's prisons and found that it was much different than life in male prisons. The fIrst two of these important works (Ward and Kassebaum; Giallombardo) discussed a prison social structure based on family, traditional sex-roles, and same-sex relations. In *Women's Prison: Sex and Social Structure,* Ward and Kassebaum found the women in prison felt a loss of control over their lives and anxiety over the course of their prison term. In order to alleviate these feelings, women participated in a prisoner social system to regain a sense of control and belonging while in prison. Included in these feelings of loss were "affectional starvation" resulting from their loss of family and male partners. Ward and Kassebaum suggested women prisoners developed the "pseudo family" and relationships with other prisoners to make up for this loss. Giallombardo's *Society of Women* also described the world of imprisoned women based on sex-role adaptation and family or kinship structures. She stated that the social order of women's prison is based on an adaptation of traditional feminine roles, such as mother, daughter, and wife. Masculine sex roles find expression in the prison social roles of the "stud." Giallombardo argued that the family or kinship structure of the women's prison is also based on this sex-role framework. In a third classic study, *Making It in Prison: The Square, the Cool, and the Life,* Heffernan described how women prisoners organize their prison identities around two things: their preprison identities and their differential adaptation to the prison subculture. Women who did not define themselves as serious criminals prior to prison adopted "the Square" orientation to prison life, and continued to hold conventional behaviors and attitudes during their imprisonment. In contrast, women who adapted to prison life as "the Cool" became heavily invested in a prison-based identity and developed a form of doing time that was based on prison values. Finally, some women retained their street identity of the petty criminal and adopted "the Life" as their style of doing time. These three studies found remarkable similarities: Prison culture among women was tied to gender expectations of sexuality and family relationships and these expectations also shaped the way women developed their lives within prison.

Decades later, *In the Mix: Struggle and Survival in a Women's Prison* described the daily life of the women's prison, with an emphasis on the gendered nature of its social structure, roles, and normative frameworks. Owen also found that prison culture for women was tied directly to the role of women in society as well as to a dynamic social structure that was shaped by the conditions of womens lives in prison and in the "free world." Like Heffernan, *In the Mix* describes the lives of women before prison and suggests that these lives shape their adaptation to prison culture. Owen found that economic marginalization, histories of personal and substance abuse, and self-destructive behavior are defining features of inmate's lives prior to prison. She also saw that the amount of time women have to serve and their kinds of work and housing assignments affect the way women in prison "program," developing a pattern to their daily life and relationships that determines the way women adapt to prison. Since about 80 percent of the women in prison are mothers, great importance was placed on relationships with their children. Finally, Owen described "the mix" as part of prison culture that supported the rule-breaking behavior that propels women into prison. This study concluded that prison subcultures for women are very different from the violent and predatory structure of the contemporary male prison. Owen did not find the presence of gangs-a central feature of the contemporary male prison-at the prison she studied. Women experience "pains of imprisonment" but their prison culture offers them other ways to survive and adapt to these deprivations.

Population Increase

Enormous increases in population characterize prisons for women since the mid-1980s.. By 1998, this number had risen to 84,427, an almost fourfold increase in just under twenty years. In addition, approximately 64,000 women were incarcerated in local jails and over 700,000 were on probation, parole, or community supervision. In total, nearly 850,000 women were under some form of criminal justice supervision in the United States (Bureau of Justice Statistics 1999a, 1999b). In California alone, the female prison population rose dramatically from 1,316 in 1980, to almost 12,000 in 1999. During 1998, Texas incarcerated over 10,000 women, New York prisons held just under 4,000, and Florida over 3,500. In the federal system, the women's prison population almost doubled from 5,011 in 1990 to 9,186 in 1998. Between 1990 and 1998, the number of women in U.S. prisons increased 92 percent compared to 67 percent increase in the number of men (Bureau of Justice Statistics, 1999a).

This explosion in the women's prison population cannot be explained by looking at the crime rate of women only. Compared to men, women generally commit fewer crimes and their offenses tend to be less serious. A major gender difference is the low rate of violent crime committed by women. The offenses for which women are arrested and incarcerated are primarily nonviolent property and drug offenses. When women do commit acts of violence, it is most likely against a spouse or partner and in the context of self-defense. In analyzing data from the 1970-1995 Uniform Crime Reports, Steffensmeir and Allan found that drug offenses have had the most significant impact on female arrest rates. Sharp increases in the numbers of women arrested for minor property crimes, like larceny, fraud, and forgery, have also contributed to the explosion in women's imprisonment. Many women resort to minor property crime in order to support their drug use. In addition to increased prosecution of drug offenses, the lack of viable treatment and alternative community sanctions for women has contributed to this unprecedented increase in women's population (Bloom, Chesney-Lind, and Owen). Most criminologists see that the war on drugs, a drug control policy started at the federal level in the 1980s, accounts for the unprecedented rise in the imprisonment of women.

The Composition of Women's Prisons

The profile of women in prison has remained consistent: Female prisoners are primarily low income, undereducated, unskilled, and unemployed. They are mostly young and heads of households with an average of two children. At least two-thirds of incarcerated women have children under the age of eighteen. Substance abuse, compounded by poverty, unemployment, physical and mental illness, physical and sexual abuse, and homelessness also characterize the women's prison population (Owen and Bloom). Surveys conducted by the Bureau of Justice Statistics (1991b, 1994), and the American Correctional Association (1990), as well as individual state profiles (Owen and Bloom) provide information about the demographic characteristics of women in prison. These descriptions remain accurate even as the numbers of women in prison continue to surge upward. The following factors characterize this population.

Race and ethnicity. In addition to gender differences between male and female crime, women's arrest and incarceration rates vary by race (Chesney-Lind). Minority women are disproportionately represented in the U.S. prison population, with the percentage of African American women who are incarcerated growing at increasing rates. In 1991, African American women made up about 40 percent of the female prison population; by 1995, this population had grown to 48 percent. The percentage of Hispanic and Latina women is also growing at a somewhat slower rate (Bureau of Justice Statistics Washington, 1997, 1994).

In spite of this disproportionate racial and ethnic composition, racial conflict has not been a primary feature of the social order of female prisons. While racial and ethnic identity is predominant in male prison culture, these conflicts do not shape the way women do their prison time. Women in prison generally live and work in an integrated environment and form personal relationships that often cross racial lines. Racial and ethnic gangs have not yet appeared in women's prisons to the extent they are found in male prisons. While a small number of women may enter the prison with some street gang or clique affiliation, the subculture of the women's prison offers little support for these pre-prison identities. Women seeking the personal and community ties found in street gangs are likely to find substitutes within the prison families or other personal relationships (Owen).

Race relations with staff, however, are potentially more antagonistic. The majority of correctional staff is both white and male in most U.S. prisons for women. Minority women prisoners have reported race-based instances of name-calling, job and program discrimination, and unfair disciplinary practices (Owen; Bloom).

Age at first arrest and criminal history. The American Correctional Association (ACA), Washington (1990), survey found that most women in prison were first arrested at a young age. One-third of those interviewed were first arrested between fifteen and nineteen years of age, and another quarter between twenty and twenty-four years old. Just over 9 percent were arrested prior to their fourteenth birthday and just over 10 percent were arrested after age thirty-five. According to the 1994 Bureau of Justice Statistics report, Washington, over half of the women in prison were serving their first prison term. This survey also found that most women serving a second term had been convicted in the past for only nonviolent offenses. Nearly two-thirds of all female inmates had two or fewer prior convictions. Almost three-quarters of all state female prisoners had served a prior sentence to probation or incarceration, including 20 percent who had served a sentence as a juvenile.

Drug use and drug arrests. In the 1990s, substance abuse played a key role in the imprisonment of women and contributed dramatically to the increasing numbers of women prisoners. Women are more likely to use drugs, use more serious drugs more frequently, and be under the influence of drugs at the time of their crime than males (Bureau of Justice Statistics, 1994). In the national studies, over one-third of all female prisoners interviewed in 1991 reported being under the influence of some drug at the time of their offense. Around 40 percent reported daily drug use in the month before their offense. Almost one-quarter of the 1991 sample reported committing their crime to get money to buy drugs (Bureau of Justice Statistics, 1994).

Victimization. Women in prison have extensive histories of sexual and physical abuse. In the 1991 national surveys, an estimated 43 percent of women in prison reported previous physical or sexual abuse. Others found higher rates of abuse among women in prison (Owen and Bloom). Violent offenders were most likely to have previously experienced this abuse (Bureau of Crime Statistics, 1994). An estimated 50 percent of women in prison who reported abuse said they had experienced abuse at the hands of an inmate, compared to three percent of men. More than three-quarters of the female inmates who had a history of abuse reported being sexually abused. An estimates 56 percent of the abused women said that their abuse had involved a rape, and another 13 percent reported an attempted rape (Bureau of Justice Statistics, 1994). The 1990 ACA survey found that 50 percent of the women reported a history of physical abuse, with 35 percent reporting sexual abuse. This abuse was likely to be at the hands of husbands or boyfriends.

Other demographic factors. According to surveys conducted in the early 1990s, just over half of the women in prison at that time had been employed in the year prior to their arrest. Most were unmarried; 45 percent of the women prisoners had never been married and another third of female inmates were either separated or divorced. Just about 60 percent grew up in households without both parents present. Almost half (47%) had an immediate family member incarcerated at some time. About 35 percent had brothers and 10 percent had sisters who had been incarcerated. Eighty percent of the prisoners interviewed in a national survey reported incomes at or below the poverty level (Bureau of Justice Statistics, 1994).

Problems and Unmet Needs in the Contemporay Women's Prisons

Women in the contemporary prison face many problems; some resulting from their lives prior to imprisonment, others resulting from their imprisonment itself. Women in prison have experienced victimization, unstable family life, school and work failure, and substance abuse and mental health problems. Social factors that marginalize their participation in mainstream society and contribute to the rising number of women in prison include poverty, minority group member, single motherhood, and homelessness. While in U.S. prisons, women, like prisoners throughout the world, face specific pains and deprivations arising directly from their imprisonment. Criminologists have argued that the prison system is ill-equipped to deal with these problems and that theses issues are better managed outside the punitive environment of the prison (Owen and Bloom; Owen).

Without attention to these issues, women are often released from prison unprepared to manage their preexisting problems as well as those created by their imprisonment. There are several critical problems faced by women in prison; most are unmet in the prison environment.

Separation from children and significant others: National surveys of women prisoners find that three-fourths of them were mothers, with two-thirds having children under the age of eighteen. Bloom and Chesney-Lind argue that mothers in prison face multiple problems in maintaining relationships with their children and encounter obstacles created both by the correctional system and child welfare agencies. The distance between the prison and the children's homes, lack of transportation, and limited economic resources compromise a woman prisoner's ability to maintain these relationships. Children of women in prison experience many hardships. Children may be traumatized by the arrest of their mother and the sudden, forced separation imprisonment brings. Emotional reactions such as anger, anxiety, depression, and aggression have been found in the children of incarcerated mothers. While most children of imprisoned mothers live with relatives-typically grandparents-a small percentage of these children are placed in the child welfare system. These conditions compound the problem of maintaining contact with children. Over half of the women responding to Bloom and Steinhart's 1993 survey of imprisoned mothers reported never receiving visits from their children.

An estimated 4 to 9 percent of women come to prison pregnant. Women who give birth while incarcerated are rarely allowed to spend time with their child after birth. Mother-infant bonding is severely undermined by this lack of contact after birth. Bedford Hills, a women's prison in New York, is the only program in the U.S. that allows women to keep their newborns with them in a special prison program. This humane response is more common in Britain and other European nations.

Most correctional systems do not take into account the importance of the mother-child relationship in designing policy for women in prison. Some states, such as New York and California, have begun innovative programs to address these problems. Coordinating visits to the prison and support services with child welfare agencies, providing special visiting areas, developing effective parenting classes, and developing community corrections programs for mothers and their children are examples of these innovations. Termination of parental rights also affect prison mothers. About half the states have policies that address the termination of parental rights of incarcerated parents. Advocates of women in prison and their children argue that family reunification, rather than termination of the mother's parental rights, should be a priority of correctional policy for women prisoners.

Lack of substance abuse treatment: Although women offenders are very likely to have an extensive history of drug and alcohol use, a relatively small percentage of women receive any treatment within the justice system. Insufficient individual assessment, limited treatment for pregnant, mentally ill, and violent women offenders, and a lack of appropriate treatment and vocational training limit the effectiveness of the few programs that exist. These findings are supported by a 1998 study released by the National Center on Addition and Substance Abuse. The report found that women substance abusers are more prone to intense emotional distress, psychosomatic symptoms, and low self-esteem than male inmates.

Physical and mental health care: In addition to requiring basic health care, women offenders often have specific health needs related to their risky sexual and drug-using behavior prior to imprisonment. Women in prison are also at risk for infectious diseases, including HIV, tuberculosis, sexually transmitted diseases, and hepatitis B and C infections. Pregnancy and reproductive health needs are another neglected area of health care. Problems of pregnant inmates include lack of prenatal and postnatal care, inadequate education regarding childbirth and parenting, and little or no preparation for the mother's separation from the infant after delivery.

Mental health disorders are equally neglected in U.S. prisons. While the prevalence and incidence of these needs are still to be determined, estimates suggest that 25 percent to 60 percent of the female prison population require mental health services. Few prisons have adequate assessment or mental health treatment programs and often "overmedicate" women inmates in need of more intensive treatment.

The impact of physical, sexual, and emotional abuse found in the experience of women offenders also creates a significant need for counseling and therapy (pollock). This abuse has implications for their emotional and physical well-being and may be tied to drug-abusing and offending behaviors.

Vocation and educational programs: In addition to insufficient substance abuse and mental health services, educational and vocational programs are also in short supply. Several studies (Pollock-Byrne; Morash, Haarr, and Rucker) found that female prisons offered fewer vocational and education program opportunities when compared to those offered in male institutions. In general, women across the country lack training needed to obtain jobs that pay a living wage. One aspect of this inadequacy is that, like the training offered in the reformatories of the early 1990s, many vocational programs for female inmates emphasize traditional roles for women and work.

Sexual abuse: The patterns of sexual abuse and coercion established in the early days of women's imprisonment continue in the contemporary era. Human Rights Watch examined this serious problem in their review of sexual abuse in selected U.S. prisons. The damage of the abuse itself is compounded by four specific issues: (1) the inability to escape one's abuser; (2) ineffectual or nonexistent investigative and grievance procedures; (3) lack of employee accountability (either criminally or administratively); and (4) little or no public concern. The report bluntly states that the "findings indicate that being a woman in U.S. state prisons can be a terrifying experience" (p. 1).

Gender-specific treatment: The criminal justice system often fails to develop a diversity of options for dealing with the gender and culturally specific problems of female offenders. Gender-specific services should incorporate physical, psychological, emotional, spiritual, and sociopolitical issues in addressing these needs. Gender-responsive supervision and program approaches must focus on issues such as cross-gender supervision, appropriate relationships between staff and offenders, parity in programming, and appropriate interventions for women offenders. There is also a need for gender-responsive (and culturally relevant) classification tools, assessment instruments, treatment plans, and aftercare. Based on the characteristics of women offenders, their pathways to crime, how they differ from male offenders, and how the system responds to them differently, the need for gender-responsive treatment and services seems clear.

Conclusion

Women in prison are typically young, poor, from minority communities, and have experienced significant problems in their life prior to imprisonment. More simply, women in prison have been triply marginalized by race, class, and gender.

Throughout history, women have been sent to prison for offenses that differ dramatically from those of male prisoners. While the increasingly harsh treatment of the drug offender leads to the incarceration of thousands of women and men into the contemporary prison, women have been sent to prison in rates far surpassing those of men. Women are usually incarcerated for nonviolent property and drug offenses and are very often serving their first prison term. Women also "do their time" in ways different from men: The "play family" and other personalized relationships structure prison culture for women; racial and ethnic differences are less pronounced; and children remain an important part of women's lives, even while imprisoned.

There is insufficient information about programmes and policies that address the gender-specific needs of women in prison (Bloom and Covington) and little criminological theory that explains why women come to prisons (Chesney-Lind).

From the beginning, prisons in the United States were designed to punish men, with little consideration for women and their specific needs. Although the numbers of women in U.S. prisons continue to grow, programmes and policies responsive to the needs of women prisoners have not kept pace. This lack of policy and research attention only continues the tradition of neglect and inattention that characterizes the history of prisons for women.

Bibliography

BELKNAP, JOANNE. *The Invisible Woman: Gender, Crime, and Justice.* Belmont, Calif.: Wadsworth Press, 1996.

BLOOM, BARBARA, and CHESNEY-LIND, MEDA. "Women in Prison: Vengeful Equity." In *It's a Crime: Women and Criminal Justice.* Edited by R. Muraskin. New York: Prentice Hall, 2000. Pages 183-204.

BLOOM, BARBARA; CHESNEY-LIND, MEDA; and OWEN, BARBARA. *Women in California Prisons: Hidden Victims of the War on Drugs.* San Francisco, Calif.: Center on Juvenile and Criminal Justice, 1994.

CHESNEY-LIND, MEDA. *The Female Offender: Girls, Women, and Crime.* Thousand Oaks, Calif.: Sage, 1997.

DOBASH, RUSSELL; DOBASH, REBECCA; and GUTTERIDGE, SUE. *The Imprisonment of Women.* New York: Basil Blackwell, 1986.

FREEDMAN, ESTELLE. *Their Sister's Keepers: Women's Prison Reform in America, 1830-1930.* Ann Arbor, Mich.: University of Michigan Press, 1981.

GIALLOMBARDO, ROSE. *Society of Women: A Study of a Women's Prison.* New York: John Wiley, 1966.

HEFFERNAN, ESTHER. *Making It in Prison: The Square, the Cool, and the Life.* New York: John Wiley, 1972.

Human Rights Watch. *All Too Familiar: Sexual Abuse of Women in Us. Prisons.* New York: Human Rights Watch, 1996.

JOHNSON, ROBERT. "Race, Gender, and the American Prison." In *Prisons: Today and Tomorrow.* Edited by Joycelyn Pollock. Gaithersburg, Md.: Aspen Press, 1997. Pages 26—51.

KLIEN, SUE. "A Profile of Female Offenders in State and Federal Prisons." In *Female Offenders: Meeting the Needs of a Neglected Population.* Baltimore, Md.: United Book Press, 1993.

KURSHAN, NANCY. "Women and Imprisonment in the U.S." In *Cages of St‹ el.* Edited by W. Churchill and J. J. Vander Wall. Washington, D.C.: Maisonneuve Press, 1992.

MANN, CORA MAE. "Women of Color in the Criminal Justice System." In *The Criminal Justice System and Women.* Edited by B. Price and N. Skoloff. New York: McGraw Hill, 1995. Pages 118-135.

MORASH, MERRY; HAARR, ROBIN; and RUCKER, LILA. "A Comparison of Programming for Women and Men and U.S. Prisons in the 1980s." *Crime and Delinquency* 40, no. 2 (1994): 197-221.

OWEN, BARBARA. *In the Mix: Struggle and Survival in a Women's Prison.* Albany, N.Y.: SUNY Press, 1998.

OWEN, BARBARA, and BLOOM, BARBARA. "Profiling Women Prisoners: Findings from National Survey and a California Sample." *The Prison Journal* 75, no. 2 (1995): 165-185.

POLLOCK-BYRNE, JOY. *Women, Prison, and Crime-* Pacific Grove, Calif.: Brooks/Cole. 1990.

RAFTER, NICOLE. *Partial Justice: Women in State Prisons 1800-1935.* Boston: Northeastern University Press, 1985.

STEFFENSMEIR, DARRELL, and ALLAN, EMILIE. "The Nature of Female Offending: Patterns and Explanations." In *Female Offendkrs: Critical Perspectives and Interventions.* Edited by R. Zupan. Gaithersbtitg, Md.: Aspen Publishing, 1998. Pages 5-30.

WARD, DAVID, and KASSEBAUM, GENE. *Women's Prison: Sex and Social Structure.* Chicago: Aldine-Atherton, 1965.

WATTERSON, KATHRYN. *Women in Prison: Inside the Concrete Womb.* Boston: Northeastern University Press, 1996.

14

Prison Visiting System in India

One of the main objectives of incarceration, right from the inception of this concept in a sovereign state, was to curtail the liberty of movement and the freedom of initiative of a person, if he was found to have violated the established law of the land. Prisons took shape as institutions of state retribution as a natural outcome of the materialization of this objective.

Resultant segregation of offenders from the society, and the obligation of prison guards to restraint their movement against escape from lawful custody, constrained the architects of prison buildings to burden them with high walls, narrow galleries, shutters, locks, chains, fetters, cells and places of solitary confmement. This physical structure of prisons and the archaic rules of management of these punitive institutions endowed them with a cover of obscurity in which fundamental human rights could be unofficially violated and officially denied.

Prisons grew to be places of low visibility where inhuman and even cruel conditions could prevail. The possibility of inflicting injury and injustice on inmates always lurked in these closed institutions. State supervision over day-to-day happenings within such institutions became a mere formality and the surveillance of the society was conspicuous by its absence.

In spite of the fact that prison system has, during the past some decades, undergone a massive change both in its objectives and in its physical structure, the basic character of prisons — as closed institutions with little public scrutiny — continues to this day. The need for non-government intervention in prisons was recognized as early as 1894 when the Prisons Act accepted that a system of visitors would be of value in providing humanitarian aid to prison inmates secluded from the society. The Cardew Committee appointed by the British Government in that year devoted a whole chapter to making this system more effective and efficacious.

As a result the concept of non-government intervention in the management of prisons was for the first time conceived in The Prisons Act of 1894. Although this concept did not find place in the body of main provisions of the Act, but in Section 59, which speaks of powers to frame rules consistent with this Act, the State Governments were empowered to make rules for the appointment and guidance of visitors of prisons in sub-section (25). The present provisions for official and nonofficial visitors in Prison Manuals of various states are the result of this sub-section (25) of section 59 of The Prisons Act of 1894.

The first comprehensive work of studying prison conditions and of making remarkably suitable recommendations for the reformation of both prisons and prisoners was done by the Indian Jails Committee, 1919-20 appointed on the 28th day of April, 1919 under the chairmanship of Sir Alexander G. Cardew, ICS, Member of the Executive Council, Madras, with six distinguished members. Quite a large number of recommendations made by this committee. This Committee devoted a whole chapter (Chapter XXVIII) to the improvement in the system of Visitors of prisons.

Addressing the need for external supervision on prisons the Committee wrote:

The plan of appointing persons, official and non-official, to serve as visitors to jails seems to us to form a very valuable part of the Indian system of jail administration. In the first place, it insures the existence of a body of free and unbiased observers, whose visits serve as a guarantee to the Government and to the public, that the rules of the Prisons Act and Prison Manuals are duly observed, and that abuses, if they were to spring up, would be speedily brought to light. In this respect the Indian system is, we think, superior to that followed in other countries where the visitors become a part of the prison organization, with definite powers and duties, and so become more or less identified with the prison administration. In India, they remain impartial and independent. In the second place, the existence of non-official visitors is specially valuable as supplying a training ground where members of the public can obtain an insight into jail problems and learn to take an interest in prisons and prisoners. It is of great importance to create such an interest in the public mind and the appointment of non-officials is one of the best methods of promoting this end. Although, therefore, some of our witnesses have criticized the system, we think it has only to be extended and improved in order to be productive of even greater advantages in the future than in the past. (Report of the Indian Jails Committee, 1919-20. para. 511.)

Legal Provisions

Sub-section (25) of section 59 of The Prisons Act, 1894, the current basic law for the management of prisons in the country provides for the framing of rules for the appointment and guidance of visitors of prisons. The Indian Jail Committee, 1919- 20, had laid down guidelines for the appointment of prison visitors stating that, *The person selected for the position of a non-official visitor of a jail should be chosen on the ground of definite qualifications, such as an interest in prison matters or other social work, or ability and willingness to assist in finding work for prisoners on release. .. Selection should not be made solely on the ground of social position, wealth or political influence, but on the basis of special fitness..* (515 . Report of the IJC- 19-20)

Only a few states of independent India incorporated these guidelines as legal provisions for the appointment of non-official visitors. One such state was Maharashtra. Rule 6 of Chapter XV . Prison Visitors. of the Prison Manual of Maharashtra dealing with .Appointment of Non-official Visitors. says:

The appointment of non-official visitors (other than members of the Maharashtra Legislature) shall, subject to the provisions of sub-rule (4), *be made by the State Government from amongst persons who in its opinion, are interested in the administration of prisons and are likely to take interest in the prisoners and their welfare both while they are in prison and after their release.*

These guidelines and some of the other rules governing the operation of prison visiting system in Maharashtra need to be emulated by other states. Rules in most of the other states of the country do not specify any qualification for a person to be eligible for appointment as non-official visitor of a prison. They empower the State Government to appoint non-official visitors, six for each Central Prison, three for each district prison and two for each lock-up jail, on the recommendations of the Divisional Commissioner or Collector and District Magistrate of the district in which the jail or lock-up is situated :

Inter alia these rules provide for the duties of visitors, procedure for the removal of a non-official visitor and the powers of the District Magistrate to cause the preparation of a Roster for monthly visits and to form a Board of Visitors for each prison in the concerned district. A visitor, so long as he retains his official connections with the jail, is precluded from giving publicity in the press or otherwise to matters connected with its administration.

The rules also provide detailed guidelines on the points to be noticed by visitors during their visit to prisons, but, unlike the rules of Maharashtra, there is no mandate about giving a copy of these rules to non-official visitors at the time of their appointment.

Duties and Functions of Prison Visitors

Prison Rules of various states prescribe what the prison visitors should do and what they should not. Generally speaking these duties and restrictions are as follows:

Do's

- It is the duty of a visitor to satisfy himself that the law and rules regulating the management of prisons and prisoners are duly carried out in the prison;
- To visit all part of the prison and to see all prisoners;
- To hear and inquire into any complaint(s) that any prisoner may make; he may for this purpose talk to any prisoner out of the hearing but in the full sight of the officer accompanying him;
- To see, if necessary, any book, paper or record (other than those of confidential nature) connected with the administration of the prison;

Don' ts

- No visitor may issue any order or instruction to any subordinate jail officer;
- No visitor shall touch prisoners. rations in the kitchen, but he can taste the food if he so desires.
- Non-official visitors (NOV) may not visit prisoners on hunger strike or prisoners who are ill and are not allowed to be interviewed on medical grounds or those detained under the Preventive Detention Act.
- Non-official lady visitors shall not visit men's portion of the prison and shall confine themselves only to the women's section;
- Non-official or official visitors shall not, without the previous sanction of the Superintendent, hold

conversation with any under-trial who may happen to be their client or relation.

Now, there are some provisions which are out-dated and do not fit in the present democratic system. Why should an NOV be debarred from visiting a prisoner on hunger strike? May be that this prisoner has taken resort to hunger strike as a last option for seeking redress to some unresolved complaint, and a non-official visitor has a right to listen to such complaint. Similarly, the restriction on non-official visitors to meet prisoners kept under the Preventive Detention Act (or any such preventive law) is also an archaic provision that suited the British rule in India, and should now be lifted.

Even the bans on visitors to touch rations in the kitchen or on lady non-official visitors to visit the men's section are uncalled for. If a visitor properly washes his hands, why should he not be allowed to touch and feel the quality of rations? And, in an age when there are women superintendents at men's jail, why should lady visitors be not allowed to visit the entire prison with appropriate security arrangements.

There is yet another controversial provision in rules which says that a visitor, so long as he retains his official connections with the jail, is precluded from giving publicity in the press or otherwise to matters connected with prison administration. There is a strong argument that this provision is a violation of the fundamental right of speech and expression that every citizen enjoys under the Constitution and it cannot be withdrawn from a person only because he has been appointed a visitor of prison. Such restriction could perhaps be permissible or even justifiable a hundred years ago when it served the interests of British Rule because the visitors provided a cross check on prison administration and the government did not want any criticism to pass to the media without proper censor. Democratic principles had not come into play then, and the government wanted all infirmities to be kept within the system created by it. But, in a democratic set-up, any flaw in administration or neglect on the part of concerned authorities that deserves public notice for an accelerated remedial measure should be brought to light through media, particularly when we have accepted the principles of transparency in administration through citizens' charters and the right to information. And, if the institution of prison visitors (official or non-official) that has been introduced to break the obscurity of prisons is forced under law to conserve the same obscurity, the very purpose of its institution shall be defeated.

Matters in this respect shall automatically improve if the qualifications, antecedents, experience and social status of persons appointed as prison visitors are duly considered at appropriate levels and nominations are made strictly according to the procedure laid down in the rules.

Board of Visitors

Obscurity to society has perhaps been the main reason why it has been so difficult and sluggish to bring about improvement in prison conditions. This obscurity results partly from the basic nature of prison institutions and partly from the predisposition of management combined with the complete disinterest of society in general. This was perhaps foreseen by the framers of the Prisons Act a hundred years ago and therefore they slid a provision in the Prisons Act to bring about the institution of prison visitors. It is also for this reason that some kind of extra-departmental and social intervention has been sought through the appointment of visitors of prison from out side the prison set-up.

The formation and involvement of a board of visitors by the state is the only area where the prison bumps into society. The way, state provided for the formation and functioning of the board of visitors tells us something about the nature of the role it expected society to play in the process of the management of prisons. Rules provide for the constitution of .Board of Visitors. Through the office of the District Magistrate/Divisional

Commissioner. The purpose of the constitution of these Boards is :

- To regulate prison visits by official and non-official visitors through the roster of visitors,
- To ensure at least one visit of the prison per month by an agency other than the officials of the department,
- To involve all persons nominated as official or non-official visitors and to give each one of them some occasions of visiting prison, and
- To provide a forum for discussing problems of prisons and prisoners outside the intervention of the prison department.

All non-official visitors of a jail except those debarred by the Government are eligible to be on the Board of Visitors. Rules provide that a Board of Visitors shall be selected biennially by the Collector and District Magistrate of the concerned district from amongst the official and non-official visitors of each prison and this Board (in entirety) shall inspect the prison twice a year on dates to be fixed by the superintendent in consultation with the President and members of the Board. The Board shall consist of two official and two non-official members, one of whom shall be nominated Chairman by the Collector and District Magistrate. At the District level, the Collector himself is the chairperson of this Board but at lock-ups (sub-jails) the Sub-divisional Officer, City Magistrate, Extra-Magistrate or Judicial Magistrate is the Chairperson. A meeting of the Board of Visitors is required to be held once in a quarter.

In Sunil Batra case the Supreme Court expressed that the Board of Visitors comes in handy for the protection of the rights of prisoners. It thought that the board, which includes judicial officers and people from varied social backgrounds and is vested with visitorial powers, could be instant administrative grievance mechanism to protect the rights of prisoners. It specifically cautioned visitors that the pressure of warders or officials were inhibitive and must be avoided. It also suspected that open inquiry of prisoners in the presence of the prison official would lead to reprisal. Whatever have been the directions of the court, the prison department has been following only the colonial document of prison manual in the manner it conceived and has structured the role and scope for intervention of society and judiciary in its own way.

The prison manual explicitly and in unambiguous terms subjects all possible means of communication between the prisoners and the outside society to restrictions. It conferred unbridled and unguided powers to the level of absurdity in the hands of prison superintendent. These rules fail to stand the test of articles 14, 19 and 21, of the Constitution, which subject the actions of state to non-arbitrariness, reasonableness and principles of natural justice. This draconian document based on the notions of 19th century criminality, is yet be revised. It continues to be applicable as it still serves the purpose of present state. A look into the kind of social arrangement made in the prison by the law gives us a hint about the true nature of its functioning in the society.

Court Rulings on the Role of Prison Visitors

The role of prison visitors as independent observers of the functioning of prisons has been repeatedly recognized by the higher and apex judiciary. It came into sharp focus in Ranchod Vs. State of M.P. (1986 16 Reports M.P. 147) in which the callous behaviour of jail doctors, maltreatment by jail staff and tampering of jail records came up for judicial scrutiny. All this went on for years with the Prison Visitors and Visiting Boards apparently oblivious of it all. According to the facts of the case an inmate of the Central Prison of Indore had died of utter negligence on the part of prison administration and the medical staff posted there. A letter written by two co-inmates of the deceased was admitted by the High Court of Madhya Pradesh as a writ petition and was decided by Hon.ble Justice V.D.Gyani and Justice B.B.L Shrivastava. Reacting sharply to the facts on record Justice V.D. Gyani, Judge of M.P. High Court observed:

The petition has many facets exposing the negligence of authorities, callous disregard to duty by all concerned, including the jail staff, the Executive Magistrate, the Visitors to jail appointed by the State Government, the District Judge, the police and the unethical conduct of doctors..

This letter petition brings into sharp focus and throws light on many other ills besetting the system. Do our District and Sessions Judges, who are ex-officio visitors to the jail within their respective jurisdiction, the Director of Health Services, the Civil Surgeon or Medical Officers, the representatives of people representing particular urban or rural constituency in the State Legislature and the non-official visitors, as appointed ..do they satisfy themselves that the law, rules regulating the management of prisons and prisoners are duly carried out? Their duties are enumerated in..the Jail Manual. They can call for and inspect any book or other record in the jail. Have they regularly visited the jail so as to apprise themselves of the genuine problems the prisoners are facing and their grievances. The non-official visitors to the jail, appointed by the State Government, have they justified their appointment by getting themselves acquainted with the prisoners. problems and making efforts for amelioration of their lot, within the framework of the Jail Manual itself; if all this had been going on smoothly, as is expected and sought to be, possibly there was no need for this letter petition. The question looms large, who bothers..

In spite of such eye opening judgments and judicial aspersions, prison conditions in the country continue to be appalling. The system of prison visitors is still considered by prison staff as an un-necessary intrusion in their work, and Non-official visitors reduce their functions to mere clerical formality in the absence of any accountability. In order to shun the erective attitude of prison staff NOV s prefer not to visit the prison at all. After all what do they lose if they knowingly evade uncomfortable situations that could arise in confronting a non-cooperative prison staff. If they have to wait for long to meet a prison superintendent who thinks it a waste of time to cause his jailor to take them round the prison on a lawful visit, it is better to avoid visiting such jail.

Even the visits of ex-officio visitors of prison are not as regular and purposeful as intended in the rules. Hon'ble Justice J.S. Verma, former Chief Justice of India and later Chairperson of the National Human Rights Commission, addressing a letter to the Chief Justices of all High Courts with regard to human rights in prisons, wrote on January 1, 2000 :

The state Prison Manuals contain provisions for District and Sessions Judges to function as ex-officio visitors to jail within their jurisdiction so as to ensure that prison inmates are not denied certain basic minimum standards of health, hygiene and institutional treatment. The prisoners are in judicial custody and hence it is incumbent upon the Sessions Judges to monitor their living conditions and ensure that humane conditions prevail within the prison walls also. Justice Krishna lyer has aptly remarked that the prison gates are not an iron curtain between the prisoner and human rights. In addition the Supreme Court specifically directed that the District and Sessions Judges must visit prisons for this purpose and consider this part of duty as an essential function attached to their office. They should make expeditious enquiries into the grievances of the prisoners and take suitable corrective measures. During visits to various district prisons, the Commission has been informed that the Sessions Judges are not regular in visiting prisons and the District Committee headed by Sessions Judge / District Magistrate and comprised of senior Superintendent of Police is not meeting at regular intervals to review the conditions of the prisoners..

He implored Chief Justices to consider giving appropriate instructions to the District and Sessions Judges to take necessary steps to resolve this acute problem as it has the impact of violating a human right which is given the status of constitutional guarantee.

The NegativeViewpoint

Even today one could find a significant number of persons working in the criminal justice system, or in the open society, who hold the view that the image of a prison must inspire awe and fear in the minds of offenders. They try to convince that the life in prisons should be demonstrably torturous to deter a prospective criminal. Reformation of a criminal, they say, is impossible and that rehabilitation is a hollow imagination of some non-practical persons. In order to generalize their perception they have a few examples to quote. They forget that their views are more sentimental than scientific. Studies in social science have proved beyond doubt that harshness of punishment has never been a deterrent to a prospective law breaker. While the continuance of death penalty for murder has not been a curb on the rate of the incidence of homicides, the abolition of this harsh punishment in a large number of federating states in the U.S.A. has not increased the number of murders there. The loss of liberty by itself is sufficient to prevent a common man from indulging into violation of rules of the society. We all know that the society itself plays an important role in inducing some people into deviant behaviour, and that a large number of prisoners do not commit the second crime after their release because they have had the lesson of their life in a single incarceration. According to the statistics gathered by the National Crime Records Bureau, MHA, the number of inmates in prisons who had two or more previous convictions at the end of the year 2002 was only 2.7% of the total prison population in the country.

To those who do not believe in improving prison conditions or in the conservation of basic human rights in custody, Pandit Jawaharlal Nehru wrote in *India and the World* ..Prison Land. (pp.108-129).

Another error which people indulge in is the fear that if *jail* conditions are improved people will flock in ! This shows a singular ignorance of human nature. No one wants to go to prison however good the prison might be. To be deprived of liberty and family life and friends and home surroundings is a terrible thing. It is well known that the Indian peasant will prefer to stick to his ancestral soil and starve rather than go elsewhere to better his condition. *To improve prison conditions does not mean that prison life should be made soft; it means that it should be made human and sensible.*

Cruelty does generate cruelty. It undoubtedly has the tendency to squeeze all compassion out of a person and to make him unsocial. Prison conditions must therefore adhere to certain norms in which an inmate could be prevented from being dehumanized. It is for restoring prisons to these basic minimum norms that the institution of Prison Visitors is so necessary and useful.

How the decay has set in

In spite of all meticulousness in the procedural details of prison rules, transparency in the management of these impermeable institutions has always been lacking. Since secure custody of inmates is the basic function of prisons, anything that is a threat (or *supposed* to be, or even *presumed* to be a threat) to security is laid off. How prison management can be transparent, it is argued, when secrecy is the keyword of security. High walls and wards and cells and locks and keys and stringent rules are all for keeping inmates out of the reach of their kin and the society. Easy access to public eye could infringe upon this age-old system of segregation and obliterate the very purpose for which prisons were conceived.

Secure management has thus slowly but consciously slipped into *obscure* management and, once transparency is shadowed, accountability becomes a farce. Prison management could, if it so preferred, become repressive and yet pass unnoticed. No inmate could complain of repression for fear of more repression. How can one dare to harness enmity with the system in which one has to live a substantial period of life in seclusion from the society.

It is common knowledge that this obscurity becomes the breeding ground of several evils. If atrocities, corruption and irregularities go un-noticed, they flourish. Misuse of authority for unlawful gain becomes the order of the day. One can create discomfiture and charge for ease. *(It is well known about certain prisons in the country where inmates have to pay for stretching their legs for a comfortable sleep at night.)*

Cliques are formed in which old-time inmates become party with the staff and run an unholy .business. The gains of which are distributed among stakeholders, who, in fact, have nothing at stake except their conscience. The network spreads. The higher it goes, the more it is necessary to extract, and therefore new methodologies are evolved to keep the game plan going. Those few, who prefer to keep away from this degradation, are ridiculed. They are disdained, isolated, rejected, placed in unimportant positions and sometimes punished on false grounds.

But atrocities in prisons are not all of the making of prison staff. A substantially large number of them result from the system itself and the neglect to which it is subjected by all concerned - the courts, the police, the probation system, district administration, the PWD and so on.

Physical and psychological torture resulting from overcrowding, lack of space for segregation of sick, stinking toilets for want of proper supply of water, lack of proper bedding, restrictions on movement resulting from shortage of staff, parading of women through men's wards for lack of proper separation, non-production of undertrial prisoners in courts, inadequate medical facilities, neglect in the grant of parole, rejection of pre-mature release on flimsy grounds, and several such afflictions result not from any malfeasance of the prison staff but from the collective neglect of the whole system. Those who can deliver goods do not know. Those who know have no means to remedy the ills. There is lack of effective communication. Those who communicate lack perseverance. There is no accountability for non-performance. There is no linkage, no monitoring, no deadlines, no evaluation and therefore no result.

Reformation: the change is slow but obvious

In spite of the fact that there are several maladies in the prison system in the country, it would not be appropriate to totally condemn the whole set-up. Obviously, there are difficulties of man-power, funds, training and right kind of attitude to deal with socially handicapped inmates, but all these ills need to be corrected with the joint effort of the government, the people and the staff manning prison institutions. Some prisons are an example of the best utilization of the resources available, and it is educative to see them. Prison visitors of different states should be given an opportunity to visit such prisons to see how they function and how those conditions can be emulated in other prisons.

Housed in comparatively new buildings constructed on the principles laid down with regard to minimum space per person, and having appropriately provided facilities of sanitation, medical care, hygienic kitchens, play grounds, separate entrance for women section, space for vocational training and prison factories, adequate staff quarters, and suitable dormitories for single-person security staff, these prisons present an image of a scientifically built custodial institution.

Reformative programmes are regularly conducted in these prisons with the help of local non-government agencies and philanthropic organizations. 'Vipasyana', spiritual discourses, lectures and preaching on issues of healthy social life, literacy classes and de-addiction programmes, adult education classes, non-government agencies, are some of the regular features of the prison. Services of educated prisoners are availed to promote literacy and to hold regular education classes for those who wish to appear at Board or University examinations as private candidates. All fees and other expenses on the education of these inmates is borne by voluntary organizations such as Rotary Club, Lions Club or by public welfare section of established banking institutions. All these activities are geared and monitored by prison management with the personal efforts of some well-intentioned prison personnel supported by active and effective prison visitors. Such correctional programmes not only break the monotony of prison setting but charge the atmosphere with an urge for betterment.

These prisons do not present a dismal picture of human beings languishing in idle confmement, but are places buzzing with activity, both administrative and correctional.

There appears to be a horizontal coordination of prison officials with the officers of other departments and with functionaries of other organs of the criminal justice system. The jail Superintendents and other staff have amiable informal relations with other district level local officers. This facilitates their official functioning. They leave no occasion, official or informal, to meet these district level officials and invite them to all functions held at the prison. Problems of prison are introduced to concerned officials during courtesy meetings to draw their appropriate attention and an early solution. Such congenial ambiance prevents unnecessary delay of bureaucratic procedures in getting things done for the prison and prisoners. One can visualize here that a purposeful and constructive local cooperation of officials of prison, police and the judiciary can go a long way in ameliorating the sufferings of prison inmates. And, if some well-meaning non-government social organizations are involved in the corrective process of prisons, it can make the rehabilitation of offenders after their release, much smooth.

It is in the creation of this congenial atmosphere that the role of Prison Visitors. both official and non- official can be best appreciated and obtained. It is they who can best (and in the spirit of constructive approach) bring to the notice of the government, the deficiencies of the system at appropriate time so that they do not accumulate or grow to unmanageable proportions. It is they who can help prison administration in securing the cooperation of non-government agencies engaged in philanthropic work for extending their activities within prison walls where a neglected mass of human beings waits for the support of society. It is they, again, who can prepare the society in shedding off their rejective prejudices for casual offenders who make mistakes in haste and repent at leisure.

The institution of Prison Visitors is, thus, not only desirable but essential for the development of a correctional atmosphere in prisons. It has to be retained and reinforced, if we want to open a casement on prisons for involving the society in general to improve prison conditions and help the prisoners in captivity to make their period of incarceration less dehumanizing and more productive.

Prison Statistics, India

SNAPSHOTS-2003

Total Number of Jails in the country: 1,140
Central Jails: 107, District Jails: 268, Sub Jails: 678, Women Jails: 14, Other Jails: 73

Total Capacity of Jails in the country: 2,33,543
Central Jails: 1,07,484 (46.0%) ,District Jails: 76,663 (32.8%)
Sub Jails: 34,851 (14.9%), Women Jails: 2,085 (0.9%), Other Jails: 12,460 (5.3%)

Total Number of Jail Inmates: 3,26,519
Male: 3,13,739 (96.1%), Female: 12,780 (3.9%)

Convicts: 91,766 (28.1 % of total inmates),

Undertrial Prisoners: 2,17,658 (66.7% of total inmates)
Male: 96.3% of total convicts, Male: 96.5% oftotal undertrials Female: 3.7% of total convicts, Female: 3.5% oftotal undertrials

Detenues: 4,008 (1.2% of total inmates) Others: 13,087 (4.00/0 of total inmates)
Male: 95.8% of total detenues, Male: 88.3% of total others Female: 4.2% of total detenues, Female: 11.7% of total others

Foreigners

Convicts: 585 Undertrials : 1,490 Detenues : 124

(Male: 433, Female: 152) (Male: 1268, Female: 222) (Male: 123, Female: 1)

- The highest number of 50, 531 inmates (49,410 male: 1,121 female) were reported from Uttar Pradesh (15.5%) followed by Bihar 37,323 (36,274 male: 1,049 female) at the end of the year 2003.
- D&N Haveli reported the highest overcrowding of prisons (344.0%) followed by Delhi (305.3%) while. the least occupancy was reported from Lakshadweep (6.3%) followed by Daman & Diu (27.5%).
- 339 Women Convicts with their 334 children and 1,132 Women undertrials with their 1,131 children were reported in the country.
- Maximum number of 12,780 (12,235 male: 545 female) Convicts were reported from Madhya Pradesh (13.9% of total convicts in the country) followed by Maharashtra 8,215 (7,825 male: 390 female) accounting for 8.9% of the total convicts at the end of the year 2003.
- The highest number of Graduate and Post Graduate Convicts were reported from Punjab (648) and Uttar Pradesh (137) respectively at the end of the year 2003.
- Murder alone accounted for 58.6% of the total Convicts under IPC Crimes. The highest number of 6,909 Murder Convicts were reported from Madhya Pradesh (15.0% oftotal Murder convicts) followed by Maharashtra (9.2% oftotal Murder convicts) at the end of the year 2003.
- The highest percentage (28.3%) of undertrials were charged with Murder. Among States, Bihar reported the highest number of 7,680 Undertrials (16.5%) followed by Uttar Pradesh 7,286 (15.6%).
- 333 Convicts including 4 Women were awaiting execution in the country at the end of the year 2003.

- 48,334 Convicts were undergoing sentences for Life Imprisonment accounting for 52.7% of total Convicts in the country at the end of the year 2003.
- 1,481 Undertrials (0.7% of total undertrials) were detained in jails for more than 5 years at the end of the year 2003.
0 16,798 Convicts were habitual offenders which accounted for 7.3% of total convicts admitted during the year.
- The highest earning by inmates trained in various vocational programmes was reported from Maharashtra (Rs. 1,398.2 lakh) followed by Bihar (Rs.652.9 lakh) during the year 2003.
- The highest earning per inmate was reported from Maharashtra (Rs.5,843.1) followed by Gujarat (Rs.5,267.0) as against All-India average of Rs. 1,392.1 during the year 2003.
- Out of the total 50,787 staff manning jails in the country, 2,806 (i.e. 5.5%) were women during the year 2003.
- The highest expenditure per inmate was reported from Manipur (Rs.71,992.2) as against All-India average of Rs.11,901.3 during the year 2003-04.

Bibliography

Books

Abrahamsen David, "The Psychology of Crime", Columbia University Press, New York, 1960.

Adler Freda, "Sisters in Crime: A Rise of the New Female Criminal", McGraw Hill, New York, 1977.

Ahuja Ram, "Female Offenders in India", Meenakshi Prakashan, Meerut, 1969.

Ahuja Ram, "Women and Crime" in 'Crime and Corrections in India' eds. J.J. Panakal and S.D. Gokhale, Tata Institute of Social Sciences, Mumbai, 1989.

Bajpai Anju and Bajpai P.K, "Female Criminality in India", Rawat Publications, Jaipur, 2000.

Becker Howard, "Outsiders", University of London Press, London, 1963.

Bhanot M.L. and Mishra S. "Criminality among Women in India", Bureau of Police Research and Development, New Delhi, 1979.

Bonger, M., "Criminality and Economic Conditions", Little Brown and Company, Boston, 1916.

Bowker L.H., "Women and Crime in America", McMillan Company, New York, 1981.

Broom and Selznick, "Sociology" , Harper and Row Publishers, New York, 1968.

Caldwell Robert, "Criminology" , University of Pennsylvania Press, New York, 1956.

Cloward Richard and Ohlin L.E., "Delinquency and Opportunity", Routledge and Kegan Paul, London, 1961.

Cohen Albert K., "Delinquent Boys: The Culture of the Gang", Free Press, New York, 1955.

Cohen Albert K., "Deviance and Control", Prentice Hall of India Pvt. Ltd., New Delhi, 1970.

Devasia L. and Devasia V.V., "Female Criminals and Female Victims: An Indinn Perspective", Dattson Publishers, Nagpur, 1989.

Durkheim Emile, "Suicide", translated by I.A. Spaulding, Free Press, New York, 1951.

Ghosh S.K., "Female Criminals in India", Uppal Publishing House, New Delhi 1986.

Gote-Gavhane S., "Female Criminality and Sociological Theories", South Asian Social Research Publication, Aurangabad, 1997.

Hall Jerome, "General Principles of Criminal Law", Free Press, New York, 1947.

Hirschi Travish, "Causes of Delinquency", University of California Press, Berkely, 1969.

Lemert C., "Social Problem", Routledge & Kegan Paul, London, 1958.

Kaldate Sudha, "Convicted Female Offenders in Indian Prisons" in 'Female Criminals and Female Victims' ed. Devasia L. & Devasia V.V., Dattson Publishers, Nagpur, 1989.

Kerawalla Perin, "A Study in Indian Crime", Popular Book Depot, Bombay, 1959.

Landis Paul, "Social Problems", J.R. Lippincott Company, Chicago, 1959.

Lombroso C. and Ferrero W., "The Female Offender", Appleton, New York, 1903.

Merton Robert K., "Social Theory and Social Structure", Free Press, New York, 1949.

Morris R., "Female Delinquency and Relational Problems", Allen & Unwin Ltd., London, 1964.

Naffine N., "Female Crime: The construction of women in Criminology", Allen & Unwin. London, 1987.

Nagla B. K., "Women, Crime and Law", Rawat Publication, Jaipur, 1991.

Nye F. Ivan, "Family Relationship and Delinquent Behaviour", John Wiley & Sons, New York, 1958.

Parsons Talcott, "Family Structure and the Socialization of the Child" in 'Family, Socialization and Interaction Process' ed. T. Parsons & R.P. Bales, Free Press, New York, 1954.

Pollak Otto, "The Criminality of Women" , University of Pennsylvania Press, Philadelphia, 1950.

Rani Bilmoria, "Female Criminality: An Empirical Study In Andhra Pradesh", Eastern Book Company, Lucknow, 1987.

Reckless Walter, "The Crime Problem", Appleton, New York, 1967.

Reid sue Titus, "Crime and Criminology",The Drydon Press, Hinsdale, Illinois, 1976.

Sanyal S., "Female Criminals in India", Uppal Publishing House, New Delhi, 1986.

Sethna MJ., "Society and Criminals", Leaders' Press Ltd., Bombay, 1964.

Sharma B.R., "Crime and Women: A Psycho-Diagnostic Study of Female Criminality", Indian Institute of Public Administration, New Delhi, 1993.

Sidney Berman, "Anti-Social Character Disorder" in Ruth S. Cavan, Readings in Juvenile Delinquency, J.B. Lippincott & Co., Philadelphia, 1964.

Simon Rita James, "Women and Crime", D.C., U.S. Govt. Printing Press, Washington, 1975.

Smart Carol, "Women, Crime and Criminology: A Feminist Critique", Routledge & Kegan Paul, London, 1976.

Smith Ann D., "Women in Prison: A Study in Penal Methods", Stevens and Sons, London, 1962.

Sohoni N.K., "Women Behind Bars", Vikas Publishing House Pvt. Ltd., New Delhi, 1989.

Sutherland Edwin H. and Cressy Donald R., "Principles of Criminology". Routledge & Kegan Paul, London, 1965.

Thomas W.I., "The Unadjusted Girl", Harper and Row, New York, 1967.

Thesis

Shekhar Sanober, "Women Prisoners: The Remand and Undertrial Experience" ,Unpublished Ph.D. thesis, T.I.S.S, Mumbai, 1989.

Journals

Bertrand M.A., "Self-Image and Delinquency: Contribution to the study of female criminality and women's image", Acta Criminologica, Jan. 1969.

Chockalingam K., "A study of relationship between Income and expenditure and past life among recidivists", Indian Journal of Criminology, Vo1.8, No.2, July 1980.

Dhanagare D.N., "Urbanism and crime", Economic and Political, Weekly, Special Number July 1969.

Glaser Daniel, "Criminality Theories and Behavioural Images", American Journal of Sociology, March 1956.

Heidensohn Frances, "The Deviance of Women: A Critique and an Enquiry", British Journal of Sociology, Vo1.l9, No.2, 1968.

Hindalang M.J., "Causes of Delinquency: A partial replication and extension", Social Problems, 20, 4, 1973.

Menon N .R.M., "Legal aid in the criminal proceedings", social defence, Vo1.l3, No.50, October 1977.

N agla B. K., "The criminality of women in India", Indian journal of Social Work, Vo1.43, No.3, October 1982.

Prasad S.K., "A study of women murderers in Tamil Nadu", Readings in Criminology, Souvenir Vol.12, No.2, Calcutta 1982.

Sanyal S. and Agarwal V., "Women Convicts in Nari Bandi Niketan",Indian Journal of criminology, Vo1.9, No. 2, July 1981.

Shastri Tara, "A study of women prisoners and their families in Maharashtra", social defence, Vol.XII, No.46, october 1976

Singh A., "Personality of Female Murrderers", Indian journal of criminology,9(2), 1980.

Reports

* Crime in India - National Crime Record Bureau (N.C.R.B.), Bureau of Police Research and Development, Ministry of Home Affairs, Govemment of India, New Delhi, Reports from 1991-2000.
* Report of National Expert Committee on Women Prisoners, Vol.I & II, 1986-87, Ministry of Human Resource Development, Department of Women and Child Development, New Delhi.
* Report of the National Workshop on Custodial Justice to Women, National Institute of Public Co-operation and Child Devolopment (NIPCCD), New Delhi, 1989.
* Extracts from the Maharashtra Prison Manual, Published by Vidhyak Sansad, Maharashtra and Human Rights Law Network, Mumbai, 1976.
* The Model Prison Manual, 1976.
* The Bombay Jail Manual, 1935.

Index

T

U

V

W